Elisa Celli's Italian Light Cooking

ELISA CELLI'S ITALIAN LIGHT COOKING

Elisa Celli

PRENTICE HALL PRESS

New York London Toronto Sydney Tokyo

All photographs by Philippe-Louis Houzé

Published by Prentice Hall Press
A Division of Simon & Schuster, Inc.
Gulf+Western Building
One Gulf+Western Plaza
New York, NY 10023

PRENTICE HALL PRESS is a trademark of Simon & Schuster, Inc.

Library of Congress Cataloging-in-Publication Data

Celli, Elisa.
  Elisa Celli's Italian Light Cooking.

  Includes index.
  1. Cookery, Italian. I. Title. II. Italian
light cooking.
TX723.C444 1987   641.5945 87-11455
ISBN 0-13-273905-4

Designed by J. C. Suarès

Manufactured in the United States of America

10 9 8 7 6 5 4 3 2

I dedicate this book to the memory of my beautiful mother, Adelaide. A great lady and great Italian cook, she taught me the classic cucina Italiana *with the* sapore *of Abruzzi and the spirit for enjoying life.*

Acknowledgments

Grazie a Dio! I thank God for giving me the opportunity and talent to share the joy of good health through the right foods the Italian way, as I have featured in this book and others.

Grazie mia famiglia: brothers Lou, Joseph, and Robert, and husband, Trevor Wallace, for his support and talent. Thanks also to my *famiglia* of friends for their loyalty, especially Stan Eckstein, and to my editor, PJ Dempsey; creative director, J. C. Suarès; literary agent, Reid Boates; and manager, Eddie Elias.

My admiration and thanks also go to the "great healers": Dr. Frank Mancini, Dr. Jack Saltonoff, Dr. Ancel Keyes, Dr. Giovanni Boni, Dr. Jeffrey Fedorko, Nancy Colby, and Hans Gartner.

Bravo and *grazie*, Ciao Italia Organization in Los Angeles, to the Italian Trade Commissioner in New York, Mario Castagna, and Augusto Marchini, the director of the Italian Wine and Food Center.

And *bravo* and *grazie* to my favorite fine Italian *ristorantes* that feature classic, *la cucina Italiana,* for their inspiration of special recipes.

In Los Angeles: Perino's, Marino's, Chianti/Cucina, Nicky Blair's, Guido's, and Italia Expresso Caffe. In Beverly Hills: Osteria Romana Orsini, La Famiglia, Celestino, Madeo, Il Giardino, Il Cielo, Da Vinci, Romeo and Juliet's, and Benito's. In Hollywood: Emilio's. In Santa Monica: Valentino's and Vito's. In Malibu: Beau Rivage. In Beverly Glen Circle: Adriano's. In Corona del Mar: Carmelo's. In Westwood: La Bruschetta. And in San Clemente: Andreino's.

In New York City: Tre Scalini, Scarlatti, Il Caminetto, Sistina, Ancora, Felidia, Marcello's, Barbetta's, Toscana, Sondro's, Cipriani, Ecco, Hosteria del Buon Gustaio, Caffe Roma, Enotecca, Aloe Aloe, Pailia, Four Season, Raffaelo's, Nanni's, Il Valetto, Ruggero's, Giambelli's, Angelo's, Patsy's, and Il Nido.

And, of course, a thousand favorites in Italy!

Contents

Foreword

Eat well and be thin! It is a fact that one can enjoy delicious Italian food and still look great and remain healthy. Elisa shows the way with her selective and carefully planned recipes that bring out all the right flavors by using special herbs and their combinations, which add further nutrients to the diet.

The culinary artistry revealed throughout this book emphasizes the use of primarily natural herbs and spices and omits the typical salt-and-pepper flavors that many people cannot handle properly; it is a compliment to her knowledge of and consideration for others. Elisa has learned this talent through many years of research and experimentation. She has mastered the art of eating well, while looking and feeling great.

Her use of fresh fruit and vegetables, natural herbs, garlic, onions, and pure green olive oil assists the immune and metabolic systems. The use of mostly fresh white fish and poultry and very little red meat and pork can be very meaningful for people who suffer from high cholesterol, high blood pressure, diabetes, or cardiovascular conditions.

It is a pleasure to follow suggestions about eating well and being healthy when they come from someone who knows what she is talking about. I compliment you, Elisa, for your dedication and success earned through hard work and sincerity.

—Frank D. Mancini, D.C., M.S., C.N.C.

Preface

Like so many people all over the world, I love Italian food with such a consuming passion that I can never get enough of the wonderful tastes and exotic aromas that I knew as a child growing up in Italy.

If ever a country reflected the color and mood of its people in the food they eat, it's my Italy! Think of the fresh seafood, the fabulous pastas, the wonderful variety of crisp vegetables, *gelatas*, pizzas, and *risottos*. Imagine the bouquet of fresh herbs! Imagine pesto, the smell of fresh crushed basil, and pure green olive oil, so light and perfect in color that the sun sparkles from it, its taste made rich with fresh grated Parmesan cheese and those wonderful pignoli nuts.

Put pesto sauce over cooked capellini (angel hair pasta) cooked al dente and the result is a symphony of flavors, a true delight to the palate.

What a multitude of sumptuous dishes there are to choose from among all the luscious foods of Italy. I can remember from my childhood how the warm Adriatic sunshine ripened the vegetables while wonderfully enticing cooking smells came from my mother's kitchen. The superb Baccala alla Adriatica was made from glistening fresh codfish with a special sauce typical of Abruzzi, my family region: fresh tomatoes, crisp green celery, white onions, brown raisins, fresh Italian parsley, and Trebbiano white wine. These marvelously strong flavors rested alongside small, white, soft-skinned potatoes baked to perfection. My brothers and I loved to sneak into the kitchen, break off a piece of crisp, freshly baked bread, and dip it into the delicious, simmering sauce.

The very thought of that magically fragrant kitchen conjures up delight—I remember it so well, hung with the deep-smoked prosciuttos, strings of dried garlic, gleaming copper saucepans, and garlands of onions. It sometimes seems impossible that my mother's simple recipes could become such incredible culinary masterpieces: simple pasta with a bouquet of fresh vegetables or seafood and just the slightest accent of freshly grated Pecorino cheese, or a tender veal chop cooked with mushrooms, pungent fresh herbs, and piquant spices. It would be served with a wine like the unforgettable Montepulciano d'Abruzzi—few wines have such unbelievable character and are so easy to drink.

When I was only seven years old, barely able to reach the tabletop, my mother taught me the classic Abruzzi way of making spaghetti: Spaghetti alla Chitarra. This method is the original, and still the simplest, way of making spaghetti. Underneath an oblong, hardwood frame with a grid of guitar strings stretched tightly over it is a shallow tray. When fresh pasta dough is rolled with a rolling pin over the guitar strings and they are plucked, the fine, rolled spaghetti falls through the strings onto the tray. This very thin, fresh spaghetti is then cooked al dente and served with a sauce made from Italian plum tomatoes and basil, accented with garlic, onions, and pure green olive oil. It's a true Abruzzi classic and a favorite Italian sauce.

So many of the classic Italian dishes are so simple. Polenta is just cornmeal simmered and stirred in water until it becomes smooth and creamy. Add Mascarpone cheese with porcini mushrooms, or quail and tomato sauce to it, and you have an elegant, gourmet feast. For gourmet simplicity, try Agnello con Carciofi (baby lamb with fresh artichokes, rosemary, and garlic, enriched with a reduced herb and white wine sauce). Many of these wonderful dishes are so quick and easy to prepare and light and delicious to eat.

Yes, *true* Italian cooking is really light! Unfortunately, through the misguided attempts of uninformed cooks, our wonderful Italian *cucina* suffers from the dread image that it is high in calories. Not so! The foods of Italy are among the purest, lightest, and most natural in the world. The staples of the Italian diet are pasta, green olive oil, cheese, fruits, lots of vegetables and legumes, pure wines, and, of course, the infinite variety of seafood from the Adriatic and Mediterranean seas. The modest consumption of wine (especially red) has a preventive action against cardiovascular disease. And seafood including anchovies, herring, sardines, and tuna, and especially the abundant bluefish is rich in unsaturated fats called omega-3's, which help prevent blood-clot formation, a major cause of heart attacks.

The key in classic Italian cooking, and an underlying principle of this book, is to understand the difference between genuine Italian foods and the adulterated, pseudo-Italian foods so often served in the United States. Classic Italian food is light, lower in calories, and much healthier than we've come to expect. Adulterated Italian food, as served in some "Italian" restaurants, means heavy, saturated oils, white flour pastas, thick cream and butter sauces, and many other inferior ingredients that amount to nothing but ersatz tastes and extra calories.

In classic Italian cooking the pasta is made from 100 percent durum semolina wheat. The difference in a five ounce serving is 210 calories versus 550 calories in starchy, mushy, white flour pasta. Most classic Italian sauces are made with a dash of green olive oil, cooked onions, garlic, fresh or dried herbs, a clever combination of spices, and little or no salt (with the herbs and spices you'll never miss the taste of salt).

Genuine Italian food has so much taste and excitement that all the senses are satisfied and you need smaller portions to appease your appetite. When food is boring or bland, there's a tendency to try to replace quality with quantity and to throw on lots of salt. A little of the right pasta, well prepared, can be infinitely more satisfying than great heaps of poorly prepared pasta.

Take heart. A comparison between two dishes, each called Fettuccine Alfredo, follows. When you've compared them, I'm sure you will look for and prepare classic Italian food—*la cucina Italiana*.

Adulterated Italian Food

Fettuccine Alfredo

5 oz. pasta noodles, cooked (white flour)	550 calories
1 cup heavy cream	650 calories
1 stick salted butter	800 calories
½ cup grated cheese (salt, chemicals, etc.)	250 calories
TOTAL	*2,250 calories*

Classic Italian

Fettuccine Alfredo

5 oz. pasta noodles, cooked (100 percent durum semolina)	210 calories
⅛ cup light cream (Half & Half)	90 calories
1 tbsp. unsalted butter	110 calories
¼ cup freshly grated Parmesan cheese	120 calories
¼ cup chopped Italian parsley	8 calories
TOTAL	*538 calories*

The difference is 1,712 fattening calories!

One of the most common causes of what medical professionals call "self-inflicted wounds" is the traditional American diet. It is lethal, and most of us suffer from it and many other self-destructive practices—mental and physical stress, crazy life-styles, long working hours, worry, and lack of proper rest. There are dozens of ways in which we can destroy our minds and our bodies. In this book you will find a perfect "livable, lifetime eating program" that is not only nutritional and slimming but is also elegant, enjoyable, and easy to incorporate into your life-style. It is proven to be one of the healthiest eating programs and is within the guidelines of the Nutritional Council, the American Heart Association, and the National Cancer Society.

This is the true Italian philosophy: "Enjoy your life with good food, good wine, and the people you love." It really does work. In Italy, people live longer and have fewer health problems. There is a lower incidence of cancer, heart problems, stress, and high blood pressure.

Italian light cooking is a great way to stay slim and healthy with lots of exciting Italian foods and wine. *Mangia bene! Vivi bene!*—eat well and live well, Italian style!

Introduction

For the past ten years, in my books and magazine articles and on television, I have been proclaiming the virtues of light, luscious Italian foods. *The Pasta Diet*, my previous book, brought to hundreds of thousands of readers the immediate benefit of a healthy fourteen-day, ten-pound weight-reduction program centered on one of the most popular yet maligned foods in the world—pasta.

Now, with everyone from the United States Department of Agriculture to the person on the street switching from heavy, harmful foods to a lighter, more natural way of eating, I know the time has come for a lively treasury of true Italian menus covering the entire "classic" *cucina Italiana*.

One of the first things to know about Italian cuisine is that it doesn't exist! First, the term *cuisine* is French. Second, Italian cooking is not a uniform way of cooking but an incredible variety of ways: Each is handed down personally and changed by the cook who thinks that perhaps this or that should be done differently. *La cucina Italiana* is regional, provincial, local, and improvised—a trove of dishes that vary from season to season and cook to cook. Passed intuitively from one generation to another, these dishes are always subject to each recipient's experiments, based on creativity or the availability of ingredients.

In some regions you will find light, refined dishes, such as those of the true Mediterranean diet: Light pastas, fish, and vegetables, are enhanced by fresh herbs and the finest green olive oil, with onions and garlic and hot peppers for a dash of excitement. Breads, cheeses, and fresh fruits with fine wines round out the menu. But you will also find dishes in *la cucina Italiana* that are among the richest fare of Europe—sauces based on butter, cream, meat, pork, and goose, complemented by heavier pastries—depending on the region and time of year. What you will find in this book are low-calorie, high-energy, classic Italian dishes with an exciting taste and lots of visual appeal—a trademark of Italy!

An American, Dr. Ancel Keys, first made the connection between the Mediterranean and Italian diets and low rates of heart disease, cancer, obesity, diabetes, and arteriosclerosis, particularly among Italians. He made a complete study and found that the nutritive habits of the Mediterranean region, which can be traced back to the ancient eating habits of the southern Italian farmers, were considered ideal for maintaining good health and enjoying a long life. And now, many doctors and nutritionists are recognizing the important health benefits of the Italian Mediterranean lifetime eating program.

It's only natural that *Italian Light Cooking* will emphasize the quality of ingredients: Only through the right ingredients can you enjoy gourmet Italian feasts of amazing variety without gaining so much as an extra pound. In fact, although this book is not designed as a "diet" per se, the evidence shows that when the ingredients are right, classic Italian cooking actually encourages weight loss!

I must state emphatically that I have not taken Italian recipes and simply "de-calorized" them. Many of the recipes in this book have been carefully selected from my region, Abruzzi, and they truly represent the type of Italian cooking I grew up with and still practice today (while remaining a size six). I have also included recipes from all the other regions of Italy.

For some recipes, I have had to substitute products that are more readily available in American markets. The imported ingredients I use can be found in local supermarkets, gourmet shops, or Italian specialty outlets, which seem to be popping up every day.

To keep my recipes slimming and my readers healthy, I have avoided the use of some dairy products whenever possible. Just as I advocate avoiding salt, I do not recommend dairy goods because they are most often found in our markets in forms that are processed, heavy in fats, and laden with preservatives. Working with some of the very best doctors of nutrition, I have been shown repeatedly the adverse effects of some dairy products.

Remember my golden rule: Salt causes higher blood pressure and contributes to the retention of water.

Italian food without cheese? Hardly. The exceptions to my rule are high-quality, *fresh* Parmesan, skim-milk ricotta, skim-milk mozzarella, and some goat cheese, which are low in fat, low in salt, low in calories, and high in protein. I have used and can recommend these cheeses. I have carefully avoided the use of products with chemicals, preservatives, white sugar, salt, and cream.

You'll be amazed at how alive with flavor my recipes can be without these problem ingredients. The "secret" is in natural herbs and spices, wine, and fresh ingredients, so that *sapore*—taste—is always my primary component.

With each recipe in this book, you will find three items listed: number of servings, preparation time, and calories.

Servings: This measurement is important for judging the portion per person. The pasta recipes are based on five ounces of cooked pasta and other foods, depending on whether the recipe is used for an appetizer or main course. The portions can be changed accordingly, since the calorie count gives you an approximate amount to judge by. Since other foods will be served, it is an amount of food that should be satisfying and not filling.

Calories: The number of calories per serving is based on the United States Department of Agriculture tables. Serving size is five ounces unless otherwise indicated. But these calorie counts should be regarded as approximate rather than actual, due to cooking reduction and types of food. They are accurate enough to give you a good idea of how low in calories each recipe is. If portions are increased, the average amount of calories can be counted. Variations will change the calorie count slightly if you are changing a vegetable or herb, but adding meat or ham will increase the calories a great deal.

Time: Most of my recipes are quick, taking from ten to twenty-five minutes to prepare. The exception will be baking, making bread, pizza, and other recipes requiring lengthy preparations. Some cooks will prepare the recipes faster, so keep in mind that the listed time is a good approximation. Preparation can sometimes take more time than cooking. To speed things up, try my quick cutting technique (see page 9). With many of my recipes, you can certainly prepare an entire meal in fifteen to twenty minutes. Most of the classic Italian recipes are quick cooking to retain the nutrients and taste of the ingredients.

In all of my recipes, I also list special variations—ideas to get your own creative juices flowing. As a result, many of these recipes won't be mine after all, but yours.

Finally, without getting formal or "preachy" about it, I want these recipes to suggest to you a new, lifetime eating pattern—a healthy, livable, fun eating program that I have prepared in consultation through the years with nutritionists and medical doctors. Although my foods can hardly assure good health, they will contribute to lower blood pressure and to reduced cholesterol levels, keeping you healthier and thinner. Even in the section on wines—a marvelous and virtually complete book in itself!—I have listed the finest, most pure wines that are available.

Italian Light Cooking can become a guide that will change your life-style, improve your health, and make you a slimmer, happier person. It can be for you and your family a successful lifetime eating program that is fun and easy!

Viva Italia!

I. *Preparing for the Recipes*

Stocking the Kitchen

It is important to have your kitchen stocked properly in order to be prepared to cook at any moment. The great thing about cooking *alla Italiana* is that it is so quick, easy, and inexpensive. If you have all the necessary ingredients and equipment on hand, many recipes take just ten to fifteen minutes to prepare.

For instance, in about ten minutes you can have a pasta dish served with salad, fresh crusty bread, and good Italian wine. Try thin spaghetti with an oil, garlic, and herb sauce sprinkled with Parmesan cheese. While the water is boiling to cook the pasta, add two tablespoons of green olive oil to a skillet and sauté a few cloves of crushed garlic. Add a dash of hot, dried red pepper flakes, some Italian herb seasoning, and let them cook for two more minutes. When the pasta is cooked al dente (about three to five minutes for thin spaghetti), drain it and add it to the skillet of oil, garlic, and seasoning; then toss and let them cook together for another few minutes. When it's ready to serve, toss with fresh, grated Parmesan cheese. Set the table with some big chunks of crusty Italian bread, a bowl of green salad in oil and light vinegar dressing, and uncork a bottle of good Italian red wine. It's a meal fit for a king! Round it off with fresh fruit and espresso and your guests will give you a medal.

The following suggestions will help you to be prepared to cook at any moment for any taste. Of course, some ingredients should always be obtained fresh on the day you need them, for example, seafood, fresh vegetables, and salad greens. Ideally such items should be bought the Italian way—shopping each day at the market. However, if it's impossible for you to do this, keep your shelves stocked with the things I list and, only when absolutely necessary, use some carefully selected frozen-food products.

FOODS TO KEEP ON HAND

Fresh Italian plum tomatoes are the small, oval Italian tomatoes with the most taste! Buy them very ripe and small for the best quality. Drop them in boiling water for a few seconds, then peel; squeeze the seeds out and dice. If fresh plum tomatoes are not available, use the canned variety of Italian plum tomatoes, whole or crushed. They have an excellent taste and are easy to store. Keep a few cans on hand so you'll always be ready to whip up a pasta sauce or a sauce for chicken, vegetables, or fish at a minute's notice.

Onions: The word *onion* will mean brown-skinned onions, also known as yellow onions, unless you are directed to use shallots or red onions.

Garlic is used a great deal in my recipes because it is very healthy and tasty. Use the big, fat cloves, not elephant garlic. Peel them in advance, and place in a jar with enough olive oil to cover them. That way you'll always have garlic ready to use. Use a garlic press. Crushed garlic helps prevent garlic breath (which comes from biting into the chunks). If you cannot digest garlic, I suggest that you use more onions, herbs, and hot pepper instead.

Green olive oil exclusively is used in my recipes. Green "extra-virgin" olive oil is considered the best because it is the first cold pressing of high-quality olives (not subjected to heat when the olive pulp is pressed to extract the oil) and subsequently not subjected to chemical refinement. Green oil is clean and pure olive oil. Look for the light green color and "virgin olive oil" if you can't find the extra-virgin olive oil, which is more expensive but worth it, since so little is used for each recipe—usually, from one to three tablespoons. The medical profession is finally recognizing the benefits of green olive oil. Green olive oil contains iron and vitamin A and is the closest in chemical composition to the fat in human milk, which makes it the most digestible and easily assimilated of all the fats and oils. Green olive oil contains no cholesterol and can contribute to maintaining a healthy cardiovascular condition. It is mono-unsaturated fat, which is important to the body in many ways, especially in keeping the arteries from clogging. America's ongoing love affair with Italian foods has also bolstered the oil's popularity; it is now widely used in the finest restaurants and sold in local supermarkets and gourmet shops. Stored in a cool place, but not in the refrigerator, it will last up to six months.

Italian herb seasoning is the perfect blend and balance of the most important Italian herbs that add *sapore* (taste) to any recipe. This premixed Italian herb seasoning containing the right balance of oregano, sage, basil, rosemary, thyme, and marjoram, is available commercially from a variety of companies. You can also make your own. The amount of each ingredient used depends on your personal taste, but go easy on the oregano, which has a very strong flavor that may overpower the other herbs. Grind the mixture in a blender or food processor, and store in an airtight jar in a cool place. Remember: Dried herbs are only good for four to six months.

Crushed red pepper: For a *piccante* (hot) taste or to slightly sharpen a recipe, use a dash to a half-teaspoon of the bottled crushed red pepper flakes. They must be added to a recipe *during* the cooking process to impart their flavor into the sauce—do not add before serving. When the oil, garlic, and onions start to sauté, add the crushed red pepper flakes. Change bottles after six months to preserve the taste.

Cayenne pepper is finely ground red pepper that is pungent and hot, yet easy to digest. Like black pepper, cayenne is neither harsh nor difficult on the digestive tract. But it is potent, so use it in small amounts, either during the cooking process or before serving.

Pasta: Buy only 100 percent durum semolina wheat pasta, which is made from the center and outer layers of the wheat, contains all the nutrients, and is low in calories. Semolina wheat also keeps the pasta firm and tasty. Regular flour (known as white flour) has been milled; it is a refined carbohydrate, and is high in calories and low in nutrients, and has a starchy, mushy texture. Italian pasta has always been made with the finest durum semolina wheat, and some American pasta manufacturers are now using the same wheat and method of making pasta. Stock your shelves with a variety of shapes and colors of dried pasta.

Rice: Keep a supply of Italian *Arborio* and brown rice.

Flour: All-purpose white, whole wheat, semolina, and self-rising flours should be on your shelves.

Eggs: Always keep a supply of large, fresh eggs.

Wine and liqueurs: Always use the finest quality because the taste determines the success of the recipe. The alcohol is burnt off in the cooking process, so only the taste remains. Buy pure wines. Italian wines are purer and lower in sugar content than other wines except private estate wines (see the extensive wine section beginning on page 221). Another bonus is that Italian wines are inexpensive, ranging from $2.50 to $7.00 for a large bottle (1.5 liters). Keep dry white and red wine on hand or use the wine you are serving your guests, since you only use one-half to one cup for the recipe. Don't buy cooking wines or use cheap wines for cooking. You will sacrifice the *taste* of the sauce and add unnecessary chemicals and calories.

Seasoning and herbs: Thyme, sage, savory, cayenne pepper, crushed red pepper flakes, rosemary, dill weed, black pepper, white pepper, dried and fresh basil and Italian parsley, and Italian herb seasoning.

Vegetables: Fresh daily if possible, but you can freeze most root vegetables (do not freeze in any kind of sauce).

Capers: Small, in a jar.

Olives: Pitted black Italian, Sicilian, and Gaeta.

Artichoke hearts: Jarred, marinated.

Tuna fish: Canned in water.

Sardines: Small, canned in olive oil.

Anchovies: Small, canned.

Beans: Canned: white, cannellini, kidney, and garbanzo; dried white.

Lentils: Dried.

Split Peas: Dried.

Cornmeal: Fine and coarse.

Pimentos: Jar.

Yeast: Dried.

Fruit: Fresh daily.

Coffee: Espresso.

Wine: See the wine section beginning on page 243 for suggestions (don't cook with cheap wine).

Basic Kitchen Equipment You Will Need

Large sauté pan with lid: Almost all sauces, preparation and sautéing of vegetables, fish, chicken, or meat can be done in a large sauté pan (frying pan, skillet, or wok). A heavy cast iron, copper, or steel pan with a nonstick surface and a lid is extremely important for proper cooking of *la cucina Italiana*. You don't need lots of utensils to cook with—or clean up. With a large sauté pan and a pasta pot you're ready to prepare a complete meal of luscious Italian food.

Pasta pot with lid: A four- to eight-quart pot is sufficient to cook one pound of pasta properly. Pasta must cook in lots of boiling water or it will stick together. Select an enamel-coated or stainless steel pot for the best results. This pot will also come in handy for cooking soups, vegetables, and stock.

Colander: Two-quart stainless steel.

Mixing bowls: Set of five sizes, not plastic.

Wooden spoons: Set of five with long handles.

Wooden forks: Two.

Grater: Four-sided box type.

Garlic crusher: Self-cleaning.

Knives: Set of six assorted sizes.

Knife sharpener: Steel is best.

Can opener: Manual is best.

Wine opener: Self-pulling type.

Baking pans: Set of three—small, medium, and large, with nonstick coating.

Pizza pans: Circular set of three—small, medium, and large.

Baking sheets: Set of two—small and large, with nonstick coating.

Skillets: Set of three—heavy, with lids.

Saucepans: Set of five in various sizes, with lids.

Cutting board: Heavy wood.

Serving dishes: Set of four in various sizes, oven-proof.

Serving spoons: Set of four—good-quality stainless steel.

Vegetable peeler: Stainless steel (double sided).

Blender: Cuisinart type recommended.

Measuring jugs: Three assorted sizes marked in cups, ounces, quarts, and metric.

Meat thermometer: Circular clock face is best.

Whisk: Hand type is quick, easy to use, and easy to clean.

Soup ladles: Three assorted sizes.

Rolling pin: Stone or marble is best.

Pastry board: Marble is best.

Preparing Food for the Recipes

This section will help you to prepare specific ingredients. When the ingredient list calls for "roasted peppers," or "soaked eggplant," or "peeled, seeded, and diced tomatoes," or "cut vegetables," use this section as your guide for food preparation.

HOW TO ROAST PEPPERS
Procedure: Wash, dry, and cut the peppers in half lengthwise. Remove the seeds and cut off the ends. Arrange the peppers, cut side down, in a single layer on a broiler pan or cookie sheet. Broil for about ten minutes or until the peppers are charred and blistered. Try to keep them about three inches from the broiler heat. You can also use the "old method" of piercing the center of the whole pepper with a fork, and then placing it over the high flame of the top burner on your stove. Char the pepper by turning the fork.

After the peppers are charred, place them in a paper bag and seal it. Let stand for fifteen minutes to steam the peppers. Remove the peppers from the bag and peel off the skins by scraping with a knife. Be careful to remove only the blackened part. If you are not using the peppers immediately, cover them with a few tablespoons of green olive oil and crushed garlic to marinate, and refrigerate overnight. Use as an appetizer, as a snack, or in recipes. Roasted peppers can be stored in a tightly sealed jar in the refrigerator for two weeks.

Red peppers have more taste than green or yellow ones, but it is a visual as well as a culinary treat to prepare a plate of three-colored roasted peppers with mozzarella and basil for a buffet or antipasto.

HOW TO PEEL, SEED, AND CRUSH FRESH TOMATOES
Types of tomatoes: Always use the freshest, ripest Italian plum tomatoes for more taste, color, and better texture. When they are not available, use the very ripe cherry tomatoes or smaller tomatoes. For certain sauces, either whole or crushed, canned Italian plum tomatoes that are peeled can be used. Be sure to strain the seeds: they add a bitter taste to the sauce.
Procedure: Place the tomatoes in a pan or bowl of boiling water for a few seconds until the skins split, then drain, cool, and remove the skins; they will peel easily. To seed the tomatoes, cut off the bottoms and squeeze them. Use a knife to pull out seeds that remain.

HOW TO PREPARE EGGPLANT (MELANZANA)
Eggplant is one of the most favored and versatile vegetables used in Italian cooking. The key to great-tasting eggplant dishes is the method of preparation and cooking.

Selecting eggplant: There are eighteen varieties of eggplant grown around the world. The less common types can be found in specialty markets and Italian and oriental markets. The small eggplants are best for sautéing, grilling, and salads. Look for the firm, heavy (for weight), purple variety that have a clear, dark, and glossy skin. Avoid eggplants that are scarred, shriveled, soft, or have dark spots. Eggplants are very sensitive to extremes in temperature. Store them in a tightly sealed plastic bag away from fruits, and they will keep for up to four days in the refrigerator.

Frying: Peel and cut the eggplant into one-inch-thick slices, sprinkle with one tablespoon of salt, and place in a large pan of cold water. Soak for ten minutes, changing the water two or three times (the water will become brown). Drain the eggplant and dry. I have found that when a pound of eggplant that had not been salted and soaked was fried in oil, it absorbed up to ten tablespoons of oil. When soaked and salted, it absorbed only three tablespoons. Note: Salting and soaking needs to be done only if you are frying the eggplant.

Grilling or broiling: Peel and cut the eggplant into one-inch cubes and sprinkle with a few tablespoons of green olive oil. Broil or grill until brown on all sides. When grilling or broiling the large slices needed for eggplant lasagna or eggplant parmesan, scrub the skins (do not peel) and slice the eggplant very thin. Brush with green olive oil and sprinkle with Italian herb seasoning, crushed garlic, and chopped Italian parsley.

Baking: For stuffed eggplant or for making eggplant caviar, bake the eggplant whole for fifteen to twenty minutes at 350°F. Slice it in half and scoop out the center.

DRIED MUSHROOMS

It is important to soak dried mushrooms properly to get the full flavor and texture. Use a small bowl to soak about one cup of dried mushrooms in two cups of water. For more taste, use dry white, red, or marsala wine. Mushrooms should soak for a minimum of a half hour to twenty-four hours. They should be covered but not refrigerated. Drain the mushrooms, and then dry and dice them. Save the liquid to use when cooking a sauce.

Dried mushrooms have 50 percent more taste than fresh mushrooms and can really make the difference in a recipe. Dried Italian porcini mushrooms are the best. They can be found in specialty stores and local markets.

After reconstituting and dicing, cover the mushrooms with olive oil and store them in a small jar in the refrigerator, so that you are always ready to use the pungent, classic dried porcini mushrooms.

HOW TO ROAST ASPARAGUS

This method of roasting asparagus will bring out the flavor much more than the traditional method of steaming, while maintaining a pleasingly firm texture. Roasted asparagus is excellent for pasta sauces, *risotto*, and pizzas, and as an appetizer, as part of the main course, or as a cocktail food wrapped with prosciutto or cheese. It's also delicious as a salad with roasted red peppers.

Ingredients: You will need one pound of fresh, firm asparagus, trimmed and peeled halfway up from the bottom; two tablespoons of green olive oil; one medium-size lemon, cut into wedges; and freshly ground pepper to taste.

Preparation: Clean and prepare the asparagus. Place the spears on a baking sheet or pan and drizzle with the olive oil. Roast in a preheated 500°F oven for ten minutes, turning the spears to brown on all sides; avoid dark browning—roast to a light brown color. When crisp, remove the spears and sprinkle with lemon. Crush the black pepper over the asparagus. If they are dry, add more olive oil. Use them immediately or store in the refrigerator.

Use a small amount of green olive oil in the cooking process and add the raw oil (only a few drops) to the top of the dish. Remember, cooked olive oil is harder to digest than raw. If you prefer, you can use safflower oil for cooking and add green olive oil just before serving.

The National Heart Association recommends margarine for cooking. Dr. Frank Mancini suggests using safflower unsalted margarine. It is pure, easy to digest, low in calories, and unsalted, making it a healthier product than regular margarines.

All three choices are light and healthy methods of cooking and living.

CELLI'S QUICK CUTTING TECHNIQUE

I created this technique some years ago, when I had to prepare recipes quickly on my television show. It saves time, eliminates the need for constant washing and cleaning of the cutting space, and it's fun. It is done with a wrist action movement and a sharp small knife. Hold the ingredient to be cut in one hand and the knife in the other. Turn your wrist from side to side as you use the knife in the same motion, cutting the ingredient into chopped or diced pieces directly into the pan. Use the same technique to cut fruit into a bowl or salad ingredients directly into a serving bowl. It will take a few practice sessions to refine this technique, but when you want to cook and cut something quickly, it's great.

Five Secrets of the Great Cooks

If the *sauce* needs *more taste*, add cayenne pepper, Italian herb seasoning, fresh herbs, a dash of mustard, or a quarter cup of dry wine or liqueur.

If the *sauce* gets *too dry*, add more oil, wine, water, tomato sauce, or stock.

If the *spaghetti sticks*, you didn't use a large enough pot with lots of boiling water and didn't stir the pasta as you added it to the water and a few times as it was cooking. Remove, toss with cold water, and toss with olive oil to keep from sticking. Spaghetti can be stored in the refrigerator covered for four to five days. If the spaghetti is too hard to unstick, it's better to cook a new batch.

If the pasta *sauce* is *bland* or *thin*, add more grated Parmesan cheese or pepper. If it's dry, add more green olive oil and toss, or add more sauce. Add a quarter cup of arrowroot or a mashed potato to thicken.

If *soups need zip*, add cayenne pepper, Italian seasoning, and a half-cup of grated Parmesan cheese.

Capon, Mushrooms, Arugula, and Red Pepper Salad (page 156). *This salad of white capon meat, red peppers, arugula, diced artichokes, and mushrooms in an herb, onion, and mustard sauce is a visually exciting addition to any lunch or dinner party or buffet.*

**Tuscan Zuppa
D'Minestrone (page 95).**
*Truly a meal in itself,
Tuscan minestrone soup
is a luscious blend of
fresh vegetables, pasta,
beans, herbs, spices, and
prosciutto.*

**Seafood and Vegetables
alla Grill (page 139).**
*Fresh mixed seafood
marinated in green olive
oil, garlic, herbs, and
lemon, grilled with
zucchini, peppers, and
tomatoes.*

Spaghetti alla Malibu (page 79). *This dish is made with thin spaghetti tossed with a mixture of seafood cooked in a wine, tomato, and herb sauce.*

PREVIOUS PAGES: Roast Leg of Lamb with Rosemary and Fresh Mint Sauce (page 176). *A magnificent, slightly pink leg of lamb stuffed with garlic and rosemary and cooked in dry white wine. A tart rosemary and mint sauce complements this dish.*

This variation on Poached Pears with Amaretto Chocolate Cream Sauce (page 215) is done with a raspberry sauce.

The makings of a savory buffet (below) and the end product (next page). From left to right: Vitello Ripieno (page 166), stuffed veal roast with fennel and tomatoes; Torte Festiva (page 131), a vegetable torte of Swiss chard, ricotta, and roasted red peppers, covered with whole wheat pastry dough and served with two sauces (Basic Pesto and Red Pepper and Tomato Sauce); Mini-Pizzas (page 19), topped with basil, roasted eggplant, red peppers, pesto, and seafood; and a variation on Fettuccine Verde con Pommodore al Capra (page 77), tomato in the center stuffed with goat cheese and herb sauce, using green and white noodles with a garlic, olive oil, and herb sauce. Montepulciano d'Abruzzi by Emidio Peppe, and Brut sparkling wine, by Berlucci.

The author putting finishing touches on Eggplant and Pasta Rolls (page 124).

II. *The Recipes*

ANTIPASTI
Appetizers & Cocktail Foods

M O Z Z A R E L L A   I S C H I A

Hot Mozzarella with Basil, Tomatoes, Olives, and Red Peppers

3 lb. small, fresh individual mozzarellas
¼ cup green olive oil
4 cloves of garlic, crushed
1 cup Italian parsley, chopped
2 tsp. balsamic vinegar
1 cup red onions, chopped
20 olives of Gaeta or small black Italian olives
½ tsp. Italian herb seasoning
6 ripe medium-size tomatoes, each cut in 6 wedges
36 fresh basil leaves
½ cup fresh-squeezed lemon juice
4 medium-size red bell peppers, roasted and sliced julienne (see page 7)

Servings:
12
Time:
20 *min.*
Calories:
395 *per serving*

Preheat the oven at 400°F.
Place the individual mozzarellas in a baking dish and bake for 5 minutes.
  In a large bowl, mix all the other ingredients together, except the peppers, olives, onions, tomatoes, and basil, and toss to blend well.
  Place the individual mozzarellas on a single serving dish and decorate first with the roasted peppers in a crisscross fashion across the mozzarellas. Then place the basil leaves and tomatoes around the sides, and arrange the olives and onions on the top and on the sides for a beautiful visual presentation. Drizzle a small amount of dressing over each dish and serve immediately.

VARIATION
* Use goat cheese or add fresh mushrooms.

MELANZANA NUNZIE

Grilled Eggplant Slices Stuffed with Red Peppers,
Ricotta Cheese, and Olives

Servings:
4
Time:
20 *min.*
Calories:
354 *per serving*

1 large eggplant (2 lb.)
1 tbsp. salt
1 cup black olives, diced
6 fresh basil leaves, chopped (or ¼ tsp. dried crushed basil)
2 cloves of garlic, crushed
½ tsp. Italian herb seasoning
1 cup fresh Italian parsley, chopped
3 medium-size red bell peppers, roasted and finely chopped (see page 7)
Dash of cayenne pepper
¼ cup Parmesan cheese, freshly grated
1½ cups of skim-milk ricotta cheese
2 tbsp. green olive oil
2 tbsp. balsamic vinegar or red wine vinegar

Preheat the grill or broiler.

Slice the eggplant into 1-inch slices, leaving the skins on.

Soak the eggplant in the salt and cold water for 15 minutes.

Use a large mixing bowl and thoroughly blend the following ingredients: black olives, basil leaves, garlic, Italian herb seasoning, parsley, red peppers, cayenne pepper, Parmesan cheese, ricotta cheese, and 1 tablespoon of the green olive oil.

Drain and dry the eggplant slices.

Brush them with olive oil and vinegar, and sprinkle with parsley.

Grill the eggplant slices for just a few minutes on each side, until slightly browned (don't overgrill—the slices will get tough).

Brush with more olive oil, on one side only.

Line the slices on a flat surface, oiled side up.

Add about 2 tablespoons of the filling to the center of each slice and take the side closest to you and place it over the edge of the filling. Do the same with the opposite side, and fasten with a toothpick. Do not roll the eggplant slice with the filling or it will squeeze out of the sides.

Place the stuffed eggplant rolls in a serving dish, and sprinkle with parsley and Parmesan cheese.

Serve at room temperature.

VARIATIONS

* Use 1 cup of goat cheese instead of ricotta cheese.
* Try diced, seeded, and drained tomatoes instead of peppers.
* Mix 1 red and 1 green pepper.
* Use ½ teaspoon of ground sage in the filling, for an herb taste.

For cocktail foods or antipasto, cut the slices in half and place a toothpick at the top of each halved eggplant roll.

If serving as an appetizer, remove the toothpicks before serving.

This dish can be made in advance and stored in the refrigerator. Remove 1 hour before serving.

ZUCCHINI AND TOMATO CAVIAR

Antipasto, Stuffing, or Sauce

3 medium-size zucchini (2 lbs.)
⅛ cup green olive oil
2 tbsp. fresh lemon juice
2 small cloves of garlic, crushed
1 cup green bell pepper, finely chopped
1 large ripe tomato, peeled, seeded, and chopped very fine
½ cup green onions, minced
⅓ cup fresh Italian parsley, chopped
¼ tsp. pepper (black or cayenne)
1 cup fresh mushrooms, finely chopped
½ cup black olives, finely diced

Yield:
4 *cups*
Time:
15 *min.*
Calories:
13 *per tbsp.*

Add zucchini to rapidly boiling water in a 4-quart saucepan. Cover and cook for 10 minutes. Drain and cool.

Chop the zucchini finely with a sharp knife or in a food processor using an on-off motion. Put the zucchini in a fine sieve to drain; press out all juices. There should be about 2 to 3 cups of mashed, drained zucchini.

Combine the oil, lemon juice, garlic, and pepper; mix well.

In another bowl, mix the zucchini with the remaining ingredients, and then toss with the oil and lemon juice mixture.

VARIATIONS
* Try ½ cup freshly grated Parmesan cheese.
* Use diced black olives.

Can be served immediately or stored in the refrigerator for up to 4 days.

Great as an appetizer, or spread over squares of garlic-toasted bread.

Also delicious as a sauce over fish, chicken, or pasta, or in hollowed-out tomatoes, pepper, zucchini, or eggplant.

E G G P L A N T   C A V I A R   S A L A

Dip for Vegetables or Crackers

Yield:
2½ *cups*
Time:
8 *min.*
Calories:
54 *per tbsp.*

1 large eggplant (2 lbs.)
2 tbsp. green olive oil
2 cloves of garlic, crushed
6 shallots, peeled and diced
Dash of cayenne pepper
3 tbsp. lemon juice
¼ cup fresh Italian parsley, chopped

Place the halved eggplant on a cookie sheet skin side down and broil for 5 minutes. Scoop out the pulp and cool for a few minutes.

Use a sauté pan and add the oil, garlic, shallots, and pepper and cook for 5 minutes.

Put this mixture in a blender with the lemon juice, parsley, and eggplant pulp and blend for a few seconds, until smooth.

Chill until ready to serve. Before serving, bring the dip to room temperature for more taste and better spreading consistency.

VARIATIONS
* Add one roasted red pepper, diced and sautéed, to the mixture.
* Add 1 tablespoon of mustard (Dijon type).

Serve as a spread over wheat crackers or as a dip with raw vegetables or grilled garlic toasts.

The eggplant dip can also be used as a sauce over fish, chicken, veal, or pasta—just heat for a few minutes and serve.

M I N I - P O L E N T A   P I Z Z A S

Servings:
26 *mini-pizzas*
Time:
70 *min. plus refrigeration time*
Calories:
86 *per serving*

BASE (to be prepared first)
4 cups cold water
2 cups fine cornmeal
½ cup Parmesan cheese, freshly grated
1 medium egg

TOPPING

2 tbsp. green olive oil
2 cups fresh tomatoes, peeled and chopped
1 cup Parmesan cheese, freshly grated
3 cups fresh mushrooms, thinly sliced
¾ cup black olives, diced
½ tsp. Italian herb seasoning
1 cup green pepper, chopped

THE BASE

Boil 2½ cups of water in a medium-size saucepan.

In a separate bowl, mix the cornmeal with 1½ cups of cold water, stirring to a smooth, thick paste. Add this mixture to the boiling water, stirring constantly for about 5 minutes. Reduce the heat and simmer gently for another 15 minutes or until the polenta mixture is thick, smooth, and soft.

Remove the mixture from the heat and add the Parmesan cheese; blend through until well mixed and smooth. Allow the polenta to cool a little, then beat in the egg.

Spoon the mixture into two lightly oiled, 8-inch round pizza pans. Store in the bottom of the refrigerator for several hours until a crust has formed and the surface is fairly dry.

TO BAKE

Preheat the oven at 375°F.

Brush the surface of the two polenta pizzas with half of the olive oil. Cover with the tomatoes and the Parmesan cheese. Top with mushroom slices, olives, Italian herb seasoning, and green peppers. Sprinkle pizzas with the remaining oil and bake for 45 minutes. Remove the pizzas, cool for a few minutes, and serve.

For mini-pizzas, use a large, round cookie cutter to cut out circular pieces. Place them on a baking sheet or serving dish to serve immediately.

To reheat, place under the broiler for a few minutes.

VARIATIONS

* Try different toppings made from seafood, zucchini strips, or shredded mozzarella cheese.
* Add a dash of cayenne pepper and fresh minced basil leaves.

This certainly will please and surprise your guests instead of the usual cocktail food or antipasto. As an appetizer, serve three different mini-polenta pizzas.

PEPPERS STUFFED WITH PASTA ADEE

Peppers Stuffed with Pasta in Caper and Anchovy Sauce

Servings:
4
Time:
20 *min.*
Calories:
400 *per serving*

½ lb. thin spaghetti
4 large green peppers (whole)
4 large red peppers (whole)
1 cup onions, chopped
3 cloves of garlic, crushed
1 anchovy filet, rinsed and mashed
½ tsp. Italian herb seasoning
2 tbsp. green olive oil
2 cups fresh plum tomatoes, diced; or 1 cup canned, crushed and drained
Dash of pepper, black or cayenne
2 tbsp. small capers, rinsed
¼ cup black olives, diced
½ cup fresh Italian parsley, chopped
¼ cup Parmesan cheese, freshly grated

Preheat oven at 350°F. Boil water to cook the pasta.

Wash the peppers and remove the tops and the insides, leaving a clean shell. Drop shells in boiling water for 3 minutes. Remove and drain.

Sauté the onions, garlic, anchovies, and Italian herb seasoning in the oil for 2 to 3 minutes; add the tomatoes, pepper, capers, olives, and parsley and cook for 5 minutes.

Drain the pasta, and transfer it to a large pasta bowl.

Pour the sauce over the pasta and mix thoroughly. Sprinkle the Parmesan cheese over the pasta and toss through.

Put a tablespoon of olive oil on the bottom of a large baking dish and place the pepper shells in it. Use a small fork and fill each pepper shell to the top with the pasta and sauce mixture.

Decorate each stuffed pepper with a slice of olive and a parsley leaf. Bake in the oven for 8 minutes, then remove and serve immediately.

VARIATIONS

* Use large, raw, hollowed-out tomatoes instead of peppers.
* Eliminate the Parmesan cheese and use ½ cup of crumbled goat cheese or ricotta cheese.
* Mix the pasta with 1 cup of mixed seafood or chicken.
* Use tuna, capers, olives, and marinated sliced artichoke hearts in place of the sauce, or stuff with chopped spinach and ricotta, instead of the pasta.

Also perfect for a main course, two stuffed peppers per person.
Great for lunch, brunch, buffets, or outdoor parties.

C R O S T I N I ' S   A S S O R T I

Browned Italian Bread Squares with Vegetables, Seafood,
Cheese, Pesto, or Olive Pâté

1 long, slender loaf of crisp-crusted Italian bread (white or wheat)
4 tbsp. green olive oil
5 cloves of garlic, crushed
2 cups diced vegetables (fresh plum tomatoes, eggplant, red pepper, or
    mushrooms)
    or 2 cups diced seafood (shrimp, crab, clams, or white fish)
    or 1 cup ricotta cheese mixed with 1 cup Parmesan cheese, freshly grated
    or 1 cup Basic Pesto Sauce (see page 197)
    or 2 cups black olive purée or olives of Gaeta (small purple), chopped
1 cup onions, chopped
½ cup fresh basil leaves, minced
1 cup fresh Italian parsley, chopped
¼ tsp. cayenne pepper

> *Servings:*
> **15**
> *Time:*
> **20** *min.*
> *Calories:*
> **127** *to* **210**
> *per slice,*
> *depending on*
> *topping**

Cut the bread into thin, ¼-inch slices. Brush with olive oil and crushed garlic, and place under the broiler or on the grill until browned.

DICED VEGETABLE TOPPING
Dice the vegetables and sauté with oil, garlic, and onions. Top with basil and parsley (tomatoes can be served raw with herbs).

SEAFOOD TOPPING
Seafood should be sautéed for only a few minutes in 2 tablespoons of oil, with onions (no garlic) and a dash of cayenne pepper.

CHEESE TOPPING
Mix the ricotta cheese and the Parmesan cheese in a small bowl. Add the herbs, a dash of cayenne pepper, 1 tablespoon of green olive oil, and 1 tablespoon of crushed garlic. Put in a blender and blend until smooth and well mixed.

PESTO SAUCE
Follow the recipe for Basic Pesto Sauce on page 197.

OLIVE PURÉE PÂTÉ TOPPING
Chop the olives. Put in a blender with 1 tablespoon of olive oil, 1 tablespoon of garlic, parsley, and dash of cayenne pepper.

Spread topping on the browned, garlic-oiled bread to serve. You can broil the cheese and seafood for a few minutes . . . it is best to serve the toasts hot.

*Calories will vary depending on topping: vegetables, 127 per slice; seafood, 160 per slice; cheese, 180 per slice; pesto, 210 per slice; olive pâté, 160 per slice.

VARIATIONS

* Use shredded skim-milk mozzarella cheese as an addition to the olive, Pesto Sauce, and vegetable toppings.
* Add crumbled goat cheese.
* Mix the Pesto Sauce with the seafood or vegetable toppings.
* Use 1 cup boiled mashed chicken livers, sautéed with oil, onions, garlic, and herbs and serve on toast (this is popular in Florence, Italy).
* Use red pepper (roasted) purée (see page 7) with sautéed mushrooms.
* Use eggplant with red pepper and mushroom purée.
* Use tomatoes with mushrooms and herbs.
* Use seafood with fresh or sun-dried tomatoes or mushrooms.

Use all of the toppings and serve an assortment. Serve as cocktail food, appetizers, or for brunch or as the first-course appetizer.

ANTIPASTO — MINI-PIZZAS

Yield:
26 *mini-pizzas*
Time:
25 *min.*
Calories:
26 *per slice,*
low-calorie crust;
75 *per slice,*
regular pizza
bread dough

Low-calorie pizza crust, pizza bread dough, or regular pizza dough
Toppings (see pizza section beginning on page 102)

Preheat oven at 425°F.
Bake the pizza crusts for 10 to 15 minutes. Remove from oven and cover with selected pizza topping.
Use a large, round cookie cutter and cut the individual mini-pizzas. Place them on a baking sheet.
Return to oven and bake for 5 to 8 minutes (depending on topping).
Serve immediately.

VARIATIONS

* Use large, square cookie cutters or mix the shapes for interest.
* Add Red Pepper and Tomato Sauce (see page 193) to some for a red pizza dough, and Basic Pesto Sauce (page 197) to others for a green pizza dough to make a colorful presentation.

Can be made ahead of time. After cutting circular pizzas, place them on cooking sheet and store until ready to serve. Bake 5 to 8 minutes and serve hot.

POTATO - SEMOLINA
GNOCCHI

2 lb. baking potatoes (whole)
5 egg yolks
1½ cups all-purpose flour
½ cup fine semolina
½ cup unsalted butter (room temperature)

Servings:
Makes about **26**
Time:
25 *min. plus*
refrigeration time
Calories:
103 *per serving*

Boil the potatoes until tender. Drain and peel. Press through a sieve into a large bowl. Add the remaining ingredients and beat until smooth. Chill until firm (½ hour in the freezer, 1 hour in the refrigerator).

Boil water to cook the gnocchi.

Shape the dough into long, thin ¾-inch rolls. Cut into 1-inch-thick pieces and cook in boiling water, in small groups, for about 10 minutes, until the pieces are light enough to come to the surface.

Remove gnocchi from the water with a large, slotted spoon and place them in a large warm bowl. Add sauce and cheese of your choice and toss. Serve immediately.

VARIATIONS

* Add ½ cup cooked, chopped spinach (drained very well).
* Add ½ cup Romano cheese.
* Eliminate the potatoes and use 1 cup ricotta cheese.

Excellent as an appetizer, lunch, brunch, or main course with a great variety of sauces.

C L A M S   C O L O R O S S I

Baked, Stuffed Clams

Servings:
6 *(4 clams per person)*
Time:
25 *min.*
Calories:
293 *per serving*

24 cherrystone clams, well washed
¼ cup champagne (or dry spumante)
½ stick of unsalted butter
3 tbsp. shallots, finely chopped
3 cloves of garlic, finely chopped
¼ cup panchetta (or prosciutto), finely diced
1 tsp. fresh basil, minced
1 cup unseasoned bread crumbs
½ cup crumbled goat cheese
1 tbsp. green olive oil
Black or cayenne pepper to taste
48 thin strips of dried tomatoes (or red peppers)

Preheat oven at 375°F.

Open the clams and separate them by draining the juice in one bowl and the clams in another. Strain the juice through a fine strainer to remove all grit, and set aside 24 well-washed shells for stuffing.

Place the clam juice and champagne in a saucepan and heat to reduce to ½ cup of liquid. Set aside to cool.

Coarsely chop the clam meat and place it in a bowl, adding and mixing all the other ingredients except the dried tomatoes.

Spoon portions of the mixture into the clam shells. Brush lightly with green olive oil, and decorate with crisscrosses of dried tomatoes.

Bake the stuffed clam shells for 15 to 18 minutes, or until they start to brown. Serve immediately.

VARIATION

* Use shredded mozzarella cheese or ricotta instead of goat cheese.

P E P P E R O N A T A   K A R I N A

Peppers, Olives, Capers, Tomatoes, and Eggs

2 large hard-boiled eggs
1 tbsp. green olive oil
1 small white onion, chopped
4 small bell peppers, 2 red and 2 green, diced
3 cloves of garlic, crushed
Dash of pepper
1 cup fresh mushrooms, diced
1 tbsp. balsamic vinegar, or red wine vinegar
2 very ripe plum tomatoes, or 6 cherry tomatoes, chopped
1 tbsp. small capers
12 lettuce leaves for garnish
¼ cup fresh Italian parsley, minced
6 small black olives, chopped

Servings:	**2**
Time:	**10** *min.*
Calories:	**222** *per serving*

Boil water to cook the eggs.

In a large frying pan, combine the oil, onion, peppers, garlic, and seasoning, and cook, covered, for 5 minutes.

Add the mushrooms, vinegar, tomatoes, and capers; cook for 3 to 4 minutes (uncovered).

Remove the cooked eggs, and cover them with cold water to cool.

Remove the shells and slice each egg into 4 wedges.

Decorate 2 plates with lettuce leaves. Divide the pepper mixture, place a portion in the center of each plate, and sprinkle with parsley.

Place 4 egg wedges around the dish and sprinkle with parsley.

Place 3 olives around each plate.

Serve at room temperature. The mixture can be prepared ahead of time and refrigerated; remove 1 hour before serving.

VARIATIONS

* Leave off the capers and vinegar if too tart; use a dash of Italian herb seasoning.
* Add a small amount of crumbled goat cheese on top, or a sprinkling of Romano or Parmesan cheese.
* For a strong peppery taste, roast the peppers first (see page 7); then seed and dice them, and toss with olive oil, hot pepper, and crushed garlic.

Perfect for lunch, brunch, and as an appetizer or a snack with crisp Italian bread and a good red wine. Also good with a small slice of hard white cheese.

If watching cholesterol, leave out the eggs and use asparagus tips or mix with shredded zucchini.

EMILIO'S RICOTTA PUFFS

Ricotta Balls with Prosciutto, Eggs, and Herbs

Servings:
8
Time:
15 *min.*
Calories:
265 *per serving*

2 cups skim-milk ricotta cheese
¼ cup prosciutto, diced
½ tsp. nutmeg
½ cup Italian parsley, finely chopped
3 eggs
2 cups safflower oil
1 cup toasted plain breadcrumbs
¼ cup Parmesan cheese, freshly grated

Mix all ingredients except breadcrumbs, oil, and Parmesan cheese, in a large bowl. Form into small balls.

Roll in breadcrumbs that are mixed with 3 tablespoons of Parmesan cheese.

Heat the oil in a saucepan; when hot, drop in the ricotta balls. Cook for 3 minutes, and place on paper towels to drain.

Place the balls on a serving platter. Serve with a choice of Red Pepper and Tomato Sauce (page 193), Basic Pesto Sauce, (page 197), or Ricotta Cheesy Sauce (page 194).

VARIATIONS
* Mix ricotta with sautéed, diced mushrooms and zucchini instead of prosciutto.
* Use diced tomatoes and basil, or diced roasted red and green peppers (see page 7) with the ricotta.
* Roll ricotta balls in just Parmesan cheese (no breadcrumbs).

BRUSCHETTA ALLA DANIEL

Toasted Bread with Pesto, Peppers, and Cheese

Servings:
10
(2 brushchettas per person)
Time:
15 *min.*
Calories:
275 *per serving*

Loaf of crusty Italian or French bread
1 cup Basic Pesto Sauce (see page 197)
1 red pepper, roasted and diced (see page 7)
¼ cup goat cheese
½ cup arugula or mache leaves, chopped
Dash of cayenne pepper

Cut two 5-inch pieces from the loaf of bread. Cut each piece in half lengthwise. Toast under a broiler for about 1 minute.

Spread with pesto sauce and top with diced red pepper, cheese, and arugula. Sprinkle with pepper.

Cut into 1-inch-thick slices, and serve warm.

VARIATIONS

* Use chopped black olives or sautéed, sliced mushrooms.
* Peeled and seeded fresh tomatoes (diced) can be substituted for red peppers.

Seafood can be diced and mixed with the pesto for a topping, so this dish can be used as an appetizer as well as cocktail food. Place 3 in a dish and decorate with arugula leaves.

G A M B E R I   C O N   A G L I O

Shrimp with Garlic Sauce

¼ cup green olive oil
4 cloves of garlic, crushed
1½ lb. medium shrimp, shelled and deveined
1 tbsp. of fresh-squeezed lemon juice
½ cup dry white wine
½ cup fresh Italian parsley, chopped

Servings:
6 *(4 shrimp per person)*
Time:
15 *min.*
Calories:
180 *per serving*

In a large frying pan, combine the oil and garlic; sauté for a few minutes. Add the shrimp, lemon juice, and wine and toss. Cook the shrimp for a few minutes.

Sprinkle with the parsley and toss through the sauce. Remove from heat.

Serve immediately alone, or with rice or pasta of your choice.

VARIATIONS

* Red wine can be substituted for white wine.
* Use 1 tablespoon of crushed red pepper.
* 1 cup of fresh sliced mushrooms can be added.

This dish can be used as an appetizer or as a main course.

RED PEPPER, BASIL GRANITA

Servings:
8
Time:
20 min.
Calories:
32 per serving

2 lb. red bell peppers, roasted (see page 7)
1 cup water
1 6-oz. can tomato juice
Dash of cayenne pepper
½ cup fresh basil leaves, minced
2 tbsp. lemon juice
8 celery stalks
8 parsley sprigs

Set aside roasted peppers.

Combine the water, tomato juice, cayenne pepper, basil leaves, and lemon juice in a saucepan; bring to a boil.

Cool the mixture, and combine it with the peppers in a blender or food processor and purée.

Pour the mixture into an 8-inch saucepan and cool to room temperature.

Freeze it on the flat surface of the freezer for up to 4 hours; stir every 20 minutes.

When ready to serve, place the mixture in the refrigerator for 15 minutes. Garnish with celery stalks and parsley sprigs.

VARIATION

* Use minced Italian parsley if fresh basil is not available.

Great between courses as intermezzo or as an appetizer with puréed zucchini.

PASTA

The Essence of Italy: Pasta!

Passionate about pasta? I am. Isn't everyone? Pasta is an Italian passion that has spread throughout the world. For many reasons, pasta has become the "in food": It is a wonderful combination of exciting tastes and high fiber; it's a high-energy food; an appetite suppressant that's low in calories; quick, easy, and economical to cook; and unbelievably versatile. After fifteen years of writing books and articles and talking about pasta on hundreds of television programs, I'm delighted to see that pasta has at last come into its own and been vindicated.

Pasta was first served in Italy during the days of the Roman Empire. Disregard the claims that Marco Polo discovered pasta in China. He only brought back a thinner noodle made from rice flour. In 1279, Italians in Rome, Padua, and Genoa were eating ravioli and fettuccine. Marco Polo didn't get back from China until 1295!

Pasta is a simple, basic food, but *warda!* what a cook can do with it. Pasta can be molded, layered, rolled, stuffed, sautéed, fried, boiled, and baked. It can even be colored with anything from squid ink to puréed herbs or vegetables. It can be served hot, cold, or sweet as a dessert. You can store it in the refrigerator, heat it up, and rehash it with a new sauce.

You can purchase pasta in dozens of shapes, colors, types, and brands. It comes fresh, frozen, dried, precooked, and canned (I don't recommend the latter). Pasta offers even the humblest of cooks the joy of being creative: There are millions of enticing sauce combinations that are quick and easy to make.

You can entertain with wonderful pasta buffets, from the very simple tomato, onion, and garlic sauce to the very elaborate and expensive sauces made from caviar, porcini mushrooms, lobster, salmon, scampi, goat cheese, or Gorgonzola.

In restaurants, pasta costs from $3 to more than $20 per serving, depending on the class of restaurant and the sauce you order. Pasta itself is cheap: In the supermarket, even the best brands seldom cost more than $1.50 per pound. You can get a usable, semolina wheat noodle for as little as $.50 per pound. Beware: If you're looking for bargains, don't make the mistake of buying the cheapest before you're sure it is made from 100 percent durum semolina wheat. Remember, white flour pasta is mushy when cooked, very high in calories, and void of nutrients.

Fresh pastas are more expensive, mainly because of the time it takes to make them, and very often they are made with a white flour–semolina mixture. Because of the time, expense, and work involved, most pasta aficionados don't make their own pasta, except for special occasions or a special type of pasta.

Pasta is the food of people who are conscious of their health and diet. It's a staple food of athletes. As an actress, I can assure you that almost all the famous movie stars I have worked with are pasta zealots. I quickly converted those who were not. Pasta is the perfect high-energy, low-fat, low-calorie food for celebrities, as well as for people who need lots of stamina and who need to look good and stay slim.

A luscious plate of pasta communicates a visual promise of seductive pleasure in the eating, a promise that is succulently fulfilled with each gently resistant, salacious bite. It's the manna of the aristocrat and the life blood of the masses—truly a food for all seasons.

The pasta chapter is the longest one in this book. There is so much to say, so much to show, and such an enormous variety of recipes to choose from: classic, creative, trendy. They're all included!

Bravo for pasta! Eat it and stay slim and healthy.

All About Pasta

It's crucial to always use the right kind of pasta. Make sure the package reads: "Made from 100 percent durum semolina wheat." Beware: Read the small print if it just says "made from durum wheat" but does not specify the proportions. The ingredients are always printed on both the American and imported Italian brands that you find in your supermarkets. The only exception to this rule may be certain Italian brands found only in gourmet specialty shops. If you like to make your own pasta, you should buy semolina wheat and blend it with a small amount of white flour. Some people prefer whole wheat pasta; it certainly is nutritious, but the hard texture and taste do not appeal to everyone.

The colored pastas you see in the markets are made from vegetable purées; tomatoes and many other vegetables are used. You may even see a black pasta made from squid ink. They, too, should be made with durum semolina wheat.

Dried pastas should be stored in a cool place in a sealed container. Fresh pastas should be wrapped in wax paper and stored in the freezer or refrigerator.

SAUCES

It is important to select the right sauce for the right pasta. Thin sauces should be used with thin pasta: Thin spaghetti, capellini (angel hair), or linguine go best with Basic Marinara Sauce or Basic Pesto Sauce. Thick pasta, such as penne, ziti, rigatoni, or other short shapes, as well as fettuccine, are best with chicken, meat, fish, chunky vegetables, and cheese sauces.

The amount of sauce is equally important: It should be proportionate to the amount of pasta. Italians insist that pasta has its own delicate, distinctive flavor, and the sauce should complement that flavor, not overpower and destroy it. Not to mention all the unnecessary calories that come with using too much sauce. Using the proper amount of sauce means that no sauce, or very little, will be left on the plate.

The type of sauce you choose determines the amount of calories. Heavy buttery, cheesy, creamy, and meat sauce bases are high in calories and hard to digest. For cheese sauces, use skim-milk ricotta, goat cheese, or shredded skim-milk mozzarella cheese. These are low in fat, salt, and cream and high in protein. For fresh grated cheese, use only Parmesan, Romano, or Pecorino cheese. Don't use prepackaged grated cheeses, which are high in calories, salt, chemicals, and preservatives. And their taste and texture are nothing like the real thing.

Some restaurants offer cheese with all pasta sauces because the customers request it. It is a matter of taste; however, for classic Italian cooking, the sauces with fish are served without cheese. Always use cheese sparingly so the delicate tastes of the sauce will not be overpowered by the cheese.

COOKING PASTA

A four-quart pot is sufficient to cook one pound of pasta properly. Use a larger pot when cooking more than one pound. Fill the pot to about three inches from the top with cold water. Cover the pot and bring the water to a boil. (There is no need to add oil to the water; the addition of salt is optional.) When the water boils, add the pasta and, using a wooden fork, stir it immediately to prevent sticking.

Pasta should *always* be cooked and served al dente. *Al dente* refers to the firmness of the cooked pasta. Cooking pasta properly to keep this firmness will depend on the timing. Test the pasta by biting into a piece to see whether it has the firmness you want. "Mushy" pasta is a disaster: It is too overcooked for the perfect taste and texture of pasta.

You will learn quickly that two to three minutes is perfect timing for the very thin angel hair (capellini) pasta; the thin spaghetti takes a few minutes longer. Shapes like penne, rigatoni, rotini, and fettuccine noodles will require five to eight minutes. *Al dente* means "firm to the bite"; therefore, keep the pasta firm, not mushy. If you do this, the right pasta and the perfect sauce can be appreciated.

THE "SEGRETTO METHOD" OF COOKING PASTA

My mother taught me to use this "secret method" when we entertained guests. When you have many courses to serve, and the pasta must be served at a certain time, this method will be very helpful. It keeps the pasta and the sauce "on hold" until you are ready to serve them. This method doesn't apply to all sauces because some sauces are so delicate that they must be served immediately. However, it works very well with tomato, vegetable, herb, chicken, and meat sauces. Seafood sauces get tough and change taste quickly, so they must be served as soon as the sauce is ready. Creamy sauces separate; they should be mixed and served quickly. For entertaining, choose a sauce that will fit the "Segretto Method," and you will be assured of the right timing and taste.

Segretto Method: Undercook the pasta by a minute. Rinse in cold water to stop the cooking process, and drain well. Mix the pasta with the sauce, which also needs another minute to cook and finish. When ready to serve the pasta and sauce, heat and cook for another one to two minutes, and serve immediately. The mixed pasta and sauce can sit on the back of the stove a short time before heating and cooking, or can be stored in the refrigerator for longer periods of time.

EATING PASTA

The best way to eat pasta is to lift the fork with four or five strands of pasta on it, and slant it against the edge or flat space on the dish. Roll with the fork pointed straight up, not slanted, so the strands will not unravel. Then lift the fork directly to your mouth, as you lean into the dish. Rolling the pasta with the fork straight up ensures an even amount around the fork. If the sauce is chunky, use the same procedure, but, after you first twirl the strands, spear a piece of meat, fish, vegetable, or chicken as your twirl the pasta around the fork.

Using a spoon, instead of the dish, to twirl the pasta around the fork, and lifting both the spoon and fork to your mouth is another method of eating pasta. This method works especially well with thinner sauces because it helps you to taste the sauce with the pasta.

You are now ready to enjoy all the joys of eating pasta. *Saluta*, pasta!

PASTA ALLA SCHIAPPA

Pasta with Wild Mushrooms, Peas, Prosciutto, *and Sun-Dried Tomatoes*

Servings:
6
Time:
20 *min.*
Calories:
427 *per serving*

1 lb. thin spaghetti
2 oz. dried porcini mushrooms (soaked in water ½ hour)
1 tbsp. green olive oil
1 cup onion, chopped
½ cup prosciutto, diced
½ tsp. Italian herb seasoning
1 cup fresh or frozen peas
½ cup sun-dried red tomatoes (marinated in olive oil and garlic), diced
3 cloves of garlic, crushed
Dash of black or cayenne pepper
¼ cup Parmesan cheese, freshly grated
½ cup fresh Italian parsley, chopped

Boil the water to cook the pasta.

Dry the presoaked mushrooms.

In a large frying pan, combine the olive oil, onion, prosciutto, mushrooms, Italian herb seasoning, peas, sun-dried tomatoes, garlic, and pepper and sauté for 5 minutes over medium heat, stirring often.

Drain the pasta, and place it in a large pasta bowl. Add the Parmesan cheese and parsley.

Add the sauce and blend thoroughly. Serve immediately.

VARIATIONS

* Use roasted red peppers (see page 7) instead of sun-dried tomatoes.
* Try chicken instead of prosciutto.

Great as a first course or a main course at a lunch, brunch, dinner party, or buffet with short pasta. It's visually pleasing, and tastes luscious.

PASTA CON LIMONE ALLA STEFANO ORSINI

Pasta in Lemon Sauce

1 lb. thin spaghetti
½ cup lemon juice, freshly squeezed
2 tbsp. lemon rind, grated
¼ cup Romano cheese, freshly grated
2 tbsp. Italian parsley, chopped
4 tbsp. unsalted butter

Servings:
4
Time:
10 *min.*
Calories:
550 *per serving*

Boil water to cook the pasta.

Mix the lemon juice and lemon rind.

Cook the pasta al dente, drain, and place in a frying pan over a low flame. Toss the pasta with the butter for a few minutes. Add the lemon juice and stir thoroughly.

Add the Romano cheese and parsley and toss to mix well. Serve immediately.

VARIATION

* Add thinly sliced mushrooms.

Great light pasta dish for an appetizer or main course.

GIUSEPPE'S PASTA SICILIA

Sicilian-Style Pasta with Broccoli, Raisins, and Pignoli

Servings:
8
Time:
10 *to* **15** *min.*
Calories:
475 *per serving*

1 lb. short-shape pasta (penne, rigatoni, rotini, or fusilli)
2 lb. broccoli (florets only)
4 tbsp. green olive oil
2 cups onion, chopped
6 cloves of garlic, crushed
1 tbsp. Italian herb seasoning
1 tbsp. crushed red pepper
2 lb. ripe tomatoes, peeled, seeded, and coarsely chopped (preferably plum tomatoes); or, if fresh is unavailable, use 2 large cans crushed Italian plum tomatoes
1 cup small red raisins
½ cup pignoli nuts
2 cups fresh Italian parsley, chopped
½ cup Parmesan cheese, freshly grated

Boil water to cook pasta.
Cut broccoli florets into 2-inch pieces.
In a large, heavy skillet or frying pan, combine the oil, onion, garlic, broccoli, Italian herb seasoning, and pepper and cook covered for 8 minutes.
Add the tomatoes and cook for 5 minutes, stirring occasionally.
Add the raisins, pine nuts, and parsley and cook for 5 minutes.
Drain the pasta, and put it in a large pan or a large pasta bowl.
Pour the sauce over the pasta in small amounts and toss thoroughly until all the sauce has been used in the pasta.
Add the Parmesan cheese and mix thoroughly. Serve immediately.

VARIATIONS
* Use colored rotini only, or, use only small penne.
* Add diced almonds instead of pignoli nuts.
* Try more hot pepper for a spicy yet sweet (from the raisins) taste.
* Use red pepper instead of tomatoes (2 cups chopped).

If made in advance for a buffet, use the "Segretto Method" (see page 28). Undercook the pasta and sauce. Drain the pasta and rinse in cold water to stop the cooking process, then add to the sauce. (Use a large pan or two to reheat when needed for a few minutes.) If the pasta seems dry, add a few tablespoons of olive oil when heating. Serve warm.

This is an ideal buffet dish: It is visually pleasing—two shapes of pasta and the green and red colors mixed with raisins and nuts.

PASTA DIO

Chicken, Red Peppers, and Arugula

4 medium-size chicken breasts, deboned and diced
1 lb. short-shape pasta (penne, rigatoni, ziti, or rotini)
3 tbsp. green olive oil
1 cup shallots or onions, chopped
3 red peppers, roasted and diced (see page 7)
3 cloves of garlic, crushed
¼ tsp. red pepper, crushed
2 cups arugula leaves, diced into 1-inch pieces (or spinach, rapini, or swiss chard)
½ tsp. Italian herb seasoning
¼ tsp. thyme
4 tbsp. Romano cheese, freshly grated

Servings:
6
Time:
15 *min.*
Calories:
558 *per serving*

Flatten and dice the chicken breasts into ½-inch cubes.

Boil the water for the pasta.

In a large frying pan or wok, combine the oil, onions, peppers, garlic, and chicken cubes. Sauté for about 5 minutes, stirring often.

Add crushed pepper, arugula leaves, Italian herb seasoning, and thyme. Cook for another 3 to 5 minutes, stirring to blend thoroughly.

Cook the pasta and drain; transfer it to a big pasta bowl or to a wok. Stir in the sauce and Romano cheese, and blend well. Serve immediately.

VARIATIONS
* Add mushrooms.
* Use fish or turkey cubes instead of chicken.

Very colorful, tasty, and light, this dish is perfect as a appetizer or main course, and is excellent for buffets.

PASTA ALLA EMILIO

Tomato and Herb Sauce

Servings:
6
Time:
15 *min.*
Calories:
342 *per serving*

1 lb. pasta capellini or thin spaghetti
½ cup leeks (ends, only), diced
4 cloves of garlic, crushed
2 tbsp. green olive oil
½ tsp. crushed red pepper flakes
½ cup dry Italian white wine
1 10-oz. can Italian imported tomatoes, seeded, diced, drained
2 bay leaves
8 fresh basil leaves, minced

Boil water to cook the pasta.

In a large frying pan or skillet, sauté the leeks, garlic, oil, and pepper together for a few minutes. Add the wine and cook for 1 minute. Then add the tomatoes and bay leaves and cook for 5 minutes. Add the basil and toss thoroughly. Remove the bay leaves.

Slightly undercook the pasta and drain.

Add the pasta to the pan with the sauce and cook for another 2 minutes, mixing the pasta and sauce thoroughly.

Serve immediately. Do *not* add cheese to this sauce because it may upset the delicate taste and special balance of the sauce.

VARIATIONS
* Serve the sauce over fish, chicken, or veal instead of pasta.
* Serve with Emilio's Ricotta Puffs, (see page 22), as an appetizer.
* Serve as cocktail food on Bruschetta (see page 22). For this recipe, the canned tomatoes have more taste than fresh tomatoes.
* Add mushrooms for variety.

S P A G H E T T I   S A L S A
V E R D E   E N R I C O

1 lb. thin spaghetti
3 tightly packed cups of fresh basil leaves
1 bunch of Italian parsley, chopped
3 large cloves of garlic, crushed
2 anchovies, washed, drained, mashed
¼ cup green olive oil
3 tbsp. lemon juice
Pepper to taste
2 6½-oz. cans of white chunky tuna in water (drained)

Servings:
6
Time:
20 min.
Calories:
409 per serving

Boil water to cook the pasta.

In a food processor (or blender), process basil, parsley, and garlic until finely chopped. Add anchovies, oil, lemon juice, and pepper. Purée to a smooth paste.

Carefully flake the tuna into a large bowl and gently fold in the mixture.

Cook the spaghetti until al dente. Drain and rinse, return to pan, and add 3 tablespoons of olive oil.

Over a moderate flame, heat the spaghetti, tossing with oil until hot. Add the tuna mixture and toss lightly. Serve immediately. (Add Parmesan cheese if desired.)

VARIATIONS
* Use whitefish, shrimp, or calamari instead of tuna.
* Use minced pimentos for color.

PASTA PINO — EGGPLANT, TOMATOES, RICOTTA

Servings:
4
Time:
15 *min. (15 min. to soak the eggplant)*
Calories:
468 *per serving*

¾ lb. Orecchiette pasta or penne
1 medium-size eggplant
1 tbsp. salt
2 tbsp. green olive oil
1 cup onion, diced
3 cloves of garlic, crushed
½ cup sun-dried tomatoes, diced
½ cup fresh Italian parsley, chopped
¼ tsp. Italian herb seasoning
Dash of black pepper
¼ cup skim-milk ricotta cheese

Boil water to cook the pasta.

Peel the eggplant; dice it and soak in cold water with 1 tablespoon of salt for 15 minutes. Rinse it two or three times and dry with paper towels.

In a large sauté pan, combine the oil, onion, garlic, and eggplant; sauté 3 to 5 minutes. Add the sun-dried tomatoes, parsley, and Italian herb seasoning. Cook for 3 minutes.

Drain the pasta and transfer it to a warm, large bowl.

Mix the pasta with the sauce and add the ricotta cheese and pepper. Blend the pasta and sauce mixture thoroughly. Serve immediately.

VARIATIONS
* Add porcini mushrooms or crushed hot pepper flakes.
* Use goat cheese instead of ricotta.
* Add fresh, diced plum tomatoes instead of sun-dried tomatoes.
* Add fresh, diced basil leaves.

S P A G H E T T I N I A L L A
C H I T A R R A A B R U Z Z I

Pasta with Traditional Abruzzi Tomato Sauce

½ lb. Chitarra pasta, capellini, or thin spaghetti
1 medium-size onion, chopped
2 cloves of garlic, crushed
3 tbsp. green olive oil
10 ripe plum Italian tomatoes, peeled and diced; or 2½ cups canned plum
   tomatoes, crushed and drained
¼ cup fresh Italian parsley, chopped
6 fresh basil leaves, minced; or ¼ tsp. dried basil
4 tbsp. Pecorino cheese, freshly grated (if you can't find Pecorino cheese, use
   Parmesan cheese)
Black pepper to taste

Servings:
6
Time:
15 *min., store-bought pasta;* **2** *hours, homemade pasta*
Calories: store-bought pasta: **280** *per serving; homemade pasta:* **375** *per serving*

Boil water to cook the pasta.

In a large frying pan, sauté the onions and garlic in oil for a few minutes.

Add the tomatoes and simmer for 6 to 8 minutes. Add the parsley and basil and cook for 2 more minutes.

Cook the homemade or thin packaged pasta only a few minutes and drain. Transfer it to a large warm pasta bowl.

Toss with the sauce and the Pecorino cheese, pepper to taste, and serve immediately.

VARIATION
* Add 1 teaspoon of crushed red pepper for a hotter sauce.

This very light, thin pasta with a superb, traditional Abruzzi tomato sauce was the first pasta I learned to make, at the age of seven. This is a pasta specialty of Abruzzi and the original method of making pasta.

L I N G U I N E M A D E O

Linguine with Mushrooms, Dried Tomatoes, and Zucchini

Servings:
6
Time:
20 *min.*
Calories:
400 *per serving*

1 lb. linguine
4 small, choice zucchini, chopped
3 tbsp. green olive oil
1 cup onion, finely chopped
4 cloves of garlic, crushed
½ tsp. Italian herb seasoning
2 cups fresh mushrooms, sliced
½ tsp. red pepper, crushed
½ cup dried tomatoes, cut in strips
¼ cup fresh basil, chopped
1 cup fresh Italian parsley, finely chopped
¼ cup Parmesan cheese, freshly grated

Boil water to cook the pasta.

Scrub the zucchini. After soaking in very cold water for about 10 minutes, cut the zucchini into ¼-inch rings, and place in a colander to drain. When completely drained, dry off all remaining moisture with a paper towel and set aside.

Cook the linguine until al dente and drain at once.

Heat the olive oil for 1 minute in a large skillet; add the dry zucchini and stir briskly until they are lightly brown on both sides. Add the chopped onion and garlic and cook for 2 minutes. Then add the Italian herb seasoning, mushrooms, and hot pepper, and cook for 3 more minutes. Add the dried tomatoes, basil, and parsley, and turn off the flame.

Add the pasta to the cooked sauce and toss lightly. Sprinkle with the Parmesan cheese and serve immediately.

VARIATIONS

* Use 1 cup of crushed canned Italian tomatoes instead of the dried tomatoes.
* Try eggplant or asparagus instead of zucchini.

FETTUCCINE CON SALMONE E VEGETALE

Fettuccine with Salmon, Zucchini, Tomatoes, and Olives

1½ lb. fettuccine noodles
1 cup onion, chopped
1 large green pepper, chopped
½ cup Italian black olives, diced
3 tbsp. green olive oil
2 cups fresh zucchini, diced
2 cups fresh plum tomatoes, diced, peeled, and seeded
2 tbsp. small capers, rinsed
½ tsp. Italian herb seasoning
3 tbsp. fresh basil, minced; or ½ tsp. dried, crushed basil
½ cup fresh Italian parsley, chopped
Dash of black pepper
2 lb. fresh salmon, poached; or 1 15½-oz can of red salmon, rinsed

Servings:
8
Time:
15 *min.*
Calories:
661 *per serving*

Boil water to cook the pasta.

In a large frying pan, sauté the onion, pepper, and olives for 5 minutes in the olive oil.

Add the zucchini, tomatoes, capers, Italian herb seasoning, basil, parsley, and black pepper, and sauté 5 minutes.

Mash the salmon and add it to the mixture; cook 4 minutes, stirring to blend the sauce thoroughly.

Drain the fettuccine noodles, and put them in a pasta bowl. Pour the sauce over the fettuccine noodles and toss thoroughly. Serve immediately.

VARIATIONS

* Use 1 cup of sliced fresh mushrooms instead of tomatoes.
* Add asparagus tips or red pepper instead of tomatoes.
* Use 1 cup of Mustard Dill Caper Sauce (see page 201) instead of tomatoes.
* Use tuna or other seafood instead of salmon.

This dish makes a beautiful presentation. It's perfect for dinner parties and can be made for buffets with rotini pasta.

P A S T A   D E L I A H

Eggplant, Spinach, Gorgonzola Cheese, and Sun-Dried Tomatoes

Servings:
4
Time:
20 *min.*
Calories:
525 *per serving*

¾ lb. thin spaghetti or short-shape pasta (penne, fusilli, or rotini)
1 medium-size eggplant (2 lb.)
1 tbsp. salt
2 tbsp. green olive oil
½ cup onion, chopped
3 cloves of garlic, crushed
¼ lb. fresh spinach (4 cups chopped)
1 cup fresh Italian parsley, chopped
3 tbsp. sun-dried tomatoes, minced
½ tsp. Italian herb seasoning
⅓ cup crumbled Gorgonzola cheese
¼ cup Parmesan cheese, freshly grated

Boil the water to cook the pasta.

Peel and slice the eggplant into 1-inch slices. Soak in cold water and 1 tablespoon of salt for 10 minutes; drain the water often. Rinse and pat dry. Dice into 4-inch cubes.

In a large frying pan, sauté the oil, onion, and garlic for a few minutes.

Place the eggplant cubes on a baking sheet and brown for 2 to 3 minutes in the broiler.

Add the eggplant and spinach to the onion and garlic sauce and cook for 8 minutes. Add the parsley, sun-dried tomatoes, and Italian herb seasoning, and cook for 3 minutes.

Drain the pasta and put it in a large pasta bowl. Toss with the Gorgonzola and Parmesan cheeses. Add the eggplant sauce and mix thoroughly.

Serve with more Parmesan cheese on top.

VARIATIONS

* Substitute arugula for spinach.
* Use goat cheese instead of Gorgonzola cheese.
* Add roasted peppers (see page 7) instead of sun-dried tomatoes.
* Add ½ cup of dried or fresh mushrooms.
* Add ½ teaspoon of crushed red hot pepper.

This is a great dish to make when entertaining—it's colorful, tasty, and unusual.

Eliminate the Gorgonzola cheese and use only Parmesan cheese for fewer calories and less cholesterol.

LASAGNA VERDE

Lasagna with Spinach, Mushroom, Ricotta, and Pimento Filling

1 lb. green lasagna noodles
6 shallots; or 1 cup onion, diced
3 cloves of garlic, crushed
2 cups fresh mushrooms, sliced
2 tbsp. green olive oil
2 lb. fresh spinach leaves, without stems
1 tsp. Italian herb seasoning
⅓ tsp. grated nutmeg
¼ tsp. cayenne pepper
1 cup skim-milk ricotta cheese
½ cup Parmesan cheese, freshly grated
1 cup pimentos, minced (plus 4 tablespoons for the topping)
1 cup fresh Italian parsley, chopped
½ cup mozzarella cheese, shredded

Servings:
8
Time:
30 *min.*
Calories:
378 *per serving*

Preheat the oven at 350°F.
Boil water to cook the pasta in a large pan.
In a large frying pan, sauté the shallots, garlic, and mushrooms in the oil for 3 minutes. Add the spinach leaves, Italian herb seasoning, nutmeg, and cayenne pepper, and continue cooking covered for 5 minutes. Remove from the flame.
Put the ricotta cheese, Parmesan cheese, and pimentos in a large bowl and blend thoroughly with the parsley until well mixed.
Drain the lasagna noodles and rinse in cold water. Line the noodles on a flat surface. (Have a bowl with cold water nearby in which you can dip your hands when the dough gets too hot.)
Layer the noodles in a 2-quart baking dish (or long baking dish). Spoon a layer of the spinach mixture over the noodles, and then a layer of about ¼ cup of the ricotta mixture and 2 tablespoons of Parmesan cheese. Make three layers of lasagna noodles, spinach sauce, and ricotta mixture with Parmesan cheese.
After layering the lasagna noodles and sauce, top with the shredded mozzarella and pimento bits.
Bake for 8 to 10 minutes.
Let the lasagna set and cool for 10 minutes before cutting and serving.

VARIATIONS
* Use white lasagna noodles, or alternate green and white noodles.
* Use tomato sauce on alternating layers.
* Use roasted red peppers (see page 7) instead of pimentos.
* Use black or wild mushrooms for more taste instead of fresh mushrooms.

* Eliminate cheeses, except Parmesan, and use cooked mixed vegetables or chopped, cooked lean meat, shredded chicken, or turkey.

This is a great, visual, and unusual type of lasagna to serve for dinner parties or buffets—or supper. Also great for brunch.

TIMBALLO MISTO MARE *

Pasta Layers with Vegetables and Seafood

Servings:
8
Time:
25 min.
Calories:
308 per serving

1 lb. lasagna noodles
12 shallots, diced; or 1 cup onion, diced
2 cups cooked mixed vegetables, chopped (mushrooms, zucchini, broccoli, eggplant, red and green peppers, asparagus, spinach)
3 cloves of garlic, crushed
1 tsp. Italian herb seasoning
¼ tsp. crushed red pepper
3 tbsp. green olive oil
2 cups canned tomatoes, drained and crushed
1 cup fresh Italian parsley, chopped
1 cup cooked mixed seafood, chopped (shrimp, lobster, crab, or whitefish)
½ cup zucchini, grated

Preheat the oven at 350°F.

Boil water to cook the lasagna noodles.

In a large frying pan or wok, sauté the shallots, all of the vegetables except zucchini, garlic, Italian herb seasoning, and red pepper in the oil for 5 minutes. Add the tomatoes and ½ of the portion of parsley and cook for 5 minutes. Add the diced seafood to the tomato-vegetable mixture and cook for just 3 minutes (so the seafood will not get tough).

Drain the pasta and rinse in cold water.

Line the lasagna noodles on a large, flat working surface and cut the wrinkled edges off.

Put some olive oil on the bottom of a large, round baking dish and cover with one line of the lasagna noodles. Layer with the sauce and sprinkle with parsley

*Timballo is similar to lasagna, but it is made in a round baking dish and cut into wedges like a pie. Usually it has more layers than lasagna.

and zucchini. Continue to layer. Cover the top with sauce, parsley, and zucchini.
Bake for 8 to 10 minutes. Let the dish set and cool before cutting into wedges.

VARIATIONS
* Vary the green and white lasagna noodles for visual presentation.
* Use cooked chicken, shredded, or turkey or ground beef.
* Add 1 cup skim-milk ricotta cheese instead of meat or fish to the tomato-vegetable mixture.

This dish can be made in advance, although it is best not to freeze seafood. Use cooked chicken, turkey, beef, or pork as a variation (they can be frozen).
Timballo is great for entertaining—it's visually pleasing and delicious.

FETTUCCINE CON TRE FORMAGGIO

Green Fettuccine Noodles with Gorgonzola, Ricotta, and Parmesan Cheese Sauce

1½ lb. green fettuccine noodles
½ cup water
1 cup skim-milk ricotta cheese
½ cup Parmesan cheese, freshly grated (plus 4 tbsp. to toss with the pasta)
½ tsp. Italian herb seasoning
Dash of cayenne pepper
3 tbsp. fresh Italian parsley, minced
¼ cup Gorgonzola cheese

Servings:
8
Time:
10 *min.*
Calories:
416 *per serving*

Boil water to cook the pasta.
In a large saucepan, combine the water, ricotta and Parmesan cheeses, Italian herb seasoning, and the cayenne pepper; heat over a low flame and stir constantly for about 5 minutes to keep smooth. Add the parsley and stir another 2 minutes.
Drain the pasta and put it in a large pasta bowl.
Toss the pasta with Parmesan cheese, and pour the cheese sauce over it; blend thoroughly. Sprinkle with Gorgonzola cheese. Add cayenne pepper to taste. Serve immediately.

VARIATIONS

* For color, add diced fresh tomatoes, chopped pimentos, red roasted peppers (see page 7), or black olives over the prepared pasta and sauce.
* Use Romano cheese instead of Parmesan cheese and substitute goat cheese for ricotta cheese.

PASTA NUOVA ALLA CELESTINO

Roasted Asparagus, Arugula, and Red Pepper Sauce

Servings:
4
Time:
15 *min.*
Calories:
468 *per serving*

¾ lb. short-shape pasta (penne, rotini, rigatoni)
2 red bell peppers, roasted and diced
8 medium-size asparagus
3 tbsp. green olive oil
1 cup onion, chopped
3 cloves of garlic, crushed
2 cups of fresh arugula leaves, loosely packed (use fresh spinach leaves, if arugula is unavailable)
½ tsp. Italian herb seasoning
Pinch of cayenne pepper
½ cup fresh Italian parsley, chopped
⅓ cup Romano cheese, freshly grated

Boil water to cook the pasta.

Roast the red peppers and asparagus. Place on a baking sheet and broil until the skins of the peppers are charred all over—about 10 minutes. Asparagus will roast in only 5 minutes; turn often and drizzle on a few drops of olive oil to keep from drying.

Remove the asparagus first and let cool. Remove the skins from the asparagus and cut into 2-inch pieces, removing the tough ends.

When the red peppers are roasted, wrap them in foil or put them in a paper bag and let stand for 10 minutes (to steam). Then remove the charred skins and chop.

In a large frying pan or wok, sauté onions, the garlic, and red peppers in the oil for 5 minutes; stir often.

Remove the stems from the arugula leaves and break into small pieces. Add the asparagus, Italian herb seasoning, and cayenne pepper to the garlic and red pepper mixture, and sauté for 3 minutes. Add the arugula leaves and parsley and stir thoroughly. Cook for one more minute.

Drain the pasta; toss with the grated Romano cheese in a large pasta bowl. Add the sauce and blend thoroughly. Add a little more Romano cheese to the top and serve immediately.

VARIATIONS
* Use tomatoes instead of red peppers.
* Use spinach, swiss chard, or broccoli instead of arugula leaves.
* Add fresh sliced mushrooms during the last 5 minutes of cooking.

P A S T A   A L L A   T R E V I

Grilled Chicken and Fusilli Pasta with Pesto Sauce

1 lb. fusilli pasta, or penne, ziti, or rotini
1½ lb. raw boneless chicken breast, cut into 1-inch cubes
3 tbsp. green olive oil
1 tsp. balsamic vinegar or red wine vinegar
½ tsp. Italian herb seasoning
3 cloves of garlic, crushed
Dash of cayenne pepper
12 cherry tomatoes, cut in half
4 small squash (2 zucchini, 2 yellow squash), cut into 1-inch cubes
1 cup onion, diced
¼ cup fresh Italian parsley, chopped
1 cup Basic Pesto Sauce (see page 197)

Servings:
6
Time
20 *min. plus*
marinating time
Calories:
711 *per serving*

Heat the grill to medium hot.

Boil water to cook the pasta.

In a large bowl, combine the diced chicken cubes, 1 tablespoon of olive oil, vinegar, Italian herb seasoning, garlic, cayenne pepper, tomatoes, and squash. Marinate (15 to 30 minutes, or overnight).

Put the chicken cubes on skewers. Put the squash cubes on separate skewers.

Brush the squash and chicken cubes with marinade. Grill the squash for a few minutes until it's charred and tender. Grill the chicken until it's slightly charred, about 3 minutes per side, keeping moist with the marinade (avoid overcooking— it will get tough quickly). Place to one side.

In a large frying pan, sauté onion and tomatoes in the oil for a few minutes. Sauté the chicken and squash cubes, parsley, and marinade juices together for 3 to 5 minutes.

Drain the pasta, put it in a large pasta bowl, and toss with pesto sauce. Then pour the chicken sauce over the pasta.

Mix the pasta and chicken sauce thoroughly, blending with the pesto sauce.

VARIATIONS

* Grill radicchio leaves and some green and red peppers or mushrooms with the squash.
* Use swordfish, turkey, lamb, or just vegetables: eggplant, zucchini, peppers, and onions. (All vegetables are lower in calories and easier to digest.)

This dish is visually fabulous. The blend of two sauces with the grilled chicken and vegetables makes for a great taste.

This very chic food combination is great for dinner parties. Must be served immediately.

ROTINI VEGETABLE AND CHICKEN SALAD

Servings:
4
Time:
15 *min.*
Calories:
521 *per serving*

1 lb. rotini pasta (white or colored)
¼ cup fresh green onion, shallots, or red onion, diced
3 cloves of garlic, crushed
1 medium-size green pepper, chopped
3 tbsp. green olive oil
1 cup cooked chicken or turkey, cubed
¼ tsp. Italian herb seasoning
Pepper to taste (cayenne or black)
1 cup fresh or frozen peas
½ cup black olives, diced
1 cup fresh tomatoes, diced
6 fresh basil leaves, minced; or ½ tsp. dried basil
1 cup marinated artichoke hearts, diced
1 cup fresh green beans, broken into 2-inch pieces
1 tbsp. safflower oil
2 tbsp. balsamic vinegar or red wine vinegar
½ cup shredded mozzarella cheese or Parmesan cheese

Boil water to cook the pasta.

In a large sauté pan, sauté the onion, garlic, and green pepper in 2 tablespoons of the olive oil for 3 to 4 minutes. Add the cubed chicken, Italian herb seasoning, and black or cayenne pepper, and cook for 5 minutes, stirring often with a wooden spoon. Add the peas, cover, and cook for 3 to 4 minutes.

Drain the cooked pasta and rinse in cold water if serving as a pasta salad. Place the pasta in a large bowl. Add the chicken mixture; then the diced olives, tomatoes, basil leaves, artichoke hearts, green beans, olive or safflower oil, vinegar, and cheese.

Mix thoroughly. Serve hot or at room temperature.

VARIATIONS

* Use tuna or cooked seafood.
* Add asparagus or eggplant cubes, cooked and diced.
* Use diced zucchini or red pepper instead of tomatoes.
* Use penne or ziti pasta instead of rotini.
* Marinate vegetables in oil, vinegar, garlic, and Italian herb seasoning. This will give them a robust, pungent taste; marinate overnight.

This dish can be stored in the refrigerator until ready to serve.
Remove 1 hour before serving. Serve at room temperature to blend the flavors.
If dry, toss and add a drop of oil or lemon juice and serve.

PASTA LA
BRUSCHETTA

Pasta with Red Peppers, Mushrooms, Spinach, and Prosciutto

¾ lb. linguine
½ tbsp. sweet, unsalted butter
1 tbsp. green olive oil
1 cup onion, chopped
2 cups fresh mushrooms, chopped
3 cloves of garlic, finely chopped
½ tsp. Italian herb seasoning
½ cup fresh Italian parsley, chopped
2 bunches of spinach, chopped; or 1 packet of chopped spinach, thawed and
   drained
1 cup red pepper, diced
2 slices of prosciutto, diced (trim off fat)
½ cup Parmesan cheese, freshly grated

Servings:
4
Time:
20 *min.*
Calories:
492 *per serving*

Boil water for the pasta.

Melt the butter with the olive oil in a large skillet, and sauté the onion, mushrooms, and garlic. Add the Italian herb seasoning, parsley, spinach, and red pepper (if you are using frozen spinach, drain off any surplus liquid). Add the diced prosciutto and sauté together for 5 to 8 minutes.

Cook the linguine pasta al dente. Drain the cooked pasta in a colander and add it to the sauce in the skillet. (If you are not going to use the pasta immediately, rinse it under cold water.)

Toss the pasta in the sauce and sprinkle with Parmesan cheese. Serve immediately.

VARIATIONS

* Use other green vegetables, asparagus, or chard.
* Add green peppers and ham instead of prosciutto and red pepper.

SPAGHETTI ALLA SERGIO

Pasta with Chicken, Mushrooms, Olives, and Eggplant

Servings:
6
Time:
25 min.
Calories:
506 per serving

1 lb. thin spaghetti
1 medium-size eggplant (2 lb.)
1 tbsp. salt
1 cup onion, diced
3 cloves of garlic, crushed
2 raw boneless and skinless chicken breasts, cut into 1-inch cubes
3 tbsp. green olive oil
¼ tsp. crushed red pepper
¼ tsp. Italian herb seasoning
4 Italian black olives, pitted and sliced
½ cup fresh Italian parsley, chopped
6 large mushrooms, sliced
⅓ cup Romano cheese, freshly grated

Boil water to cook the pasta.

Slice the eggplant and soak in cold water and 1 tablespoon of salt for 10 minutes, rinsing often.

In a large skillet or wok, sauté the onion, garlic, and chicken cubes in oil for 5 minutes with the crushed pepper and Italian herb seasoning.

Drain and dry the eggplant. Cut into small cubes and add to a baking sheet. Broil for 5 minutes to brown.

Add the eggplant to the chicken mixture with the olives, parsley, and mushrooms, and sauté 3 to 5 minutes.

Drain the spaghetti; add it to the sauce and mix thoroughly. Sprinkle with the Romano cheese. Serve immediately.

VARIATIONS
* Add diced red peppers or tomatoes.
* Use short-shape pasta and serve for buffet.
* Substitute diced zucchini instead of mushrooms.
* Eliminate hot pepper and add whole pignoli nuts or roasted almonds.

P A S T A   P R E S T O   A L L A
B E R T H A

Tomato, Garlic, Cheese, and Herb Sauce

½ lb. thin spaghetti or capellini (angel hair)
1 tbsp. green olive oil
2 cloves of garlic, crushed
2 ripe tomatoes, peeled and diced (preferably plum tomatoes)
¼ tsp. Italian herb seasoning
Dash of hot pepper (cayenne or crushed red pepper)
¼ cup Parmesan cheese, freshly grated

Servings:
2
Time:
10 *min.*
Calories:
563 *per serving*

Boil water to cook the pasta.

In a large frying pan, sauté the oil and crushed garlic for a minute. Add the diced tomatoes, Italian herb seasoning, and hot pepper, and cook for 6 to 8 minutes. Stir often with a wooden spoon.

Drain the pasta. Place it in a bowl and pour the sauce over it. Mix the sauce and pasta thoroughly, with two forks.

Sprinkle on the grated Parmesan cheese and again toss thoroughly. Serve while it is hot.

VARIATIONS
* Use short-shape pasta (rigatoni, ziti, penne) instead of spaghetti.
* Add diced vegetables or leftover cooked diced chicken, turkey, or meat. Add about one cup of uncooked, diced seafood (clams, shrimp, lobster, crabmeat, or whitefish) to the tomatoes and cook 5 to 8 minutes.

P A S T A   N E P T U N E
A L L A   I T A L I A

Fresh Tomatoes, Tuna, Olives, and Anchovies

Servings:
4
Time:
10 *min.*
Calories:
472 *per serving*

¾ lb. short-shape pasta (penne, fusilli, rotini, or rigatoni)
1 cup onion, chopped
2 anchovy filets, rinsed and minced
2 cloves of garlic, crushed
2 tbsp. green olive oil
1 lb. fresh plum tomatoes, skinned, seeded, and chopped; or 1 cup canned plum
   tomatoes, crushed
12 Italian black olives, chopped
1 6-oz. can of tuna in water, drained and mashed
¼ tsp. Italian herb seasoning
Black or cayenne pepper
½ cup fresh Italian parsley, chopped

Boil water to cook the pasta.

In a large frying pan, sauté onions, anchovies, and garlic in the oil for a few minutes. Add the tomatoes and olives, and cook for 5 minutes. Add the tuna fish, Italian herb seasoning, and pepper, and cook for another 4 minutes. Add the parsley and stir thoroughly.

Drain the pasta; put it in a large pasta bowl and pour the sauce over the top. Blend the pasta and sauce thoroughly. Serve immediately.

VARIATIONS

* Add mushrooms, diced celery, pimentos, or roasted peppers, and a touch of balsamic or red wine vinegar.
* Use salmon, whitefish, calamari, shrimp, crabmeat, lobster, or scallops instead of tuna.

This sauce can be served as a "pasta salad" with an uncooked sauce at room temperature. It's great during summer, and for entertaining or for a casual picnic.

Purée the tomatoes and pour them over the cooked pasta, which has been rinsed in cold water; toss with 1 tablespoon of olive oil. Then add the mashed tuna, diced anchovies, crushed garlic, olive oil, olives, pepper, and parsley. (Eliminate the onions and the Italian herb seasoning.)

Serve hot or cold.

PASTA ALLA DAVINCI

Asparagus, Mushroom, Tomato, and Cheese Sauce

½ lb. white fettuccine noodles or short-shape pasta
1 lb. fresh asparagus or frozen asparagus tips
3 cloves of garlic, crushed
½ cup onion, diced
1 tbsp. green olive oil
1 cup fresh mushrooms, sliced
¼ tsp. Italian herb seasoning
½ cup fresh Italian parsley, chopped
½ cup fresh tomatoes, diced
Dash of cayenne pepper
¼ cup mozzarella cheese, shredded

Servings:
2
Time:
10 *min.*
Calories:
633 *per serving*

Boil water to cook the pasta.

In a large skillet, sauté the asparagus, garlic, and onion in the oil over medium heat, covered, for 5 minutes. Add the mushrooms, Italian herb seasoning, parsley, tomatoes, and pepper; cook uncovered, for 5 minutes.

Drain the pasta, and put it in a large bowl or place it in the pan with the sauce; toss thoroughly. Add the shredded mozzarella cheese and mix. Serve immediately.

VARIATIONS
* Eliminate the tomatoes.
* Use porcini or wild mushrooms, even two kinds of mushrooms.
* Use red peppers or diced black olives. Add cooked fish or chicken, cubed.

COCHIGLIE CON ZUCCHINE MANCINI

Pasta Shells with Zucchini, Tomatoes, and Cheese

Servings:
7
Time:
15 *min.*
Calories:
375 *per serving*

1 lb. medium-size pasta shells
1 cup onion, diced
4 cloves of garlic, crushed
¼ tsp. crushed red pepper
8 small zucchini, sliced very thin (save one for grating)
3 tbsp. green olive oil
4 ripe plum tomatoes, peeled, seeded, diced
¼ tsp. Italian herb seasoning
½ cup Parmesan cheese, freshly grated
¼ cup mozzarella cheese, shredded

Boil water to cook the pasta.

In a large skillet, frying pan, or wok, sauté the onion, garlic, hot pepper, and zucchini in the oil for 5 minutes. Add the tomatoes and Italian herb seasoning and cook 3 to 4 minutes.

Drain the pasta, and put it in a large pasta bowl. Pour the sauce over the pasta and mix thoroughly. Sprinkle the Parmesan and mozzarella cheeses over the pasta and toss quickly. Grate the zucchini on top, using the large-holed side of the grater. Serve immediately.

VARIATIONS
* Use diced tomatoes for color.
* Add mushrooms.
* Bake with cheese on top at 350°F for 10 minutes.
* Add leftover turkey, chicken, or meats (calories increase).

Serve as a casserole—perfect for brunch, lunch, or dinner with a salad.

ORECCHIETTE WITH BROCCOLI RAPPINI AND ANCHOVY SAUCE

Pasta with Italian Bitter Broccoli

1 lb. orechiette pasta (if unavailable, use any short-shape pasta, such as penne, fusilli, or rigatoni)
3 garlic cloves, crushed
2 anchovy filets, rinsed and minced
¼ tsp. crushed red pepper
1 lb. broccoli rappini (also known as rabe—if unavailable, use fresh broccoli florets and some stems)
½ tsp. Italian herb seasoning
3 tbsp. green olive oil
¼ cup cold water
½ cup Parmesan cheese, freshly grated

Servings:
6
Time:
15 *min.*
Calories:
402 *per serving*

Boil water to cook the pasta.

In a large sauté pan, sauté the garlic, anchovy pieces, red pepper, broccoli, and Italian herb seasoning in the oil and water for 8 minutes, covered over medium heat.

Drain the pasta, put it in a large warm bowl, and pour the sauce over it. Mix the sauce thoroughly with the pasta. Sprinkle with the Parmesan cheese, toss thoroughly, and serve immediately.

VARIATIONS

* Eliminate the anchovies for less salt and fewer calories.
* Increase the hot pepper taste by adding a touch of color with diced red pepper or tomatoes.

This is a classic (great as it is!).

Broccoli rabe, also known as rappini, *is more bitter-tasting than broccoli, but delicious. Quite a delicacy, it is becoming very popular in restaurants and is found in many supermarkets.*

FUSILLI WITH RAPPINI ALLA MARINO'S

Swirl Pasta with Italian Broccoli

Servings:
6
Time:
15 *min.*
Calories:
387 *per serving*

1 lb. fusilli pasta (or other short-shape pasta)
1 lb. broccoli rappini (also known as rabe or Italian broccoli)
2 cloves of garlic, crushed
Dash of red hot pepper, crushed
3 tbsp. green olive oil
½ cup sharp Romano or Parmesan cheese, freshly grated

Boil water to cook the pasta.

Chop the rappini stems off to about 3 inches and discard (before the floret tips); cut the florets into 1-inch sections.

In a large frying pan, sauté the garlic, rabe, and hot pepper in the oil for 5 minutes. Cover and stir often.

Drain the pasta. Put it in a large, warm bowl, cover with the rappini sauce, and toss with Romano or Parmesan cheese. Serve immediately.

VARIATIONS

* Use regular broccoli florets, if you do not like the bitter taste of the rabe. (But, if you try rappini cooked in this manner, I know you will like them.)
* Reduce the pepper and eliminate the cheese, to really taste the *rappini*.

Great as a side dish and in a pasta sauce.

LASAGNA ROLLS FILLED WITH CHEESE AND PEPPERS

Eggplant Sauce Topping

FILLING

½ cup Parmesan cheese, freshly grated
1 cup skim-milk ricotta cheese
½ cup fresh Italian parsley, chopped
Dash of cayenne or white pepper; or 6 fresh basil leaves, minced; or ½ tsp. dried basil
1 green pepper, roasted (see page 7) and diced
1 red pepper, roasted (see page 7) and diced

SAUCE

1 lb. lasagna noodles (thin)
1 medium-size eggplant (2 lb.), diced
1 tbsp. salt
1 cup onion, diced
3 cloves of garlic, crushed
2 tbsp. green olive oil
1 cup canned Italian plum tomatoes, crushed and drained
½ tsp. Italian herb seasoning
½ cup fresh Italian parsley, chopped
Dash of cayenne pepper

Servings:
8
Time:
20 *min.*
Calories:
360 *per serving*

Preheat oven at 300°F.

Boil water to cook the pasta.

Soak the diced eggplant in cold water and 1 tablespoon of salt.

Mix the filling in a large bowl. Combine the Parmesan and ricotta cheeses, parsley, herbs of choice, green pepper, and diced, roasted red peppers, and mix thoroughly. Set aside.

Drain the eggplant and dry. In a sauté pan, sauté the onion, garlic, and eggplant in the oil for 5 minutes. Add the tomatoes, Italian herb seasoning, parsley, and cayenne pepper, and cook for 5 to 8 minutes.

Drain the lasagna noodles. Rinse them in cold water and lay flat on a large working surface. Cut the curly edges off.

Add about 2 tablespoons of the cheese and pepper filling to each noodle, and roll carefully. Put some eggplant sauce on the bottom of a large baking dish. Line the lasagna rolls upright. Place the rolls very close together to prevent unraveling. Bake for 10 minutes.

To serve, put eggplant sauce on the bottom of each dish and lay the lasagna rolls in the center. Sprinkle some grated Parmesan cheese on top. Serve hot.

VARIATIONS

* Add ground beef to the cheese mixture instead of peppers.
* Use green and white lasagna noodles.
* Cover with Ricotta Cheesy Sauce or Basic Pesto Sauce (see pages 194 and 197).
* Leave the curly edges on the lasagna noodles if you like a wider lasagna roll.

This dish is great for entertaining—visually fabulous!
Also, it can be made in advance and stored in the refrigerator.

M A N I C O T T I   A N N A

Manicotti Stuffed with Cheese, Spinach, Eggplant, Mushrooms, and
Pignoli Nuts with a Tomato Sauce Topping

Servings:
6
Time:
20 *min.*
Calories:
300 *per serving*

12 manicotti pasta shells
1 eggplant (2 lb.), sliced
1 tbsp. salt
1 cup onion, chopped
2 cups fresh spinach, chopped, or frozen spinach, drained and chopped
1 cup fresh mushrooms, sliced
¼ tsp. crushed red pepper
3 tbsp. green olive oil
3 cloves of garlic, crushed
2 cups canned Italian plum tomatoes, crushed
½ tsp. Italian herb seasoning
½ cup fresh Italian parsley, chopped
¼ cup pignoli nuts, toasted
¼ cup Parmesan cheese, freshly grated
½ cup skim-milk mozzarella cheese, shredded

Preheat oven at 300°F.

Boil water to cook the pasta.

Soak the eggplant, peeled and cut into 1-inch slices with 1 tablespoon of salt in cold water, for about 10 minutes.

In a large frying pan, sauté the onion, spinach, mushrooms, and hot pepper in the oil for 5 minutes, stirring often.

Drain and dry the eggplant. Place the slices under a broiler for 5 minutes per side.

To prepare the tomato sauce, sauté the garlic for 2 minutes in 1 tablespoon of oil; add the tomatoes, Italian herb seasoning, and parsley, and cook for 5 minutes.

Drain the manicotti pasta shells and rinse in cold water. Dry with paper towels. Mix the eggplant with the spinach-mushroom mixture and add the pignoli nuts; cook for 5 more minutes. Let cool for 1 minute.

Spoon the eggplant stuffing into the manicotti shells (use a teaspoon). Use just enough to fill: Do not overstuff or the pasta will tear.

Put the tomato sauce on the bottom of a deep baking dish, and line the stuffed manicotti shells close to one another.

Cover the manicotti with the tomato sauce, Parmesan cheese, and shredded mozzarella. Bake for 10 minutes.

Remove each manicotti carefully. Use a large spatula to prevent the filling from falling out. Serve warm.

VARIATIONS

* Use vegetables, seafood, minced cooked chicken, or turkey with vegetables as a filling.
* Use only spinach and ricotta cheese with tomato sauce, or red pepper filling with cheese topping.

This dish is perfect for entertaining—dinner parties or buffets. For variety, you can make half of the portion with the eggplant filling and half with a ricotta-mozzarella filling.

You can create your own fillings and toppings. You can freeze the manicotti. It's not advisable to freeze seafood.

You can make the manicotti a day in advance and keep refrigerated.

P A S T A   G I A M B E L L I

Pasta with Arugula, Goat Cheese, and Roasted Red Peppers

¾ lb. green and white fettuccine noodles
½ cup shallots, diced; or 1 cup onion, diced
¼ tsp. crushed red pepper
3 cloves of garlic, crushed
4 roasted red bell peppers, cut into strips (see page 7)
2 tbsp. green olive oil
½ tsp. Italian herb seasoning
¼ cup fresh Italian parsley, chopped
3 cups arugula leaves, chopped
½ cup fresh goat cheese

Servings:
4
Time:
15 *min.*
Calories:
514 *per serving*

Boil water to cook the pasta.

In a large frying pan, sauté the shallots, red pepper flakes, garlic, and roasted red peppers in the oil for 5 minutes.

Add the Italian herb seasoning, parsley, and arugula leaves, and sauté 2 to 3 minutes, stirring often.

Drain the pasta, and put it in a warm pasta bowl. Pour the sauce over the pasta. Crumble the goat cheese on top and stir thoroughly. Serve immediately.

VARIATIONS

* Try sun-dried tomatoes or 1 cup diced cherry tomatoes instead of red peppers.
* Use diced black olives.
* Use spinach leaves instead of arugula leaves.

P E N N E
A L L ' A R R A B B I A T A

Classic Hot Pepper Sauce with Pasta

Servings:
4
Time:
15 *min.*
Calories:
440 *per serving*

¾ lb. short-shape pasta (penne)
3–4 cloves of garlic, crushed
½ tsp. crushed red pepper
2 tbsp. green olive oil
1 lb. fresh ripe tomatoes, peeled, seeded, chopped; or canned imported Italian plum tomatoes (14-oz. can), crushed and drained
½ cup fresh Italian parsley, chopped
½ cup Pecorino or Romano cheese, freshly grated

Boil water to cook the pasta.

In a large frying pan, sauté garlic and hot pepper in the oil for 1 minute. Add the tomatoes and cook for 5 minutes. Add the parsley and cook for 2 minutes.

Drain the pasta, and transfer it to a large pasta bowl. Pour the sauce over the pasta and toss with the Pecorino or Romano cheese.

Mix the pasta and sauce thoroughly. Serve immediately.

VARIATIONS

* Add more or less pepper to taste.
* Add onions or more garlic to taste.

This simple, quick, inexpensive sauce has a great piccante taste.

SPAGHETTI ALLA PUTTANESCA

Classic Sauce of Tomatoes, Olives, Capers, Hot Peppers, and Anchovies

1 lb. thin spaghetti
2 tbsp. green olive oil
3 cloves of garlic, crushed
¼ tsp. crushed red pepper
1 cup plum tomatoes, freshly diced; or 1 cup canned Italian tomatoes, drained and crushed
½ tsp. Italian herb seasoning
3 tbsp. small capers, drained and rinsed
2 anchovy fillets, rinsed, drained, and minced
¼ cup fresh Italian parsley, chopped
6 black Italian olives, pitted and sliced
½ cup Pecorino or sharp Romano cheese, freshly grated

Servings:
6
Time:
10 *min.*
Calories:
362 *per serving*

Boil water to cook the pasta.

In a large sauté pan, cook the oil, garlic, and pepper for 3 to 4 minutes. Add the tomatoes, Italian herb seasoning, capers, anchovies, parsley, and olives, and cook for 5 to 8 minutes.

Drain the pasta and put it in a bowl. Mix the pasta with the sauce and sprinkle with the Pecorino or Romano cheese. Serve immediately.

VARIATIONS
* Serve without the tomatoes.
* Use porcini or wild black mushrooms instead of regular fresh mushrooms (more taste).

This quick, pungent, piccante sauce zaps up the energy and spirit. It was named after "the girls of Via Veneto" in Rome.

PASTA QUATRO FORMAGGI CIRA

Pasta with Four Cheeses

Servings:
6
Time:
10 *min.*
Calories:
396 *per serving*

1 lb. rotelle or penne pasta
½ cup skim-milk ricotta cheese
¼ cup Fontina cheese, cut into ¼-inch pieces
3 tbsp. Gorgonzola cheese, crumbled
Dash of white or cayenne pepper
½ cup fresh Italian parsley, minced
1 tbsp. unsalted butter
½ Parmesan cheese, freshly grated

Boil water to cook the pasta.

Mix the ricotta cheese with the Fontina and Gorgonzola cheeses, pepper, and parsley.

Drain the cooked pasta and put in a large pasta bowl. Toss the pasta with the butter and Parmesan cheese. Add the cheese mixture and blend thoroughly.

Serve immediately: Cheese sauce will not wait!

VARIATIONS

* Use shredded skim-milk mozzarella instead of Fontina and Gorgonzola cheese (fewer calories and cheaper).
* Top with fresh diced tomatoes, marinated in crushed garlic and green olive oil—two sauces blend for great taste.

BUCATINI ALLA MATRICIANA

Prosciutto, Tomato, and Garlic Sauce

Servings:
4
Time:
20 *min.*
Calories:
598 *per serving*

1 lb. bucatini pasta; or rigatoni, penne, ziti
1 cup onion, finely chopped
3 large cloves of garlic, crushed
½ cup prosciutto, diced (without fat)
2 tbsp. green olive oil
1 lb. fresh ripe plum tomatoes, peeled, seeded, and chopped (1½ cups); or 1 can (14-oz.) Italian plum tomatoes, crushed and drained

¼ cup fresh Italian parsley, chopped
Black pepper to taste
½ cup Parmesan or sharp Romano cheese, freshly grated

Boil water to cook the pasta.

In a large frying pan, sauté the onion, garlic, and prosciutto in the oil for 5 minutes. Add the tomatoes, parsley, and pepper, and cook for 5 to 8 minutes.

Drain the pasta and transfer it to a large, warmed pasta bowl. Pour the sauce over the pasta; sprinkle on grated Parmesan or Romano cheese and toss thoroughly.

Sprinkle a little more cheese on top and serve immediately.

VARIATIONS
* If you can't find prosciutto, use pieces of slab bacon without fat, or ham.
* Add a dash of hot pepper.
* Try meatless version without the prosciutto and add more garlic and onions.

C A P E L L I N I
Z I N G A R E L L A
A N D R E I N O S

Mushrooms, Tomatoes, and Prosciutto

1 lb. capellini pasta (angel hair) or thin spaghetti
3 tbsp. green olive oil
¼ lb. prosciutto, chopped
2 cloves of garlic, crushed
1 cup onion, chopped
2 packages of dried porcini mushrooms (about .8 ounces each) soaked in warm water about 15 to 30 minutes
¼ cup fresh basil, chopped; or 2 tbsp. dried basil
1 lb. (12 oz.) canned Italian-style plum tomatoes (with juice)
½ cup dry Italian white wine
¼ cup sharp Romano or Parmesan cheese, freshly grated
Black pepper to taste

Servings:
6
Time:
20 *min.*
Calories:
450 *per serving*

Boil water to cook the pasta.

Heat oil in a heavy skillet. Sauté the prosciutto and garlic for 3 minutes. Add the onion, mushrooms, and basil, and sauté for 2 minutes. Add tomatoes, wine, and black pepper. Cook for 10 minutes.

Drain the pasta and transfer it to a warm pasta bowl. Pour sauce over the pasta and toss thoroughly.

Add the Parmesan or Romano cheese and toss again. Serve immediately (thin pasta must be served quickly).

VARIATIONS

* Create your own sauce with crushed hot pepper, parsley, and fresh mushrooms.
* Eliminate the prosciutto.

S P A G H E T T I   C O N
P O M M A D O R E   C R U D O *

Spaghetti with Uncooked Tomato Sauce

Servings: **6** *Time:* **10** *min.* *Calories:* **390** *per serving*	1 lb. thin spaghetti 1 lb. very ripe plum tomatoes, peeled, seeded, and diced 2 cloves of garlic, crushed 3 tbsp. green olive oil 5 fresh basil leaves, chopped ½ cup Parmesan cheese, freshly grated Black pepper to taste

Boil water to cook the pasta.

Drop the tomatoes into a small pan of boiling water; remove the skins, seed, cord, and dice. Place in a bowl with the crushed garlic, olive oil, and diced basil leaves. Stir often to blend the tastes. (Can also be marinated, before serving, for more flavor.)

Drain the pasta and put it in a large pasta bowl. Pour the tomato sauce over the pasta, and toss with the Parmesan cheese and pepper.

Serve warm or at room temperature.

VARIATIONS

* Add less or more pepper or garlic to taste. Fresh tomatoes are a must!

*This sauce can be used with fish, chicken, and veal, or for Crostini's, pizza, or Foccacia.

This is a great, light sauce that is quick and easy to prepare. It's perfect during the warm weather and the "tomato season."

This is a popular sauce in Rome; it's often called, alla Checca.

This dish can be made ahead of time and refrigerated or frozen. It can be used with many recipes.

PASTA CON RICOTTA E POMMODORE

Ricotta Cheese and Tomato Sauce

1 lb. pasta (penne, ziti, rotini, wheels, or fettuccine noodles)
1 cup skim-milk ricotta cheese
½ cup Parmesan cheese, freshly grated
¼ cup fresh Italian parsley, chopped
4 fresh basil leaves, minced; or 1 tsp. dried basil
Dash of white or cayenne pepper
1 cup fresh tomatoes, peeled and diced

Servings:
4
Time:
10 *min.*
Calories:
570 *per serving*

Boil water to cook the pasta.

In a small saucepan, heat the ricotta and Parmesan cheeses for 3 minutes; stir often to blend the cheeses, parsley, basil, and pepper, and to keep from becoming lumpy. Remove from heat.

Drain the pasta and transfer it to a large pasta bowl. Add the tomatoes. Toss the pasta with the ricotta sauce and add more Parmesan cheese on top. Serve immediately.

VARIATIONS

* Goat cheese can be used instead of ricotta—create your own sauce.
* Serve the ricotta without the tomato.

PASTA PALERMO

Swordfish, Fennel, Wine, and Caper Sauce

Servings:
4
Time:
15 *min.*
Calories:
546 *per serving*

¾ lb. short-shape pasta (rotini, penne, or ziti)
3 tbsp. green olive oil
1 cup onion, diced
2 cloves of garlic, crushed
1 cup fresh fennel (anise celery), diced
1 medium-size red pepper, chopped
¼ tsp. Italian herb seasoning
½ lb. filet of swordfish, cubed
½ cup black Sicilian olives, chopped
2 tbsp. small capers, rinsed
½ cup dry white Italian wine
1 tbsp. pignoli nuts, roasted
½ cup fresh Italian parsley, chopped

Boil water in a large lidded pan to cook the pasta.

In a large skillet, heat the olive oil and sauté the onion, garlic, fennel, red pepper, and Italian herb seasoning for 4 minutes.

Add the cubed swordfish, olives, capers, and half the pignoli nuts; cook for 3 minutes and then add the wine. Cover the skillet and cook for another 3 minutes. (Do not overcook the fish—it will get tough.)

Cook the pasta al dente, drain, and transfer it to a large, warm pasta bowl. Add the swordfish sauce and toss gently through the pasta. Sprinkle the parsley and pignoli nuts on top and serve immediately.

VARIATION

* Use 1 cup of crushed tomatoes instead of white wine and eliminate the red peppers.

PASTA LENTICCHE SYLVESTRO

Pasta with Lentils and Vegetables

1 cup onion, chopped
4 cloves of garlic, crushed
½ cup celery, diced
1 cup carrots, diced
¼ tsp. crushed red pepper
2 tbsp. green olive oil
8 oz. lentils, cleaned and drained (soak overnight)
1 tsp. Italian herb seasoning
2 cups chicken or vegetable stock
1 cup Italian parsley, chopped
½ lb. short-shape pasta (elbows, ditali, penne)
¼ cup Romano or Parmesan cheese, freshly grated

Servings:
4
Time:
25 *min.*
Calories:
543 *per serving*

In a large skillet, sauté the onion, garlic, celery, carrots, and crushed red pepper in the oil for 5 minutes. Add the lentils, Italian herb seasoning, stock, and parsley. Cover and cook over medium heat about 20 minutes. (Taste the lentils to see if they are cooked to your taste.)

While the lentils are cooking, boil water to cook the pasta. Drain the pasta and add it to the cooked lentils. Sprinkle on Parmesan or Romano cheese and blend thoroughly. Serve immediately.

VARIATIONS
* Use other vegetables.
* Add diced ham, prosciutto, or sausage (½ cup).

This dynamite, high-energy dish is very high in protein and easier to digest than a steak.

PASTA CON ARUGULA AL POMMADORE

Pasta with Arugula Leaves and Tomatoes

Servings:
4
Time:
15 *min.*
Calories:
461 *per serving*

¾ lb. thin spaghetti
2 tbsp. green olive oil
1 cup onions, diced
3 cloves of garlic, crushed
1 cup fresh Italian plum tomatoes, peeled and diced; or 1 cup canned Italian
   plum tomatoes, crushed
2 cups arugula leaves, chopped and loosely packed
½ cup Parmesan cheese, freshly grated

In a large lidded pan, boil water to cook the pasta.

In a large skillet, heat the olive oil and sauté the onion, garlic, and tomatoes for 5 minutes. Add the arugula leaves and cook for 3 more minutes.

Drain the pasta, cooked al dente, and transfer it to a warm pasta bowl. Add the arugula tomato sauce and gently mix thoroughly. Sprinkle the Parmesan cheese on top and toss through the pasta. Serve immediately.

VARIATIONS
* Eliminate the tomatoes and use one minced anchovy.
* Use diced olives.
* Use goat cheese instead of Parmesan cheese and decorate with diced sun-dried tomatoes.

PASTA CONTADINA

Pasta with Beans, Prosciutto, and Tomatoes

Servings:
4
Time:
15 *min.*
Calories:
403 *per serving*

½ lb. short-shape pasta (elbows, penne, ziti, rotini)
2 tbsp. green olive oil
1 cup onions, chopped
3 cloves of garlic, crushed
¼ tsp. crushed red pepper
1 cup fresh Italian plum tomatoes, peeled and chopped; or 1 cup canned Italian
   plum tomatoes, crushed
1 tsp. Italian herb seasoning

½ cup fresh Italian parsley, chopped
½ cup prosciutto (ham), diced
1 cup canned white cannolini beans, rinsed and drained
¼ cup Parmesan cheese, freshly grated

In a large lidded pan, boil water to cook the pasta.

In a large skillet, heat the olive oil and sauté the onion, garlic, prosciutto, and pepper for 5 minutes. Add the tomatoes, Italian herb seasoning, and parsley, and cook for 5 more minutes; then add the beans and mix thoroughly until they are heated.

Cook the pasta al dente, drain, and transfer to a warm pasta bowl. Pour the tomato–bean sauce over the pasta, sprinkle on the Parmesan cheese, and gently mix thoroughly. Add a little more cheese to the top and serve immediately in small pasta bowls.

VARIATION
* Omit the prosciutto and replace it with tuna fish or vegetables.

This dish can be a total meal in itself—full of high protein, it's good for lunch or dinner.

P A S T A   A L   C A R T O C C I O

Pasta Cooked in Parchment Paper, in Tomato and Clam Sauce

1 lb. linguine
2 tbsp. green olive oil
4 cloves of garlic, crushed
1 cup onion, chopped
¼ tsp. crushed red pepper
1 tsp. Italian herb seasoning
1 lb. fresh ripe plum tomatoes, peeled, seeded, and diced; or 2½ cups of canned
   plum tomatoes, crushed
½ cup black olives, diced
½ cup fresh Italian parsley, chopped
½ lb. small clams (remove shells and dice)
6 pieces of parchment paper (large enough to fit the portion of linguine and
   sauce and close tightly on all sides)

Servings:
6
Time:
35 *min.*
Calories:
372 *per serving*

Preheat oven at 350°F.

Boil water to cook the pasta.

In a large skillet, cook the oil, garlic, onion, hot pepper, and Italian herb seasoning for 3 to 4 minutes. Add the tomatoes, olives, and parsley, and cook for 5 minutes. Mix in the clams and cook for 3 to 4 minutes.

Drain the pasta and add it to the sauce; mix thoroughly.

Place a portion of the pasta in the parchment paper and wrap tightly on each end and the top. Place in a large baking pan and bake for 15 minutes.

Remove the paper bundles, place on a warm plate, and serve immediately.

VARIATIONS

* Use mixed seafood, or only tomatoes, olives, and vegetables.
* Try short-shape pasta with eggplant and cheese sauce.
* Place open clams on top of the pasta for decoration; cook in the sauce for a few minutes.

Open each bundle in front of your guests with a scissors or a knife; make a long opening in the front—the steam and the smell of the sauce and the pasta . . . will be fantastic.

P A S T A   D O R A

Pasta with Tuna, Beans, Red Pepper, and Onion Sauce

Servings:
4
Time:
10 *min.*
Calories:
397 *per serving*

½ lb. short-shape pasta (elbows, penne, rotini, or farfalle)
2 tbsp. green olive oil
2 cups onion, chopped
3 cloves of garlic, crushed
1 6½-oz. can of tuna fish in water
½ tsp. Italian herb seasoning
1 small red pepper, diced
1 cup white cannellini beans (canned)
1 cup fresh Italian parsley, chopped
1 tbsp. balsamic or red wine vinegar
Dash of cayenne or hot red pepper flakes (to taste)

In a large lidded pan, boil water to cook the pasta.

Heat the olive oil in a large skillet and sauté the onion, garlic, tuna, Italian herb seasoning, and red pepper for 8 minutes; stir often. Add the beans and parsley and cook for 3 more minutes.

Drain the cooked pasta and transfer it to a heated pasta bowl. Add the tuna sauce and mix gently, blending in the balsamic vinegar. Add pepper to taste. This dish may be served hot or when it has cooled to room temperature.

VARIATIONS
* Add diced tomatoes, capers, celery, or fennel.
* Use short-shape green pasta.
* Add 1 teaspoon of dill weed.

This dish is a great appetizer, pasta salad, or a main course.

PASTA CON
SCAMPI ROBERTO

Linguini Pasta with Shrimp, Caper, Anchovy, and Tomato Sauce

1 lb. short-shape pasta (linguine, spaghetti, or farfalle)
3 tbsp. green olive oil
1 medium-size onion, chopped
1 anchovy, minced
2 cups fresh plum tomatoes, peeled and diced; or 1 cup of canned Italian plum
   tomatoes, crushed
½ tsp. Italian herb seasoning
Dash of cayenne pepper (to taste)
2 tbsp. small capers, rinsed
1 lb. fresh shrimp, cleaned and chopped
½ cup fresh Italian parsley, chopped

Servings:
6
Time:
15 *min.*
Calories:
421 *per serving*

In a large lidded pan, boil water to cook the pasta.

In a large skillet, heat the olive oil and sauté the onion and anchovy for 5 minutes. Add the tomatoes, Italian herb seasoning, pepper, and capers, and cook for 5 more minutes. Add the shrimp and cook for 3 more minutes.

Cook the pasta al dente, drain, and transfer it to a warm pasta bowl. Pour the sauce over the pasta and mix thoroughly. Sprinkle with the chopped parsley and serve immediately.

VARIATIONS
* Add green pepper and celery or dried olives.
* Try minced clams and mussels.

This dish can be served at room temperature with short-shape pasta as a pasta salad.

PASTA PRIMAVERA CELLI III

Fresh Vegetables and Herb Cheese Sauce

Servings:
6
Time:
15 *min.*
Calories:
428 *per serving*

1 lb. pasta (thin spaghetti, linguine, swirls, or other short shapes)
3 tbsp. green olive oil
4 cloves of garlic, crushed
6 shallots, diced; or 1 cup onion, diced
¼ tsp. crushed red pepper
1 tsp. Italian herb seasoning
1 cup broccoli florets or asparagus tips
2 cups fresh mushrooms, sliced very thin
4 medium-size zucchini, diced
1 lb. fresh plum tomatoes, peeled and diced; or 2 cups Italian canned tomatoes
  with juice, crushed
½ cup fresh Italian parsley, chopped
8 basil leaves, chopped
½ cup Parmesan or sharp Romano cheese, freshly grated

In a large lidded pan, boil water to cook the pasta.

In a large skillet, heat the olive oil and sauté the garlic, shallots, pepper, Italian herb seasoning, broccoli, mushrooms, and zucchini for 5 minutes with the lid on. Add the tomatoes, parsley, and basil; cook for 5 more minutes (uncovered).

Cook the pasta al dente, drain, and transfer it to a large, warm pasta bowl. Add the sauce and mix thoroughly. Sprinkle the grated Parmesan or Romano cheese over the pasta and sauce, mixing thoroughly. Add the chopped basil leaves and serve immediately.

VARIATIONS

* *Primavera* means springtime; thus, the fresh vegetables of the season should be used. You can create many versions of this sauce using eggplant; yellow squash; and red, green, and yellow peppers. Do not use carrots, peas, snow peas, or brussel sprouts. Even green beans don't work well because of their texture and taste. Rappini instead of broccoli is good, as is chopped spinach or fresh, diced artichoke hearts.
* Eliminate the tomatoes and serve only vegetables, herbs, and cheese.
* Use a cup of ricotta cheese with the grated Parmesan cheese and make a creamy sauce.
* Pesto is wonderful with a vegetable mixture and a touch of tomato.
* Serve the short-shape pastas for entertaining. Make a pasta salad by adding only vegetables and 1 tablespoon of red wine vinegar and some diced olives—great for picnics!
* Add freshly grated zucchini, roasted red pepper, goat cheese, or diced mari-

nated artichoke hearts to the top. When you cook the tomatoes, add a cup of diced, fresh seafood, cooked shredded chicken, turkey, or meat—mix them in when cooking the onion and garlic.

* Bake in a casserole with shredded mozzarella cheese instead of Parmesan cheese on top.

* Try tuna fish, sardines, or salmon; add them when cooking the tomatoes.

This is a wonderful recipe in which you can let your imagination run wild—create your own version of pasta primavera.

This dish can be used as an appetizer or as a main course for brunch, lunch, or buffets. It has a very pungent taste of vegetables and herbs. Light and easy to digest, it's perfect for a late dinner.

PASTA SHELLS STUFFED WITH PESTO AND CHEESE

Red Pepper Purée Sauce

16 large pasta shells
2 cups of skim-milk ricotta cheese
¼ cup Parmesan cheese, freshly grated
White or cayenne pepper to taste
¼ cup Basic Pesto Sauce (see page 197)
¼ cup mozzarella cheese, shredded
¼ cup Red Pepper and Tomato Sauce (see page 193)
4 sprigs of parsley

Servings:
4
Time:
20 *min.*
Calories:
847 *per serving*

Preheat oven at 325°F.

In a large lidded pan, boil water to cook the pasta.

Put the ricotta cheese, Parmesan cheese, and pepper in a bowl and mix thoroughly; add the pesto sauce to the mixture.

Cook the pasta al dente, drain, and rinse in cold water. Dry the pasta shells on a flat working surface.

Stuff each shell with 2 tablespoons of the cheese–pesto filling; do not overfill. Sprinkle with the shredded mozzarella cheese, place on an oiled baking sheet, and bake in the oven for 5 minutes.

Spoon red pepper sauce onto the bottom of 4 serving dishes and arrange 4 stuffed pasta shells on top of the sauce. Decorate with sprigs of parsley.

VARIATIONS
* Use cooked, drained, and chopped spinach instead of pesto.
* Use Basic Marinara Sauce (see page 192) instead of Red Pepper and Tomato Sauce.
* Fill the shells with cooked vegetables or ground meat.

P A S T A   A L L A   B R U N O

Red and Green Pepper Sauce

Servings:
8
Time:
15 *min.*
Calories:
460 *per serving*

1½ lb. thin spaghetti, short-shape pasta, or ziti
1½ cups onion, chopped
3 cloves of garlic, crushed
3 lb. red and green peppers, cut in ½-inch strips
½ cup black Italian olives, diced
½ tsp. crushed red pepper
¼ tsp. Italian herb seasoning
3 tbsp. green olive oil
½ cup Parmesan cheese, freshly grated
1 cup fresh Italian parsley, chopped

In a large lidded pan, boil water to cook the pasta.

In a large frying pan, sauté the onion, garlic, red and green peppers, olives, hot pepper, and Italian herb seasoning in the olive oil for 8 minutes. Add the parsley and toss thoroughly.

Cook the pasta al dente, drain, and place it in a large serving bowl. Pour the sauce over the pasta. Mix the sauce and pasta and add the Parmesan cheese and parsley. Serve at once.

VARIATIONS
* Use chopped zucchini, diced tomatoes, or mushrooms.
* Add 1 tablespoon of small, rinsed capers.
* Use goat cheese instead of Parmesan cheese.

PASTA PESCARA

Mixed Fresh Seafood Sauce

1 lb. linguine
1 medium-size onion, chopped
2 cloves of garlic, crushed
¼ cup crushed red pepper (to taste)
2 tbsp. green olive oil
½ cup Italian dry white wine
2 cups fresh tomatoes, peeled, seeded, and diced
1 tsp. Italian herb seasoning
1 cup fresh Italian parsley, chopped
3 cups fresh seafood, chopped (calamari, mussels, clams, shrimp, crabmeat,
   lobster, cod, bass, or swordfish)
2 tbsp. fresh basil, chopped

Servings:
6
Time:
25 *min.*
Calories:
447 *per serving*

In a large lidded pan, boil water to cook the pasta.

In a frying pan, sauté the onion, garlic, and crushed pepper in the olive oil for 2 minutes; add the white wine and continue cooking. After 5 more minutes, add the tomatoes, Italian herb seasoning, and parsley; cook for 5 minutes. Stir in the diced seafood and cook for 3 to 4 minutes. (Do not overcook: Seafood is better slightly underdone.) Stir in the basil and remove from the heat.

Cook the pasta al dente and drain it. Place the pasta in a large bowl; mix in the seafood sauce. Serve immediately.

VARIATIONS
* Use only one kind of fish.
* Eliminate the wine.

PASTA ALLA NORMA

Sicilian-Style Eggplant Sauce

Servings:
7
Time:
20 *min.*
Calories:
331 *per serving*

1 lb. rigatoni or penne pasta
2 lb. eggplant (1 large or 8 small eggplants)
Salt for soaking eggplant
3 cloves of garlic, crushed
2 tbsp. green olive oil
¼ cup Pecorino or Parmesan cheese, freshly grated
¼ cup fresh basil leaves, chopped (or 3 tbsp. dried basil)
Pepper to taste
½ cup fresh Italian parsley, chopped

In a large lidded pan, boil water to cook the pasta.

Wash the eggplant; cut lengthwise into long strips, leaving the skin on. Soak in cold water with 2 tablespoons of salt per quart of water. Rinse a few times, drain, and pat dry. Cut the slices into ¼-inch strips.

In a large frying pan, sauté the garlic and the eggplant strips in the oil; cook until they are soft and brown.

Cook the pasta al dente, drain, and put it in a large bowl. Toss the pasta with the cheese and herbs. Arrange the eggplant strips across the top of the pasta and sprinkle with a dash of parsley. Serve immediately.

VARIATIONS

* The cheeses change the taste; try to find *Ricotta Salata* and use sparingly.
* Use ½ cup fresh sliced mushrooms or chopped red pepper.

This classic dish was named after Bellini's opera, Norma.

PASTA CON LE SARDE TAORMINA

Pasta with Fresh Sardines, Fennel, Pignolis, and Raisins

Servings:
8
Time:
20 *min.*
Calories:
356 *per serving*

1 lb. bucatini, linguine, or penne pasta
2 tbsp. green olive oil
1 cup onion, chopped
¼ tsp. Italian herb seasoning
3 heads of wild or regular fennel

6 medium-size fresh sardines, or 2 3½-oz. cans of imported boneless sardines in olive oil
2 tbsp. pignoli nuts, roasted
½ cup dark raisins
½ cup fresh Italian parsley, chopped

In a large lidded pan, boil water to cook the pasta.

In a large skillet, heat the olive oil and sauté the onion, Italian herb seasoning, and fennel for 5 minutes. Remove the head, bones, and skins of the fresh sardines; or rinse, dry, and mash the canned sardines and add them to the skillet with the pignoli nuts, raisins, and parsley; cook for 8 more minutes.

Cook the pasta al dente, drain, and transfer it to a warm pasta bowl. Pour the sauce over the pasta and mix thoroughly. Serve immediately.

VARIATION
* Add 1 cup crushed plum tomatoes or ½ cup diced Sicilian olives.

In this classic dish, wild fennel and fresh sardines are the keys to real taste. You'll find this dish is a most unusual and luscious blend of tastes.

SPAGHETTINI BOSCO E MARE MEDITERRANEI ORSINI

1 lb. spaghettini (thin spaghetti)
1 lb. small fresh clams
2 cloves of garlic, crushed
⅛ cup green olive oil
¼ cup dry white wine
½ lb. Italian plum tomatoes, peeled, seeded, and diced
¾ lb. fresh porcini mushrooms, sliced
¼ cup fresh Italian parsley, chopped

Servings:
4
Time:
20 *min.*
Calories:
604 *per serving*

Boil water to cook the pasta.

Clean the clams; rinse well.

In a large frying pan, sauté the garlic and the clams in ½ of the oil until the clams open. Add the wine and cook for a few minutes; then add the tomatoes and cook for 3 minutes.

In a separate pan, sauté the mushrooms and another clove of garlic, crushed with the parsley, in the remaining olive oil for 3 minutes.

Cook the pasta, drain, and add it to the pan with the clams and tomato sauce. Pour over the mushroom sauce and mix together. Serve immediately.

VARIATIONS
* Use dried mushrooms; soak in 1 cup of white wine for ½ hour.
* Use fresh regular mushrooms.
* Use other seafood.

PASTA LIVORNESE

Linguine Pasta with Seafood, Tomatoes, Capers, and Olives

Servings:
6
Time:
15 *min.*
Calories:
505 *per serving*

1 lb. linguine pasta
3 cloves of garlic, crushed
1½ cups onion, chopped
2 anchovy filets, rinsed and minced
Cayenne or crushed red pepper to taste
3 tbsp. green olive oil
2 cups fresh plum tomatoes, peeled and diced; or canned Italian tomatoes, crushed
1 cup Italian Gaeta black olives, diced
2 tbsp. small capers, rinsed
½ tsp. Italian herb seasoning
3 cups fresh seafood, chopped (calamari, mussels, clams, shrimp, crabmeat, lobster, cod, or swordfish)
1 cup fresh Italian parsley, chopped

In a large lidded pan, boil water to cook the pasta.

In a large frying pan, sauté the garlic, onion, anchovies, and hot peppers in the olive oil for 3 minutes. Add the tomatoes, olives, capers, and Italian herb seasoning, and cook for 5 more minutes. Add the seafood and parsley; cook 3 to 6 minutes (keep the fish slightly undercooked).

Cook the pasta al dente, drain, and place it in a large serving bowl. Pour on the sauce and mix thoroughly. Serve immediately.

VARIATIONS
* Eliminate the anchovies.
* Add ½ cup sliced mushrooms.

F E T T U C C I N E   V E R D E
C O N   P O M M O D O R E
A L   C A P R A

Green Fettuccine with Goat Cheese and Basil-Stuffed Tomato

2 lb. green fettuccine noodles
12 small ripe tomatoes
1 cup onion, chopped
3 cloves of garlic, crushed
½ tsp. crushed red pepper flakes
½ tsp. Italian herb seasoning
¼ cup green olive oil
1 lb. goat cheese
2 cups fresh basil leaves, chopped

Servings:
12
Time:
20 *min.*
Calories:
475 *per serving*

Preheat oven at 400°F.

In a large lidded pan, boil water to cook the pasta.

Cut off a ¼-inch slice from the top of each tomato and set it aside. Scoop out the tomato seeds and pulp with a small spoon and strain off the seeds, saving the pulp for the sauce.

Set aside 3 tablespoons of olive oil and heat the remainder in a large skillet; sauté the tomato pulp, onion, 1 clove of garlic, crushed pepper, and Italian herb seasoning for 5 minutes; stir often. Place the goat cheese, olive oil, 2 cloves of crushed garlic, and the basil in a blender or food processor and blend.

Put the tomato shells in an oiled baking dish and fill them with the goat cheese mixture. Cover the tomato tops with the ¼-inch slices set aside and bake for 5 to 8 minutes.

Cook the pasta al dente, drain, and toss it with the tomato sauce. Put 2 or 3 ounces of pasta on 12 serving dishes and place a stuffed tomato in the center of each one. Decorate the top of each tomato with a small sprig of basil and serve.

VARIATIONS

* Use ricotta instead of goat cheese.
* Use colored pasta swirls.
* Toss pasta with a sauce made by sautéing 2 tablespoons of crushed garlic, 4 tablespoons of olive oil, and 1 teaspoon of Italian herb seasoning for 3 minutes, instead of tomato sauce.
* Use green and white fettuccine noodles.

R I G A T O N I   W I T H
E G G P L A N T   S A U C E
A L L A   C A R M E L O

Servings:
6
Time:
20 *min.*
Calories:
410 *per serving*

1 lb. rigatoni pasta
4 small or 2 medium-size eggplants
Salt to soak eggplant
1 cup onion, chopped
3 cloves of garlic, crushed
3 tbsp. green olive oil
6 ripe plum tomatoes, peeled and diced
4 fresh basil leaves, diced
¼ cup Pecorino cheese, freshly grated

Boil water to cook the pasta.

Dice the eggplant, soak it in cold water with salt, and rinse well.

In a large skillet, sauté the onion, garlic, and eggplant in the oil; brown the eggplant.

Add the diced tomatoes and cook for 5 minutes. Stir the tomatoes and the diced basil leaves through the sauce. Serve immediately over the pasta and toss with the Pecorino cheese.

VARIATIONS
* Use ½ cup of Parmesan cheese.
* Add ¼ cup diced fresh Italian parsley and ½ teaspoon hot pepper (crushed pepper flakes).

This is a real classic from the Calabria region of Italy. The eggplant and the Pecorino cheese make the taste.

SPAGHETTI ALLA MALIBU

Thin Spaghetti with Seafood and Vegetables

1 lb. thin spaghetti or linguine
12 mussels
12 small clams
1 lb. small shrimp
2 cups white onion, diced
3 red peppers, cut into julienne strips
2 green peppers, cut into julienne strips
2 cups marinated artichoke hearts, diced (fresh or jarred)
4 cloves of garlic, crushed
½ tsp. crushed red pepper
2 cups mushrooms, sliced
3 tbsp. green olive oil
2 cups fresh tomatoes, crushed; or canned Italian plum tomatoes with juice
1 tsp. Italian herb seasoning
1 pint bay scallops
1 cup fresh Italian parsley, chopped
Juice of 1 lemon

Servings:
6
Time:
20 *min.*
Calories:
644 *per serving*

Boil water to cook the pasta.

Scrub the mussels, clams, and shrimp well, drain, and set aside with the shells intact.

In a large skillet, sauté the onion, red and green peppers, artichokes, garlic, hot pepper, and mushrooms in the oil for 5 minutes. Add the tomatoes and Italian herb seasoning, and cook for 3 minutes.

Place all the fish in the sauce mixture and cover. Cook 3 to 4 minutes (just until shells open; do not overcook).

Remove the cover from the seafood mixture and add the parsley and lemon juice.

Cook the pasta al dente, drain, and transfer it to a large, warm bowl. Pour the seafood *misto* over the pasta and blend thoroughly. Place the seafood with the shells along the side of the bowl as a decoration. Sprinkle with more parsley and serve immediately. (The shellfish get tough when served cold.) Be sure to keep the fish slightly undercooked.

VARIATIONS

* Use a white wine sauce with the vegetables and seafood: Add 1 cup of dry white wine instead of the tomatoes.
* Use other vegetables: zucchini, broccoli, or diced black olives.
* Use only one kind of shellfish to cut the expense.

G N O C C H E T T I   D I
R I C O T T A   M A R C E L L A

Gnocchi with Ricotta Cheese

Servings:
4
Time:
45 *min.*
Calories:
398 *per serving*

1½ cups skim-milk ricotta cheese
1¼ cups all-purpose flour
½ cup Parmesan cheese, freshly grated
2 eggs, beaten
Pinch of nutmeg
½ cup fresh Italian parsley, finely chopped
Dash of white pepper
2 egg yolks

Put all the ingredients in a large bowl and blend together to form a smooth dough. Knead well. Roll the dough into 2 long, thin, "stick-shape" forms: Keep the board and your hands well floured. Cut into short pieces about ¼ inch long. Let the gnocchi stand for 30 minutes.

Cook the gnocchi in boiling water for 2 to 3 minutes. Remove from the pan with a slotted spoon and place in a warm bowl. Serve with butter and Parmesan cheese or with a Basic Marinara Sauce (see page 192), Basic Pesto Sauce (see page 197), Red Pepper and Tomato Sauce (see page 193), or Ricotta Cheesy Sauce (see page 194). Serve immediately.

VARIATIONS
* For color, add finely diced pimentos.
* Try drained, chopped spinach as a combination.

This dish can be frozen or stored in the refrigerator before serving.

PASTA ALL' AGLIO ALLA SINATRA

Garlic, Cheese, Oil, and Hot Pepper Sauce

1 lb. thin spaghetti
4 cloves of garlic, crushed
¼ tsp. crushed red pepper
3 tbsp. green olive oil
½ cup fresh Italian parsley, chopped
½ cup Parmesan cheese, freshly grated

Servings:
6
Time:
10 *min.*
Calories:
380 *per serving*

Boil water to cook the pasta.

In a large frying pan, sauté the garlic and hot pepper in the oil for 2 to 3 minutes.

Drain the pasta and add it to the pan. Toss with the oil, add the parsley and grated Parmesan cheese, and mix thoroughly. Heat for 1 minute. Serve immediately.

VARIATIONS

* Adjust the amount of garlic and hot pepper to taste. The finest oil and garlic are the key tastes.
* Add diced mushrooms and sauté.
* Add 1 cup of chopped onions.

This is one of Frank Sinatra's favorite pasta sauces: hence the name.

O R Z O   C O N   T U N A   M I S I

Orzo Pasta with Tuna Sauce

Servings:
6
Time:
15 *min.*
Calories:
434 *per serving*

2 cups orzo pasta
1 small red onion, diced
1 cup black olives, diced and pitted
2 6½-oz. cans of chunky style tuna fish (packed in water)
½ tsp. Italian herb seasoning
¼ cup green olive oil
Juice of 2 lemons
3 tbsp. small capers, rinsed
1 tsp. dry mustard
1 tsp. dill weed
½ cup dry white Italian wine
1 cup fresh Italian parsley, chopped
Pepper to taste

Boil water to cook the pasta.

In a large sauté pan, sauté the onion, olives, tuna, and Italian herb seasoning in the olive oil and lemon juice for 3 minutes. Add the capers, mustard, dill, and white wine; cook for 5 to 8 minutes, stirring often to make a creamy sauce with the tuna–mustard–wine base.

Drain the pasta and add it to the tuna sauce. Heat for 1 minute; cook thoroughly—mix the pasta and sauce. Garnish with parsley and add pepper to taste.

VARIATIONS

* Make a pasta salad: Add 1 cup of fresh cherry tomatoes, chopped—mix, do not cook.

POTATO GNOCCHI
PARMESAN

6–8 large Idaho potatoes (about 4½ lb.)
3 eggs
3 cups all-purpose flour
2 large cloves of garlic, crushed
½ cup Parmesan cheese, freshly grated
½ cup fresh Italian parsley, chopped

Servings:
11
Time:
80 *min.*
Calories:
280 *per serving*

Preheat oven at 400°F.

Scrub, then bake the potatoes until soft and tender. Cut them in half and scoop out the pulp, while still hot. Mash them thoroughly, adding the eggs. Sprinkle in ½ cup of flour. Crush the 2 cloves of garlic and add to the mixture along with the Parmesan cheese. Knead into a dough; place the dough on a work surface, gradually kneading in another 2½ cups of flour. Continue to knead until the dough is smooth and elastic, then shape into a loaf about 4 inches thick.

Cut the loaf into 1-inch strips and roll into ropes about ½ inch in diameter each. Cut the dough ropes into 1-inch pieces.

To test the dough, place 1 or 2 pieces in a large pan of fast-boiling water for about 2 to 3 minutes. If the pieces show signs of falling apart, add more flour (¼ cup at a time) and knead in, until the pieces hold together when boiled. Press the prongs of a floured fork down into each piece of gnocchi, making it curl around the fork.

Arrange each piece separately on a generously floured cloth, and allow to stand at room temperature until dry (about 3½ hours).

Add the gnocchi to a large pan of fast-boiling water and stir gently. When the gnocchi float to the surface, cook for about 2 minutes. Use a colander to drain thoroughly. Place on a platter, garnish with parsley, and serve with your favorite sauce. (See Salsas on page 190.)

VARIATIONS

* Use ricotta cheese (½ cup skim-milk ricotta, drained) instead of Parmesan cheese.
* For a zesty taste, try ¼ teaspoon of cayenne pepper.

This dish should be served warm, as an appetizer or main course.

RISOTTOS
Rice

All About Risotto

Risotto is the Italian version of rice. Italians never serve plain rice; they add a variety of ingredients to create recipes that range from the simplest *risotto* with cheese and mushrooms to a champagne, seafood, vegetable, chicken, or meat *risotto*—a meal in itself.

Risotto is known as more of a northern Italian speciality. *Risotto* is eaten more in the north of Italy; pasta is favored in southern Italy.

The special hard-grain Arborio rice grown in northern Italy is perfect because it holds an al dente texture during the long cooking process. This type of rice is very nutritious and low in calories.

For entertaining and special dinner parties, *risotto* can be very elegant. It's easy to prepare and serve. The ingredients can vary the cost factor a great deal. A base of butter, cheese, or herbs is inexpensive, but mixed seafood, caviar, champagne, porcini mushrooms, or Gorgonzola and goat cheeses can change the presentation to a very special, but expensive recipe.

Italian food markets, gourmet stores, and some supermarket chains feature Arborio rice. If Arborio rice is not available, use long-grain, brown, or wild rice.

RISOTTA FRUITA D' MARE

Italian Rice with Mixed Seafood

Servings:
4
Time:
35 *to* **50** *min.*
Calories:
467 *per serving*

2 cups onion, diced
2 cloves of garlic, crushed
½ tsp. crushed red pepper
2 tbsp. green olive oil
1½ cup Italian Arborio rice
1 cup warm water
2 cups dry white wine
1 cup Italian plum tomatoes with juice, crushed

1 tsp. Italian herb seasoning
2 cups fresh seafood, diced (clams, mussels, lobster, shrimp, crabmeat, or
    pieces of whitefish)
1 cup fresh Italian parsley, chopped

In a large casserole or skillet, sauté the onion, garlic, and pepper flakes for a
few minutes in the oil. Add the rice and ½ of the water and wine; cook the rice
for 20 minutes adding the remaining water and wine. Add the tomatoes, Italian
herb seasoning, and seafood; cook for 5 minutes stirring continuously. Do not
overcook the seafood—it will become tough and chewy. Sprinkle with parsley
and serve immediately.

VARIATIONS
* Use one kind of seafood.
* Add mushrooms or capers.
* Use lemon juice instead of water.
* Eliminate the tomatoes.

R I S O T T O   P R I M A V E R A P A R M I G I A N O

Italian Rice with Vegetables, Tomatoes, and Cheese

2 cups shallots or onion, diced
4 cloves of garlic, crushed
½ tsp. crushed red pepper
2 cups of mixed vegetables, diced (zucchini, broccoli, mushrooms, peppers,
    asparagus, eggplant, green peas, spinach, green beans)
2 tbsp. green olive oil
1 tsp. Italian herb seasoning
2½ cups Italian Arborio rice
2 cups Italian plum tomatoes with juice, crushed
1 cup warm water
1 cup fresh Italian parsley, chopped
¾ cup Parmesan cheese, freshly grated

Servings:
6
Time:
35 *to* **50** *min.*
Calories:
454 *per serving*

Preheat oven at 350°F.
In a large skillet or casserole that can be used for serving, sauté the shallots,
garlic, hot pepper, and vegetables in the oil for a few minutes, stirring often.
Add the Italian herb seasoning and the rice.

Add the crushed tomatoes in small amounts with water and stir thoroughly until the rice is cooked (about 20 minutes) and the liquid absorbed. Add the parsley and Parmesan cheese and stir thoroughly. Serve immediately, or bake, covered, before serving for 5 to 8 minutes.

VARIATIONS

* Use a wine and water base instead of tomatoes.
* Add olives, roasted red peppers, or sun-dried tomatoes.
* Use only one kind of vegetable.
* Top with mozzarella cheese and bake as a casserole.

The dish can be prepared in advance and heated by baking before serving.

R I S O T T O   A L   F U N G H I

Rice with Mushrooms, Cheese, and Herbs

Servings:
6
Time:
35 *to* **50** *min.*
Calories:
398 *per serving*

1 cup shallots, finely chopped
3 cloves of garlic, crushed
10 oz. mushrooms (porcini, dried, or fresh), thinly sliced
1 tbsp. green olive oil
1 tsp. Italian herb seasoning
½ tsp. crushed red pepper
1 cup warm water
2 cups dry Italian white wine
2 cups Italian Arborio rice
1 tbsp. unsalted butter
1 cup Parmesan-Reggiano cheese, freshly grated
1 cup fresh Italian parsley, chopped

In a large casserole (serving type) or heavy skillet, sauté the shallots, garlic, and mushrooms in the oil at medium heat for 5 minutes, stirring often. Add the Italian herb seasoning, red pepper, and ½ cup of the water and wine. Add the rice and cook, stirring constantly.

Add the remaining water and wine in small amounts as the rice mixture thickens. Cook the rice about 20 minutes; then add the butter, Parmesan-Reggiano cheese, and parsley, and stir thoroughly. Serve immediately.

VARIATION

* Add a mixture of 3 or 4 kinds of mushrooms.

RISOTTO
D'CHAMPAGNE

Rice with Italian Brut Sparkling Wine, Mushrooms, and Cheese

1 cup shallots, chopped
10 oz. porcini mushrooms, thinly sliced
2 tbsp. unsalted butter
2 cups Italian Arborio rice
1 tsp. Italian herb seasoning
1 cup warm water
3 cups Italian Brut Sparkling wine
1 cup fresh Italian parsley, chopped
1 cup Parmesan cheese, freshly grated

Servings:
6
Time:
35 *to* **50** *min.*
Calories:
398 *per serving*

In a large casserole or skillet, sauté the shallots and mushrooms in the butter for 3 minutes under medium heat. Add the rice, Italian herb seasoning, and small amounts of water and wine until the rice is cooked. Add the parsley and grated Parmesan cheese. Serve immediately.

VARIATIONS
* Use finely diced asparagus with the mushrooms.
* Use sliced fresh mushrooms if you cannot find porcini mushrooms.

RICE AND VEGETABLE MISTO STUFFED PEPPERS

Servings:
12
Time:
20 *min.*
Calories:
180 *per serving*

12 medium-size peppers (6 red, 3 green, and 3 yellow)
1 cup Italian Arborio rice, long-grain white rice, or brown rice
2 cups onion, diced
3 cloves of garlic, crushed
½ tsp. crushed red pepper
2 cups fresh mushrooms, sliced
3 tbsp. green olive oil
4 medium-size tomatoes, seeded and chopped
1 cup zucchini, diced
½ cup pitted black olives, diced
1 tsp. Italian herb seasoning
1 cup fresh Italian parsley, chopped
1 cup Parmesan cheese, freshly grated

Preheat oven at 350°F.
Boil water to cook the rice.
Cut the tops off the peppers and scoop out the centers.
In a large skillet, sauté the pulp of the peppers (not seeds or cores), onion, garlic, hot pepper, and mushrooms in the oil for 3 to 4 minutes, stirring often. Add the tomatoes, zucchini, olives, Italian herb seasoning, and parsley; cook for 5 minutes. Add the cooked rice and Parmesan cheese to this sauce and blend thoroughly.
Fill the peppers, put them in a baking dish, and bake with more cheese sprinkled on the top of each pepper for 8 minutes.

VARIATIONS
* Add diced seafood, chicken, turkey, or meat instead of the zucchini.
* Mix with Basic Pesto Sauce (see page 197).
* Use eggplant instead of the tomatoes.
* Try roasting the outside of the peppers for more taste.

INSALATA DI RISO

Dried Tomatoes, Artichokes, Peas, Mushrooms, and Rice Salad

2 cups long-grain brown rice (6 cups cooked rice)
1 tsp. green olive oil
2 14-oz. jars of marinated artichoke hearts, rinsed and chopped
1 cup mushrooms, sliced
12 sun-dried tomatoes, sliced, rinsed, and chopped
4 medium-size carrots, grated
6 green onions, thinly sliced
3 stalks of celery, diced
1½ cups cooked green peas
½ cup fresh Italian parsley, minced
½ cup black olives, pitted and sliced
1 cup Romano cheese, freshly grated

Servings:
10
Time:
25 *min.*
Calories:
375 *per serving*

MARINADE
½ cup wine vinegar
½ cup green olive oil
1 tbsp. fresh basil, chopped
1 tsp. tarragon
3 cloves of garlic, minced

Add the rice to 1½ cups of briskly boiling water containing 1 teaspoon of green olive oil and cook for exactly 20 minutes in a tightly lidded saucepan. While the rice is cooking, mix the marinade ingredients in a large, open bowl.

Drain and quarter the artichoke hearts. Place them in the bowl of marinade with the mushrooms and chopped sun-dried tomatoes and soak until the rice is cooked. When the rice is cooked, let it cool to room temperature and add the remaining ingredients, except the Romano cheese, to the marinade bowl. Mix in the cooled rice and toss thoroughly. Sprinkle on the Romano cheese and serve at room temperature.

VARIATIONS
* Add 2 cups of chopped, precooked chicken, turkey, or tuna fish.
* Add diced, roasted red peppers.
* Add minced arugula leaves.

RISOTTO ALLA LUCIANA

Clams, Mushrooms, Shrimp, and Caviar Cooked with Rice

Servings:
6
Time:
25 *min.*
Calories:
251 *per serving*

1 cup Italian Arborio rice
2 lb. small clams
12 large shrimp
⅛ cup green olive oil
1 cup mushrooms, thinly sliced
3 cloves of garlic, crushed
1 tsp. crushed hot red pepper
½ cup fresh Italian parsley, chopped
1 tsp. Italian herb seasoning
3 tbsp. caviar (quality will make the difference)

Cook the rice about 45 minutes.

Wash the clams and shrimp. Place the clams in a large skillet with 1 tablespoon of olive oil. Cover and steam over high heat (3 to 5 minutes) until the clams open. Remove from heat and separate the clams from the shells. Reserve the juice and pass it through a strainer.

Place the remainder of the oil in a large sauté pan; sauté the mushrooms, garlic, and hot pepper for a few minutes. Add the clam juice, parsley, shrimps, and the Italian herb seasoning and sauté for 3 to 5 minutes. (Do not overcook the shrimp.) Add the clams and mix thoroughly.

Remove from the heat and set aside. Add the cooked rice to the seafood mixture and blend thoroughly. Arrange the rice on serving plates and top with a dab of caviar. For decoration, put a few clams back in their shells and place on top of each dish.

VARIATIONS

* Instead of caviar, use one cup diced sun-dried tomatoes.
* Add 1 cup chopped black olives instead of caviar.
* Use about one cup of chopped, fresh tomatoes.
* Vary the seafood: Use lobster instead of clams or shrimp.
* Cook the rice in clam juice instead of water.
* Add diced red pepper while cooking the garlic to add a dash of color and taste (2 red peppers finely chopped).

C O R O N O   D I   R I S O

Rice Ring with Red Peppers and Mushrooms

Servings:
6
Time:
Arborio, **70**
min.; brown rice,
55 *minutes*
Calories:
280 *per serving*

2½ cups water or thin chicken broth
1 cup Italian Arborio rice or short-grain brown rice
¼ cup green olive oil
½ cup Parmesan cheese, freshly grated
4 medium-size red and green peppers, sliced
4 cups mushrooms
4 medium-size cloves of garlic, crushed
½ tsp. Italian herb seasoning
2 tbsp. fresh Italian parsley, chopped
Fresh ground black pepper or cayenne pepper to taste
1 large onion, finely chopped
1 8-oz. can of Italian plum tomatoes, crushed
1 small bay leaf

Preheat oven at 350°F.

In a tightly lidded pan, boil water or stock and add the rice (cook Arborio rice for 45 minutes, brown rice for 30 minutes). Do not let the rice burn.

Stir 2 tablespoons of olive oil and the Parmesan cheese into the warm, cooked rice. (If the rice is precooked, warm it.) Spoon the rice into a lightly oiled ring mold and press it down firmly. Seal the mold with foil and bake for 10 to 15 minutes.

Heat 1 tablespoon of olive oil in a large skillet, and sauté the red peppers, mushrooms, garlic, Italian herb seasoning, and parsley for 6 minutes, adding pepper to taste. While the peppers are cooking, heat the remainder of the olive oil in a separate skillet, and sauté the onion until translucent. Add the tomatoes and bay leaf and cook briskly for another 6 minutes.

To serve, turn the baked rice mold over onto a large serving platter and arrange the cooked mushrooms and peppers in the center. Remove the bay leaf from the sauce and pour it around the rice ring.

VARIATION
* Use green peppers, zucchini, or Basic Pesto Sauce (see page 197).

ZUPPAS

Soups

Italian cooking offers one of the largest selections of soups in the world. *Zuppa* specials come from every region and feature seafood, pasta, beans, lentils, meat, herbs, dumplings, rice, scrapellas, and all kinds of combinations of ingredients.

There are soups that are consommés and others that are purées. There are chunky, creamy, cheesy, hot, delicate, and spicy soups; many of them are a meal all by themselves.

Italy is a country of many climates, and the regional soups usually reflect the weather conditions of the areas from which they originate. It can get very cold in the north; thus, a full-bodied *zuppa* is popular. In the south, it's warm; therefore, a light consommé *zuppa* is the favorite. In the central regions, you'll find both full-bodied and light soups.

Zuppa should be a regular feature on your menu because of the enormous variety, simple preparation, and, of course, lightness. There are many Italian soups to choose from: Many of them are so elegant and exciting that they are ideal for entertaining as a first course, or even as a main course.

Imagine a luscious bowl of Minestrone alla Famiglia with pasta, herbs, and grated Parmesan cheese; or Pasta Fagioli Giuseppe with pasta and beans; or lentil and pasta soup. Zuppa di Merluzzo is a mixed fresh seafood soup: Serve it with fresh, crusty Italian bread, a glass of white wine, and a mixed green salad on the side, and you have the perfect meal—nutritious, light, and easy to prepare.

BASIC
VEGETABLE STOCK

Yield:
2 *qts.*
Time:
50 *min.*
Calories:
115 *per cup*

2 medium-size onions, chopped
2 large leeks, cleaned, trimmed, and diced
1 medium-size parsnip, diced
4 carrots, diced
5 stalks of celery, diced (no leaves)
2 cups fresh Italian parsley, chopped
2 medium-size white potatoes, diced
2 large turnips, diced
1 sweet potato, diced

3 large plum tomatoes, peeled and diced
6 cloves of garlic, crushed
2 tsp. Italian herb seasoning
¼ tsp. cayenne pepper
1 cup Parmesan cheese, freshly grated

Wash and prepare the vegetables. Place them with the seasonings in a 4-quart lidded pot and cover with about 2 quarts of cold water.

Bring to a boil and simmer for about 50 minutes. Mix in the Parmesan cheese. The broth may be strained through a sieve or served as is.

VARIATIONS
* Add 2 cups of diced escarole or spinach.
* Use zucchini, cabbage, green beans, and peas.

C H I C K E N   S T O C K

1 lb. shin knuckles of veal
2 chicken backs and necks
1 chicken carcass
3 quarts cold water
3 carrots, diced
3 medium-size onions, chopped
4 celery stalks, diced
3 large plum tomatoes
2 leeks (dice white part only)
6 cloves of garlic, crushed
1 bay leaf
1 small chunk of Parmesan cheese (1-inch square)
1 tbsp. of Italian herb seasoning
1 tsp. Vegit seasoning
3 cups Italian parsley, chopped
Pepper to taste.

Yield:
2 *qts.*
Time:
3½ *hrs.*
Calories:
68 *per cup*

Wash the veal bones and chicken parts and place them in a large pot. Cover them with the cold water and bring to a boil; then simmer for 30 minutes.

Skim the bone stock and then add the vegetables, seasoning, cheese, and herbs. Simmer for 3 hours. Cool and then remove fat from the surface.

Strain through a fine sieve. Remove any fat from the surface. Use as a chicken stock base for chicken, veal, game, sauces, and soup dishes.

F I S H   S T O C K

Base for Fish Soups and Sauces

Yield:
2 *qts.*
Time:
3½ *hrs.*
Calories:
58 *per cup*

2½ quarts of boiling water
2 lb. fish bones, heads trimmings, leftovers; cleaned and washed
3 cups dry white Italian wine
3 onions, diced
4 cloves of garlic, crushed
4 cups diced mixed vegetables (carrots, turnips, parsnips, leeks, etc.)
4 celery stalks, diced
3 large ripe plum tomatoes, peeled
1 small bay leaf
3 cups fresh Italian parsley, chopped
1 tbsp. Italian herb seasoning
1 tsp. Vegit seasoning
Pepper to taste

In a large lidded pan add the ingredients to boiling water. Bring to a boil again and simmer gently for 3 to 4 hours. Pour through a fine strainer into small, lidded containers and freeze until needed. (Will keep for up to 6 weeks.)

Any part of the fish can be used for a stock except the gills and viscera. Crab, lobster, clams, mussels, and shrimp add a full, rich flavor to stock. When adding herbs to your fish stock, I recommend Italian parsley and thyme, sage, Italian herb seasoning, a bay leaf, dill, fennel seeds, cayenne pepper, crushed hot pepper flakes, leeks, onions, or garlic.

After cooking fish stock for about three hours, you should carefully strain it to make sure there are no bones left. When that's done, you can freeze it in working size, lidded containers so that it is always ready for use.

To make good seafood sauces, strain and boil the stock, reducing it, and thus intensifying the flavor. Don't forget that a dash of fresh lemon juice or diced fresh parsley can do wonders for a sauce when added just before serving.

TUSCAN ZUPPA D'MINESTRONE

1 cup short-shape pasta, cooked (elbows, shells, short noodles)
2 cups onion, chopped
6 cloves of garlic, crushed
3 celery stalks, diced
4 carrots, diced
1 slice prosciutto or bacon, diced
4 soft tomatoes, peeled, seeded, and diced
4 plum tomatoes, peeled and diced
1 leek (diced, white part only)
1 cup fresh green beans, diced
1 cup savoy cabbage, chopped
1 tsp. Italian herb seasoning
½ tsp. thyme
Black pepper to taste
3 cups vegetable stock
1 cup fresh Italian parsley, chopped
1 can of white cannellini beans, drained and rinsed
½ cup Parmesan cheese, freshly grated
2 tbsp. green olive oil
4 slices of Tuscan-style, hard-crusted bread, toasted

Servings:
6
Time:
30 *min.*
Calories:
427 *per serving*

Cook the pasta. In a large skillet, sauté the onion, garlic, celery, carrots, and prosciutto for 5 minutes in the oil. Add the tomatoes, leek, green beans, cabbage, and seasonings; cover and cook over medium heat for 10 minutes with the stock. Add the parsley, beans, and Parmesan cheese and cook for 5 more minutes.

Drain the pasta and add to the soup. If the soup is thick, add some hot water and blend thoroughly. Sprinkle with a few drops of olive oil after serving, and add one piece of bread to each bowl of soup.

MINESTRONE ALLA GENOVESE ZEFFIRINO

Vegetable Soup with Pesto Sauce

Servings:
6
Time:
30 *min.*
Calories:
464 *per serving*

½ lb. short-shape pasta
2 celery stalks, diced
2 leeks, (diced, white part only)
2 carrots, diced
2 cloves of garlic, crushed
1 cup swiss chard leaves, chopped
1 cup fresh Italian parsley, chopped
2 quarts of vegetable stock
3 tbsp. tomato puree
½ tsp. of Italian seasoning
1 cup white cannellini beans (drained)
½ cup Basic Pesto Sauce (see page 197)

Cook the pasta and drain.

Put all the ingredients, except the pasta, beans, and Pesto Sauce into a large pot and cover. Cook over medium heat for 20 minutes. Add the pasta, beans, and pesto sauce, and cook for 5 minutes. Serve immediately.

VARIATIONS
* Use chicken stock instead of vegetable stock.
* Prepare without the beans; use only pasta.
* Use rice instead of pasta.

RED PEPPER AND ARUGULA SOUP WITH BRUSCHETTA

Servings:
2
Time:
25 *min.*
Calories:
290 *per serving*

4 large red bell peppers
1 cup onion, chopped
3 cloves of garlic, crushed
2 tbsp. green olive oil
½ cup chicken stock
½ cup fresh Italian parsley, chopped

¼ tsp. Italian herb seasoning
3 fresh basil leaves, minced
Dash of cayenne pepper
1 3-×-2-inch piece of Italian bread (crust removed), toasted and cut into small
   pieces
2 bunches of arugula, broken into small pieces, using leaves only (if not
   available, use watercress)

   Roast the peppers (see page 7) and dice.
   In a large skillet, sauté the onion, garlic, and peppers in the olive oil for a few
minutes. Purée the mixture for 2 minutes and return to the skillet; then add the
chicken stock, herbs, and seasonings, and cook for 15 minutes. Toast and cube
the bread; add it to the soup with the arugula leaves. Serve immediately.

VARIATIONS
* Use 1 cup of fresh mushrooms.
* Sprinkle with freshly grated Parmesan cheese.
* Add a dab of ricotta cheese or goat cheese.

This dish is great as a different soup or appetizer.

Z U P P A   D I   L E N T I C C H E

Soup of Lentils

2 cups red lentils (soaked in warm water for 1 hour)
2 quarts cold water
2 tsp. Italian herb seasoning
2 cups onion, diced
3 stalks of celery, chopped
5 cloves of garlic, crushed
3 tbsp. green olive oil
1 cup canned Italian plum tomatoes with juice, crushed
Dash of crushed hot pepper or cayenne pepper
2–3 sage leaves, minced
1 cup fresh Italian parsley, chopped
½ cup Pecorino or Parmesan cheese, freshly grated

Servings:
6
Time:
80 *min.*
Calories:
350 *per serving*

Soak the lentils for 1 hour in warm water; discard those that float to the surface and look inferior. Drain the lentils and add them to a large pan with 2 quarts of cold water, with 1 teaspoon of Italian herb seasoning, and cook for 20 minutes. In a large skillet, sauté the onion, celery, and garlic in the oil for 5 minutes. Add the tomatoes, seasonings, herbs, and parsley; cook for 8 minutes. Drain the cooked lentils and add to the tomato mixture. Cook for 5 more minutes, mixing thoroughly. Add the Pecorino or Parmesan cheese and mix thoroughly. Serve hot.

VARIATIONS
* Add 1 cup of short-shape pasta.
* Add pieces of ham.

Z U P P A   D I   M E R L U Z Z O

Soup Made with Whitefish

Servings:
4
Time:
25 *min.*
Calories:
192 *per serving*

1 cup onion, chopped
1 large leek (dice white part only)
2 cups fresh Italian parsley, chopped
1 tsp. Italian herb seasoning
1 lemon (juice only)
1 cup dry white Italian wine
3 cloves of garlic, crushed
1 tsp. red pepper flakes
1 lb. whitefish (cod, bass, flounder, whiting)
1 bay leaf
1 tsp. fennel seeds
5 oz. fresh tomatoes, peeled, seeded, and diced; or 1 cup canned Italian plum tomatoes, diced with juice
2 slices of crusty Italian bread
1 cup warm water

In a large skillet, sauté the leek, onion, garlic, and pepper in the oil for 4 minutes. Add the wine and fish and cook for 5 minutes. Add the tomatoes, bay leaf, parsley, seasoning, fennel seeds, and water, and cook for 10 minutes. Remove from the heat.

Toast the bread and cut into small squares; add to the soup. Serve warm with a salad and toasted bread that is spread with olive oil and garlic.

VARIATIONS

* Try adding 2 cups of mixed, chopped fresh vegetables.
* Make the soup without the tomatoes and add a tablespoon of Basic Pesto Sauce (see page 197) to the top of each portion served.
* Add 2 cups of thinly sliced fresh mushrooms.
* One cup of very small cooked pasta, such as ditali or small shells, can be added to the soup.

MINESTRONE ALLA FAMIGLIA

1 cup cooked short-shape pasta
2 carrots, diced
3 stalks of celery, diced
½ cup frozen peas
1 large potato, cubed
1 cup cabbage, shredded
2 leeks (diced, white part only)
2 quarts of stock, vegetable or chicken
1 tsp. Italian herb seasoning
Dash of cayenne pepper
6 ripe tomatoes, peeled, skinned, seeded, and diced
1 cup fresh Italian parsley, chopped
2 small zucchini, diced
¼ lb. fresh spinach, chopped
½ cup Parmesan cheese, freshly grated

Servings:
4
Time:
30 *min.*
Calories:
482 *per serving*

Cook the pasta.

Add all the vegetables to a large pan, except the spinach, tomatoes, zucchini, and parsley. Cook the stock with the Italian herb seasoning and pepper for 20 minutes, covered, under low heat. Add the tomatoes, parsley, zucchini, spinach, and Parmesan cheese, and cook for 8 minutes. Add the pasta.

Serve in a large, heated bowl and sprinkle with grated Parmesan cheese.

VARIATIONS

* Add Swiss chard leaves instead of spinach.
* Use green beans instead of cabbage.

MINESTRA DI RISO E PISELLI

Rice and Pea Soup

Servings:
4
Time:
25 *min.*
Calories:
390 *per serving*

1 cup shallots, diced; or 1 cup onion, diced
¼ cup ham, diced
3 cloves of garlic, crushed
¼ tsp. crushed hot pepper flakes
3 tbsp. green olive oil
1 package of frozen peas
1 tsp. Italian herb seasoning
1 cup fresh Italian parsley, chopped
1 quart vegetable stock
⅔ cup cooked rice
½ cup Romano cheese, freshly grated

In a large skillet, sauté the shallots, ham, garlic, and hot pepper in the oil for a few minutes. Add the peas, Italian herb seasoning, and parsley, and cook with the stock for 10 minutes. Add the rice and Romano cheese and cook for 3 to 5 minutes.
Serve hot.

VARIATIONS:
* Use peas only.
* Add mixed vegetables, such as carrots, celery, zucchini, and spinach leaves.
* Leave the ham out, or use prosciutto instead.

PASTA E FAGIOLI GIUSEPPE

Pasta and Bean Soup

Servings:
4
Time:
25 *min.*
Calories:
300 *per serving*

1 cup short-shape pasta (elbows or short rigatoni)
1½ cups onion, chopped
4 cloves of garlic, crushed
2 celery stalks, chopped
¼ tsp. crushed hot pepper flakes
2 tbsp. green olive oil

1 cup red kidney beans, drained
1 tsp. Italian herb seasoning
1 cup fresh plum tomatoes, seeded, peeled, and diced; or canned Italian
    tomatoes, crushed
1 cup fresh Italian parsley, chopped
¼ cup Parmesan cheese, freshly grated

Boil water to cook the pasta.

In a large skillet, sauté the onion, garlic, celery, and hot peppers in the oil for 5 minutes.

Drain the cooked pasta and set aside. Add the beans to the mixture with the Italian herb seasoning, tomatoes, and parsley, and cook for 5 minutes. Add the pasta and the Parmesan cheese and cook for 2 to 3 minutes.

Serve immediately in pasta bowls.

VARIATION

* Add pieces of ground beef, prosciutto, or ham, sautéed with onion and garlic.

ZUPPA ALL'AGLIO ALLA NANCI

Garlic Soup

1¾ pints water
16 cloves of garlic, crushed
1 cup fresh Italian parsley, chopped
1 tsp. Italian herb seasoning
¼ tsp. cayenne pepper
4 slices of hard-crusted Italian bread
Green olive oil (to spread on the bread)
½ cup Parmesan cheese, freshly grated

Servings:
4
Time:
20 *min.*
Calories:
200 *per serving*

Boil water. Add all the ingredients, except the Parmesan cheese, olive oil, and bread, and simmer for 15 minutes. Toast the bread and spread it with olive oil and crushed garlic cloves to serve with the soup. Add the Parmesan cheese to the soup and stir thoroughly.

Serve hot.

VARIATION

* Add mushrooms, shredded spinach, or diced tomatoes.

PIZZAS

Breads

The Pizza Revolution

After pasta became such a popular food with a new identity, pizza followed in its footsteps, changing its image with a new gourmet touch.

Pizza, once the simple food of the poor people in Naples, first spawned an Americanized version that quickly put it into the category of "junk" food. Now pizza has changed: It's the new "in" sensation—on every menu in every chic restaurant, café, and trattoria.

Needless to say, high-priced ingredients have pushed up the price from $6 for a simple cheese-and-tomato pizza to as high as $25 for toppings that include caviar, smoked salmon, lobster, shrimp, duck breast, goat cheese, and imported Gorgonzola.

Now pasta and pizza share the same billing as the most popular foods of the day. Pizzas can be made with many creative sauces and a wide variety of pizza crusts. But let's get back to the great basics, the old classics that never die: a thin, crisp-crusted pizza with the finest homemade mozzarella cheese, the freshest plum tomatoes, fresh basil, perfect green olive oil, and Italian herb seasoning—what a wonderful blending of tastes in this classic Italian pizza.

The simple taste of quality ingredients is still the essence of fine dining and cooking. Look underneath your pizza to be sure you are making the best pizza. The crust should be speckled with grains of browned, semolina flour. Then look at the topping. Remember, quality ingredients are so important. Use fresh, homemade mozzarella, preferably in slices or shredded, never grated. A distinguished tomato sauce—using only the finest tomatoes, olive oil, and fresh garlic—is essential. You must have fresh, crisp, snow-white mushrooms and other vegetables; the finest grated Parmesan cheese sprinkled on top; and the best, mixed Italian seasoning added. (Be careful with the oregano; it's the downfall of so many American pizza makers—too much is too overpowering.) If you are buying your pizza, keep in mind that a coal-burning oven is the best, followed by a wood-burning oven.

You'll enjoy making the following pizza recipes. They are Italian classics and great for entertaining.

I N D I V I D U A L   P I Z Z A S

PIZZA CRUST
2 cups whole-wheat flour
1 cup all-purpose flour
6 tbsp. cold butter, cut into cubes
8 tbsp. ice water

TOPPING
8 fresh plum tomatoes, sliced
6 oz. goat cheese, crumbled; or mozzarella cheese, sliced
½ tsp. Italian herb seasoning
1 yellow pepper, cut into strips
¼ cup black olives, diced
¼ cup fresh basil leaves, minced; or Italian parsley, chopped
Dash of black pepper
1 tbsp. green olive oil (per pizza)

Servings:
6
Time:
55 *min.*
Calories:
538 *per slice*

Preheat the oven at 400°F.

Make the pastry in a medium-size bowl. Combine the flours and the butter; use your fingertips to rub the flour and butter together until the mixture resembles cornmeal. Stir in the ice water until the dough holds together. Knead the dough into a ball, and wrap it in waxed paper. Refrigerate for 30 minutes.

Divide the dough into 6 equal pieces. On a lightly floured surface, roll each piece into an 8-inch circle. Place circles on ungreased cooking sheets and bake 12 to 15 minutes until lightly browned; then remove from the oven.

Place the tomatoes all around the dough. Crumble the cheese on top of the tomatoes, and sprinkle with the Italian herb seasoning. Place the yellow pepper strips all around the cheese-and-tomato topping. Place the olives all around the cheese, and sprinkle with the basil leaves or parsley. Add a dash of black pepper.

Dribble 1 tablespoon of olive oil on each pizza. Bake for 6 to 8 minutes.

VARIATION
* Select a different topping from the suggestions in this section. Or, create your own topping with what you have to work with.

Pizza is visually beautiful as well as a delicious taste sensation.
Serve it for lunch, brunch, dinner, or supper. It can also be an appetizer, with a vegetable or fish topping.

PIZZA ELISA

Servings:
8
Time:
25 *min.*
Calories:
112 *per slice*

PIZZA CRUST
½ cup whole wheat flour
3 tablespoons Parmesan cheese, freshly grated
½ teaspoon Italian herb seasoning
3 cloves of garlic, crushed
8 egg whites
Dash of white pepper
2 tablespoons green olive oil

TOPPING
2 cups fresh tomatoes, diced
¼ cup fresh basil, minced; or Italian parsley, diced
¼ cup mushrooms, chopped
⅓ cup Parmesan cheese, freshly grated

Preheat oven at 350°F.

Combine all the ingredients for the pizza crust, except the olive oil, in a large mixing bowl. Blend and pour into a greased 12-inch-diameter pizza pan. Bake for 15 minutes.

Remove the crust from the oven and sprinkle on more Italian herb seasoning; spread the olive oil over the surface of the pizza crust.

Add the diced tomatoes, basil, mushrooms, and Parmesan or mozzarella cheese. Bake for another 5 minutes. Serve immediately.

VARIATION
* Select toppings from those listed in this section.

Pizza is perfect for lunch, brunch, dinner, late supper, or snacks.

This great low-calorie pizza offers more health benefits than regular pizza: It's a better balanced source of protein, and contains all the essential amino acids for easier digestion. It's also low in cholesterol.

This pizza has a total of 300 calories per 12-inch crust versus the usual 900 calories. This is a 600 calorie saving per slice. With the topping, it is 120 calories per slice.

POTATO-CRUSTED PIZZA

PIZZA CRUST

1 lb. potatoes, peeled and cut for cooking
1½ oz. Romano cheese, freshly grated
1½ oz. mozzarella cheese, shredded
1½ tbsp. milk
2 eggs, separated
1 cup all-purpose flour

TOPPING

½ cup green olive oil
3 large cloves of garlic, crushed
½ tsp. Italian herb seasoning
1 cup mushrooms, sliced
½ cup fresh Italian parsley, chopped
6 plum tomatoes, peeled and diced
½ cup Romano cheese, freshly grated

Servings:
4
Time:
35 *min.*
Calories:
595 *per slice*

Preheat oven at 400°F.

Boil the potatoes until soft; drain the potatoes and mash smooth, free of lumps, adding the cheeses. Beat the milk and the egg yolks and stir them into the potato mix; add the flour. Beat the whites of the egg until stiff, and gently fold into the potato mixture.

Spread the mixture onto a well-oiled, 12-inch, metal pizza pan and bake until the crust is lightly browned and a fork inserted in the center comes out clean. Perforate the whole surface of the crust with a fork.

Heat the oil in a skillet; add the garlic, Italian herb seasoning, and mushrooms. Cook for about 2 minutes over medium heat. Remove from the flame and stir in the Italian parsley.

Spread the mixture over the pizza crust, top with the tomatoes, and sprinkle on the Romano cheese. Sprinkle lightly with green olive oil and place under the broiler about 6 inches from the flame. Cook until the cheese is bubbly and the crust edges are brown. Decorate with a dash of chopped parsley, cut into portions, and serve.

Pizza can be served as brunch, lunch, an appetizer, or dinner. It's also great for buffets.

Pizza Toppings

The lists of suggested toppings that follow will include ingredients only. Depending on the size of the pizza and the taste you desire from a particular ingredient, you will usually use one-half cup of chopped fresh ingredients to one-quarter cup of shredded meats and cheeses. And use lots of Italian herb seasoning (without fear of the heavy oregano taste) and lots of fresh herbs.

Cover the pizza evenly with about one-half to one cup of sauce; spread the ingredients over the sauce, covering the pizza lightly. Do not use a heavy amount of ingredients—balance the tastes. Use hot crushed pepper if you cook the ingredients; use cayenne or black pepper at the last moment.

Here is a great variety of classic and trendy ingredients. Remember, you can create your own combinations, too.

Try the following:

* Red and green strips of pepper, diced black olives, diced marinated artichoke hearts, chopped fresh Italian parsley, and a dash of hot pepper over a tomato sauce base with shredded mozzarella cheese.

* Grilled eggplant slices, mushrooms, roasted red peppers, and zucchini rounds with grated Parmesan cheese and a small amount of crumbled goat cheese.

* Freshly sliced large tomatoes, chopped fresh basil, a sprinkle of green olive oil, and a dash of Italian herb seasoning. (Optional: Sprinkle with Parmesan cheese or shredded mozzarella cheese.)

* Cooked, mixed seafood, a light tomato sauce, parsley, and Italian herb seasoning. (Add the seafood at the last minute.)

* Four cheeses—mozzarella, Parmesan, Bel Paese, and a touch of Gorgonzola—with sliced mushrooms, red onions, diced tomatoes, and Italian herb seasoning.

* Mashed garlic, onions, parsley, mozzarella slices, basil, and a sprinkling of green olive oil.

* Diced Italian sausage, with shredded mozzarella cheese over tomato sauce with Italian herb seasoning.

* Sun-dried tomatoes, mozzarella, basil, Italian herb seasoning, diced black olives, and a dribble of green olive oil.

* Ricotta cheese over Pesto Sauce, with finely chopped fresh tomatoes and Italian herb seasoning.

* Sautéed eggplant with tomatoes, black olives, shredded mozzarella cheese, black pepper, and Italian herb seasoning.

* Gorgonzola cheese, prosciutto, garlic, Italian parsley, diced fresh tomatoes, and Italian herb seasoning.

* Tomatoes, capers, tuna fish, olives, and Italian herb seasoning.

* Freshly cooked, diced spinach with goat cheese, mushrooms, pimentos, garlic, and Italian herb seasoning.
* Primavera topping—cooked, diced, fresh vegetables. Choose from among broccoli tips, zucchini rounds, mushrooms, and tomatoes. Use garlic and cayenne pepper. Sprinkle with shredded mozzarella.
* Minced anchovies, green peppers, olives, Italian herb seasoning, garlic, onions, tomatoes; sprinkle with green olive oil.
* Three mushrooms—porcini, fresh, and dried (soaked)—with tomatoes, basil, Italian herb seasoning, and crumbled goat cheese.
* Diced fennel, Fontina cheese, grilled eggplant slices, crushed garlic, parsley, diced tomatoes, and green olive oil.
* Asparagus, mushrooms, mozzarella cheese slices, tomatoes, Italian herb seasoning, and a dash of cayenne pepper.
* Zucchini rounds, mushrooms, red pepper rings, onions, garlic, Italian herb seasoning, and green olive oil.
* Tomato sauce base, prosciutto, onions, garlic, Italian herb seasoning, mozzarella slices, and chopped parsley.
* Shallots, garlic, green olive oil, black pepper, Italian herb seasoning, and chopped parsley.
* Fresh tomatoes (raw), garlic, basil, green olive oil. (Add salt and pepper after the pizza is baked with olive oil.)

PIZZA BREAD

¾ cup lukewarm water
2 tsp. granulated yeast
1¼ cup unbleached all-purpose flour
1 tbsp. milk
5 tbsp. green olive oil (plus oil for brushing the dough)
½ cup rye flour
1 cup onion, thinly sliced
4 cloves of garlic, crushed
½ tsp. Italian herb seasoning
Dash of pepper

Servings:
10
Time:
65 *min.*
Calories:
154 *per slice*

Preheat oven at 500°F.
Combine ¼ cup of lukewarm water, the yeast, and the all-purpose flour in a large mixing bowl. Blend well and cover with a towel. Let stand in a warm place for 25 minutes.

Add the remaining ½ cup of water, milk, 2 tablespoons of olive oil, and the rye flour. Mix the dough with a wooden spoon; then knead it on a lightly floured board. It will be soft and a bit sticky. Add a little more flour to the board as you knead the dough with quick, light strokes. Do not add any more flour than is absolutely necessary. Knead for another 15 minutes.

Lightly oil the inside of a mixing bowl and place the dough in it. Lightly oil the top of the crust—cover it evenly. Cover the bowl with a towel, and let the dough rise in a warm place for about 2 hours or until doubled in bulk. Punch it down and shape it into a ball; then place it back in the bowl and cover. Let rise for 40 minutes. Put a flat pizza pan on a rack in the preheated oven.

Flatten the dough on a floured board. Roll it with a rolling pin into an elongated shape with rounded ends, about ⅛ inch to ¼ inch wide and the length of your pan. Flour a baking sheet and transfer the dough onto it.

Heat 1 tablespoon of the olive oil in a skillet and cook the onion, garlic, Italian herb seasoning, and pepper for a few minutes.

Sprinkle the onion and garlic evenly over the bread dough.

Dribble 2 tablespoons of olive oil over the top of the dough; slide the dough from the baking sheet to the pizza pan and bake for 15 minutes or until golden brown and crisp. Do not bake too brown or crisp or the bread will be hard.

VARIATIONS

* Sprinkle with sautéed mushrooms, zucchini, red pepper, or tomatoes.
* Try shredded mozzarella cheese and diced tomatoes with a sprinkling of minced fresh basil or Italian parsley.
* Eliminate the onion or garlic, and serve as a white pizza bread with black pepper, a light touch of salt, and green olive oil. (This is very traditional in Italy, especially in Abruzzi, and was my mother's favorite.)

Pizza bread is perfect to serve with salad, antipasto, cheese, Pasta Fagioli soup, or as a snack.

Focaccia

Focaccia is a flat bread that was created in the north of Italy; pizza was created in the south, in Naples. *Focaccia* is usually served as a flat bread with oil, salt, and pepper, or as a light meal with toppings of grated cheese, mushrooms, roasted shallots, garlic, fresh herbs, olive oil, and roasted peppers. The toppings are usually lighter than pizza toppings, and the dough is made with dry yeast, flour, olive oil, and cornmeal.

Focaccia with a topping of green olive oil, Italian herb seasoning, garlic, roasted red peppers, or sun-dried tomatoes, and a sprinkling of goat, ricotta, or mozzarella cheese is a popular appetizer or cocktail food; just cut it into little squares.

Try serving *focaccia* with herbs and oil instead of regular bread rolls (fattening and messy) or sliced hard-crust bread (ordinary). *Focaccia* is a much more interesting addition to a meal. As a replacement for bread, it is less fattening, but more important, it is much more delicious and easy to digest.

Use a *focaccia* bread base with cheese, herbs, olives, pesto, or tomato toppings instead of thin slices of crisp Italian bread for Bruschettas (bread topped with oil, garlic herbs, and a variety of toppings). It provides great cocktail or appetizer tastes, and is small enough not to be filling or high in calories.

To make the *focaccia*, first preheat the oven at 425°F. Then cover the bread rounds with olive oil and sprinkle with black pepper. Bake the *focaccia* until golden, about 15 minutes.

If using roasted garlic on the dough, toss about 4 heads of garlic cloves with olive oil and roast them in a preheated oven at 350°F until soft, about 25 minutes. Cool and remove the skins; halve or chop the cloves and sprinkle on the dough before baking.

For fresh herb toppings, stir one-quarter cup of minced fresh herbs, such as basil, parsley, sage, or rosemary. Sprinkle on top of the dough with olive oil and bake.

For cheese toppings, try provolone, mozzarella, or Parmesan with herbs and olive oil: Don't overcook.

Tomato and basil topping should be added *after* the dough is baked. Mix the tomatoes with olive oil, basil, and crushed garlic, and marinate. Spread on the cooked focaccia before serving.

Pesto Sauce can be added to cooked *focaccia*. Olives, mushrooms, and zucchini rounds are good, too.

VARIATIONS

* Add the herbs, garlic, onion, or Parmesan cheese to the dough before cooking; add more of these ingredients to the top of the *focaccia* before baking.
* Use whole-wheat flour instead of white flour with cornmeal to add to nutrition and taste.

F O C A C C I A

Basic Dough

Servings:
4
Time:
210 *min.*
Calories:
477 *per serving*

2 cups all-purpose flour or bread flour
1 cup cornmeal, finely ground (plus extra to sprinkle on baking sheet)
1½ cups warm water
1 package active dry yeast
¼ cup green olive oil

Preheat the oven at 475°F.

Dissolve yeast and warm water; set aside until it starts to foam (15 to 20 minutes).

Beat in 1 cup of flour, cover the bowl tightly, and let the contents triple in volume (about 2 to 3 hours). Place the bowl in a warm, draft-free place and cover with a dish towel.

Add the remaining ½ cup of warm water, 2 tablespoons of olive oil, and enough of the remaining flour to form a soft but workable dough. Knead the dough on a lightly floured working surface until it is smooth and elastic, about 10 minutes.

Oil a large bowl and place the dough in it; cover loosely with plastic wrap and put it in a warm place until the dough has doubled in volume and an indentation remains when you press down gently on the dough (about 1 hour).

Sprinkle a large baking sheet with olive oil and then cornmeal. Roll the dough on a floured surface into four rounds, each about ¼-inch thick and 8 inches in diameter. Carefully slide a prepared baking pan under the dough circles and drizzle with olive oil.

POLENTA

Cornmeal

In a recent article for a national food magazine, titled *"La Cucina Povera Divendata Chic"* ("The Poor Kitchen of Italy Has Become Chic"), I wrote that the foods of the peasants are the "in foods" of today. Polenta, Pasta Fagiole, simple pastas, and vegetable combinations were originally created by the poor, who had to use the economical ingredients available in their regions.

Cornmeal is plentiful, cheap, and easy to prepare. It can be mixed with almost anything: vegetables, game, wild mushrooms, or just a little cheese. It can also be served as an appetizer, or main course, or for brunch, with eggs and tomato sauce.

When I was a child in Italy, I can remember a wonderful game my mother would play with my brothers and me. She would place on the table a huge round board spread with polenta covered in cheese and tomato sauce. In the very center of the polenta was a delicious portion of her special chicken. When we were all seated at the table with our spoons ready in hand, Mother would give the starting signal and each of us would race to eat our way through the polenta to the prize of chicken in the center. The problem for me was that my brothers had bigger mouths than I did, so I had to cheat in order to win the chicken.

The resurgence of polenta in America began with the increasing popularity of foods from the southwestern states. Cornmeal was a staple of the basic American Indian diet.

Today, polenta is served in most classic Italian restaurants and cafés; it's interesting, tasty, nutritious, low in calories, and versatile. You'll find it on the menu with exotic embellishments, such as baby quail, porcini mushrooms, grated truffles, Mascarpone cheese, and even caviar.

BASIC POLENTA

Servings:
6
Time:
40 *min.*
Calories:
275 *per serving*

2½ quarts cold water
½ lb. yellow cornmeal, coarse or stone-ground
½ lb. yellow cornmeal (regular type), finely ground
Dash of black pepper

Bring the cold water to a boil in a large pot. Add the two types of cornmeal to the boiling water in a very slow stream; stir with a wooden spoon to keep the mixture smooth, or it will become lumpy. Stir slowly for about 30 minutes.

If lumps form, push them to the side of the pot; smash the lumps with the spoon and blend with the mixture. Add pepper to taste. Serve immediately.

VARIATION

* Add grated Parmesan cheese if serving with game or meats.

If polenta is baked or used as an appetizer, remove it from the pot by scraping it from the sides and bottom. Pour it onto a smooth surface that is covered with foil. Spread the polenta out with a spatula.

When cold, cut the polenta into different shapes: squares for crostini and ½-inch strips for frying or baking. The polenta can be kept in the refrigerator for up to 5 days.

POLENTA CON QUAGLIE

Polenta with Baby Quail in Mushroom Sauce

Servings:
6
Time:
45 *min.*
Calories:
545 *per serving*

2 oz. porcini mushrooms, dried, soaked, and diced
6 small quail
2 cups shallots or onion, chopped
3 cloves of garlic, crushed
3 tbsp. green olive oil
1 cup dry Italian red wine
1 tsp. Italian herb seasoning
1 cup fresh Italian parsley, chopped

POLENTA
4 quarts chicken stock
1 lb. cornmeal, stone-ground or coarse
1 lb. finely ground cornmeal
1 cup Parmesan cheese, freshly grated

Soak the porcini mushrooms for ½ hour in lukewarm water.

Boil the stock to cook the polenta.

Clean and dry the quail.

In a large skillet, sauté the mushrooms, shallots, and garlic in the olive oil for 3 minutes. Add the quail and brown them slightly for a few minutes. Add the wine, cover, and cook for 5 minutes. Add the stock, the Italian herb seasoning, and parsley, and cook over low heat for 10 minutes.

Remove the skillet from the flame, and prepare the polenta, using the Basic Polenta recipe on page 112. Spread the cooked polenta over a large serving platter and place the quail and sauce in the center. Serve immediately.

VARIATIONS
* If you can't find quail, use small cornish hens.
* Use fresh sliced mushrooms instead of porcini mushrooms but soak them in ½ cup of brandy for ½ hour for more taste.
* Try using 3 cups of diced chicken meat instead of quail, with ½ teaspoon of crushed red pepper.

GRILLED POLENTA

Servings:
8
Time:
25 *min.*
Calories:
240 *per serving*

8 cups cold water
¼ tsp. Italian herb seasoning
Salt and pepper to taste
3 cups cornmeal, coarsely ground
2 tbsp. green olive oil

Add the water, Italian herb seasoning, salt, and pepper to a large skillet and bring to a boil. Slowly add the cornmeal in small amounts; stir constantly to keep the polenta smooth. Continue cooking for 5 to 8 minutes.

Pour the polenta into an oiled baking pan, about 8 inches square. Allow it to cool; then brush with olive oil, and grill over a hot, preheated grill until the top is brown and crisp, about 10 minutes.

If you cannot use a grill, use the broiler, or bake for 15 minutes; then brown the top under the broiler.

Cool the polenta and cut into 8 squares.

VARIATIONS
* Serve as an appetizer with a variety of sauces.
* Serve with chicken or meats as a side dish.
* Serve as a cocktail food with cheese broiled on top.

CROSTINI DI POLENTA

Squares of Polenta for Appetizers

POLENTA

Servings:
8
Time:
45 *min.*
Calories:
80 *to* **125** *per square*

½ lb. cornmeal, stone-ground or coarse
½ lb. cornmeal, finely ground
2 quarts cold water

TOPPINGS
1 cup fresh tomatoes, diced
4 fresh basil leaves, minced
2 cloves of garlic, crushed
2 tbsp. green olive oil
1 cup mozzarella cheese, shredded

½ cup sun-dried tomatoes, minced
4 oz. porcini mushrooms, soaked
½ cup red wine
2 cloves of garlic, crushed

1 cup onion, chopped
1 cup cooked chicken, shredded
1 cup roasted peppers, diced
1 cup black olives, pitted and sliced
1 cup mozzarella cheese, shredded

Preheat oven at 375°F if baking polenta.

Prepare the polenta, using the Basic Polenta recipe on page 112. Pour the polenta into a long baking dish, cool, and then cut into squares. Prepare toppings as follows:

Sauté tomatoes, basil leaves, and garlic in olive oil for 5 minutes. Serve on top of the polenta squares.

Top the polenta squares with mozzarella cheese and sun-dried tomatoes. Place under the broiler for 1 minute.

Sauté porcini mushrooms, ½ cup red wine, garlic, and onion for a few minutes; add to the polenta squares.

Top the polenta squares with the chicken, sliced black olives, roasted peppers, and 1 cup shredded mozzarella cheese.

Crostinis can be prepared in two ways: Bake in an oiled baking pan for 15 minutes, or deep fry in olive oil until golden brown, turning to brown both sides.

VARIATIONS

* Try using Basic Pesto Sauce as a topping. (See page 197.)
* Instead of chicken, use 1 cup of shredded turkey, prosciutto, or seafood. If using seafood, do not use the mozzarella cheese.

Sauces should be prepared in advance; reheat before topping the polenta squares.

Baking is the healthier and preferred method of preparing the crostinis: It adds fewer calories than frying does.

FRITTATAS

Egg Dishes

Much More than Just an Italian Omelet

The *frittata* is a very popular dish in Italy and is often served with salad, fruit, and cheese, as a main course for lunch, brunch, cocktails, dinner, or supper. *Frittatas* can even be served as a dessert!

The *frittata* looks like a flat omelet or pancake. It's cooked slightly on both sides and has a filling mixed in the batter. But it's more versatile than the omelet and much more exciting. The *frittata* can be served with a wide variety of sauces, as well as with dozens of different fillings. Let your imagination run wild and create your own favorite combinations.

For cocktail food, cut the *frittata* into small squares; fill with seafood, vegetables, cheese, or chicken; then dip it into a sauce of tomato, cheese, pesto, red pepper, or vegetables.

For a first course, blend the eggs with a mixture of either pasta, cheese, meat, or vegetables, and top with an appropriate sauce; add grated cheese or shredded mozzarella. Cut the *frittata* into wedges as you would a pie, and serve them decorated with diced tomatoes or sprigs of parsley.

For a main course, serve larger portions of *frittata* and add a seafood or chicken and vegetable combination. By browning both sides a little longer, you can even serve *frittata* as a pizza with toppings of tomato sauce, vegetables, and cheese.

As a dessert, make the *frittata* with a combination of fruit, ricotta cheese, cinnamon, nuts or dried fruits, and liqueur with Zabaglione Sauce (page 207).

The Italian *frittata* is extremely versatile and lusciously satisfying.

FRITTATA ALLA SANDI

Eggs with Red and Green Peppers, Ham, and Cheese

6 fresh eggs
½ tsp. Italian herb seasoning
Dash of cayenne pepper
1 red and 1 green pepper, finely diced
½ cup ham, diced
3 cloves of garlic, crushed
½ cup onion, chopped
2 tbsp. green olive oil
¼ cup mozzarella cheese, shredded
2 tbsp. Parmesan cheese, freshly grated
1 cup fresh Italian parsley, chopped

Servings:
4
Time:
15 *min.*
Calories:
270 *per slice*

Put the eggs in a small bowl with the Italian herb seasoning and pepper; beat slightly.

In a large frying pan, sauté the peppers, ham, garlic, and onion in the oil for 5 minutes. Add the egg mixture and cook on one side; then invert on a plate and cook the other side.

Top with the mozzarella and Parmesan cheeses. Sprinkle the parsley on top and add a drop of green olive oil to the cheese. Serve immediately.

VARIATIONS
* Add the cheese to the *frittata* and cook for a few minutes in the mixture.
* Top with a pesto sauce.
* Add mushrooms, eggplant, or asparagus.

F R I T T A T A   F A N T A S I A

Eggs with Fresh Herbs, Cheese, and Two Sauces

Servings:
4
Time:
15 *min.*
Calories:
651 *per serving*

6 fresh eggs
1 tsp. Italian herb seasoning
½ cup fresh Italian parsley, chopped
Dash of cayenne pepper
¼ cup fresh basil leaves, diced
¼ cup Parmesan cheese, freshly grated
½ cup onion, chopped
2 cloves of garlic, crushed
1 tbsp. sweet, unsalted butter
1 cup Basic Pesto Sauce (see page 197)
1 cup Red Pepper and Tomato Sauce (see page 193)

Put the eggs in a small bowl and beat lightly with the Italian herb seasoning, parsley, cayenne pepper, basil leaves, and Parmesan cheese. Sauté the onion and garlic in the butter for a few minutes. Add the egg mixture and cook on both sides.

Serve with the Pesto and Red Pepper Sauces.

VARIATIONS
* Use mushrooms, diced olives, and shredded chicken or ham.
* Use the Basic Marinara Sauce (see page 192) instead of Red Pepper Sauce.

FRITTATA TREVISO

Eggs, Zucchini, Cheese, Ham, and Tomatoes

1 cup onion, diced
3 cloves of garlic, crushed
½ cup lean prosciutto or lean ham, diced
1 cup fresh plum tomatoes, diced
6 medium-size mushrooms, diced
1 cup zucchini, sliced
1 tsp. Italian herb seasoning
2 tbsp. green olive oil
7 fresh eggs
¼ cup fresh Italian parsley, chopped
Dash of pepper
½ cup skim-milk mozzarella, shredded

Servings:
6
Time:
15 *min.*
Calories:
185 *per slice*

Preheat the broiler.

In a large skillet, sauté the onion, garlic, ham, tomatoes, mushrooms, zucchini, and Italian herb seasoning in the oil for 5 minutes.

In a medium-size bowl, beat the eggs with the parsley and pepper for a minute to blend well. Pour the eggs over the sauté mixture, and cook until the bottom is set (8 to 10 minutes).

Sprinkle the mozzarella cheese on top of the frittata, and broil for 3 minutes, until the top is melted and crisp. Cut into wedges and serve immediately.

VARIATIONS
* Cook without ham.
* Use diced peppers.

F R I T T A T A   A L L A
M O N I C A

Eggs with Onions, Mushrooms, Cheese, and Tomatoes

Servings:
4
Time:
15 *min.*
Calories:
211 *per slice*

6 fresh eggs
½ tsp. Italian herb seasoning
Dash of pepper (black or cayenne)
¼ cup fresh Italian parsley, chopped
1 tbsp. green olive oil
½ tbsp. sweet, unsalted butter
1 cup onion, diced
2 cloves of garlic, crushed
1 cup fresh mushrooms, diced
1 cup fresh tomatoes, diced
¼ cup mozzarella cheese, shredded

Put the eggs in a bowl with the Italian herb seasoning, pepper, and parsley; beat for a few minutes.

In a large frying pan, sauté the oil, butter, onion, and garlic for a few minutes. Add the mushrooms and tomatoes; cook 3 to 4 minutes. Pour the eggs over the mixture; push the sides in to let the eggs run to the side. Brown slightly.

Place a flat plate over the top of the pan and invert; slide the frittata back in the pan, and cook the other side until light brown. Sprinkle with the mozzarella cheese and more parsley, and cover for a minute. Cut into wedges, and serve immediately.

VARIATION
* Add diced green pepper, zucchini, or diced olives.

VEGETALES

Vegetables

La cucina Italiana has one of the most extensive varieties of vegetable recipes and the healthiest and lightest methods of preparation. An enormous selection of fresh vegetables that come from all the regions of Italy is available in the United States: the ripest, reddest plum tomatoes; small, tender zucchini; baby eggplants; and perfect porcini mushrooms. These vegetables offer wonderful adventures in taste, but to get the very best *sapore* they all must be cooked in the original *suffocato* method.

This special combination of steaming and sautéing is the secret to keeping color, flavor, and texture while retaining all the nutrients. You can cook to the point of true perfection! The *suffocato* method can be used for all kinds of vegetables. Use a large frying pan, skillet, or wok with a lid. Add one or two tablespoons of green olive oil and one or more cloves of crushed garlic. (The garlic is optional, but it gives a great flavor.) Put the lid on tight and cook over low to medium heat for three to five minutes, depending on your preference for texture and taste. (Remember this rule: "Any vegetable that can be eaten raw needs very little cooking.")

T O M A T O E S
A L L A   T I A N A

Tomatoes Stuffed with Mushrooms, Eggplant, and Cheese

4 firm, ripe red tomatoes
½ lb. mushrooms, diced
3 cloves of garlic, crushed
1 medium-size eggplant
2 tbsp. green olive oil
½ tsp. Italian herb seasoning
½ cup fresh Italian parsley, chopped
1 medium-size onion, diced
Cayenne pepper to taste
¼ cup Romano cheese, freshly grated

Servings:
4
Time:
20 *min.*
Calories:
159 *per serving*

Preheat over at 350°F.

Scoop out the centers, of the tomatoes and put them in a small bowl.

In a large frying pan, sauté the mushrooms, garlic, and eggplant in the olive oil for 5 to 8 minutes.

Add the tomato pulp, Italian herb seasoning, parsley, onion, dash of cayenne pepper; stir and cook together for another 5 minutes.

Place the tomato shells in an oiled baking dish and fill with the sautéed mixture.

Sprinkle with the Romano cheese and bake for 15 minutes.

VARIATION

* Use zucchini, rice, pasta, asparagus, broccoli, or peppers.

Serve hot as a side dish, with an entreé, or as an appetizer.

ZUCCHINI SCRAPELLAS

Zucchini Crêpes

Yield:
20
Time:
15 *min.*
Calories:
74 *per scrapella*

3 medium-size zucchini, shredded
1 medium-size onion, minced
1 tbsp. salt
3 fresh eggs
3 tbsp. all-purpose flour
¼ tsp. pepper (black or cayenne)
1 clove of garlic, crushed
3 tbsp. fresh Italian parsley, minced
4 tbsp. Parmesan cheese, freshly grated
1 tbsp. olive oil or safflower oil per scrapella

Put the zucchini and onion in a bowl and sprinkle with 1 tablespoon of salt. Let stand about 15 minutes; then drain the juice by pushing through a cheesecloth, sieve, or collander to drain the remaining water.

Beat the eggs in a large bowl; beat in the flour, pepper, garlic, parsley, and Parmesan cheese. Stir in the zucchini and onion mixture.

Heat about ¼ cup of oil in a deep, heavy frying pan over medium heat until hot. Drop tablespoons of the zucchini mixture into the hot oil; keep the drops several inches apart. Flatten each drop to a 3-inch oval. Fry about 1 minute per side until well browned. Place on paper towels to dry.

Serve warm with a variety of toppings and fillings.

VARIATIONS

* Fill with vegetables, fish, chicken, cheese, or ground beef.
* Top with Basic Marinara or Basic Pesto Sauce (see pages 192 and 197).

Serve as an appetizer, brunch, lunch, or main course.

C A P O N A T A   C A V A S I N O

Eggplant, Capers, Olives, and Tomatoes

1 large eggplant (about 1½ lb.)
Salt to soak eggplant
2 large green peppers, diced
2 medium-size onions, chopped
2 cloves of garlic, crushed
2 tbsp. green olive oil
3 tbsp. capers
½ tsp. Italian herb seasoning
Dash of pepper (black or cayenne)
½ Sicilian olives, diced
1 tbsp. red wine vinegar
½ lb. fresh plum tomatoes, peeled and diced
½ cup fresh Italian parsley, chopped

Servings:
10 *(½ cup each)*
Time:
20 *min.*
Calories:
71 *per ½ cup*

Wash eggplant well and cut into small cubes, leaving the skin on. Soak the cubes in cold water with 1 tablespoon of salt for each quart of water for 10 minutes. Drain, rinse, and pat dry.

In a large sauté pan, cook the peppers, onions, garlic, and eggplant in the oil for 6 to 8 minutes. Add the capers, Italian herb seasoning, black or cayenne pepper, olives, and vinegar, and cook for 2 minutes.

Cook the tomatoes and parsley for 5 more minutes. Stir and mix well. Serve warm or at room temperature.

VARIATION

* Use mushrooms instead of olives.

This is a perfect appetizer over a leaf of radicchio or regular lettuce, or with pasta, or as an accompaniment to the main course.

EGGPLANT AND PASTA ROLLS

Yield:
45 *eggplant rolls*
Time:
25 *min.*
Calories:
71 *per eggplant roll*

1 lb. short-shape pasta (rotini, elbows, or penne)
2 large purple eggplants (about 2 lb. each)
Salt to soak eggplant
3 tbsp. green olive oil
1 cup shallots or onion, chopped
3 cloves of garlic, crushed
½ tsp. Italian herb seasoning
2 cups Italian plum tomatoes, crushed (fresh or canned)
½ cup fresh Italian parsley, chopped
1 cup skim-milk ricotta cheese
½ cup Romano cheese, freshly grated
Dash of cayenne pepper

Preheat oven at 350°F.

Boil water to cook the pasta.

Slice the eggplant into ½-inch slices; soak in salt and cold water for 10 minutes. Rinse often, drain, and dry.

Put the eggplant slices on a baking dish; brown in the broiler for 4 to 8 minutes on each side. Set aside and brush with olive oil. (Or, grill with olive oil.)

In a large frying pan, sauté the chopped onion, garlic, and the Italian herb seasoning in the oil for a few minutes. Add the drained, crushed tomatoes and cook for 5 to 8 minutes; add the parsley during the last few minutes.

Mix the ricotta cheese with the Romano cheese and cayenne pepper; blend until smooth.

Cook the pasta al dente, drain, and mix with the ricotta and 1 cup of the tomato sauce.

Rub a large, shallow baking dish or two medium-size baking dishes with oil. Line the dish with the eggplant slices, and put about 3 tablespoons of the pasta and sauce in the center of each slice. Roll the slices and fasten the ends with a toothpick. Spread the remaining tomato sauce over the eggplant rolls.

Bake for 10 minutes and serve hot or at room temperature.

VARIATIONS

* Eliminate the ricotta cheese and use just tomato sauce with sautéed mushrooms as the filling with the pasta.
* Use long, thin spaghetti cut into 1-inch lengths as the filling with Basic Pesto Sauce (see page 197).
* Red Pepper and Tomato Sauce (see page 193) can be used instead of Tomato Sauce.

ZUCCHINI STUFFED WITH MUSHROOMS AND CHEESE

6 medium-size zucchini (6 oz. each)
8 shallots, chopped; or 1 cup onion, chopped
1 tsp. Italian herb seasoning
½ tsp. crushed red pepper
10 large fresh mushrooms
1 anchovy filet, rinsed and dried
3 cloves of garlic, crushed
2 tbsp. green olive oil
½ cup fresh Italian parsley, chopped
½ cup black olives, diced
2 tbsp. pimentos, chopped
¼ cup Parmesan cheese, freshly grated

Servings:
6 (2 halves each)
Time:
20 min.
Calories:
133 per serving

Preheat oven at 300°F.

Scrub and trim the zucchini; do not peel. Cut lengthwise into halves, and carefully scoop out the pulp without damaging the shells. (If zucchini are very hard, drop them into boiling water for a minute to make it easier to scoop out the centers.) Cover the shells in cold water; bring to a boil for 2 to 3 minutes; then drain and plunge into cold water. Drain the shells and place them on paper towels to dry.

In a large sauté pan, sauté the shallots, Italian herb seasoning, hot pepper, mushrooms, anchovy, garlic, and zucchini pulp in the oil for about 5 minutes.

Put this mixture in a large bowl, and mix with the parsley, olives, pimentos, and Parmesan cheese. Toss thoroughly to mix well.

Fill the zucchini shells with the mixture and place them on a baking sheet or in a shallow baking pan. Bake for 10 minutes. Serve immediately.

VARIATIONS
* Use tomato sauce instead of pimentos.
* Try about 1 cup of diced, cooked veal, beef, or chicken instead of anchovies and olives.
* Top with shredded mozzarella instead of Parmesan cheese.

This dish can be used as an appetizer, main course, or as an accompaniment to the main course.

T O M A T O E S   B R A Z Z I

Tomatoes Stuffed with Mushrooms, Olives, Eggplant, and Cheese

Servings:
4
Time:
25 *min.*
Calories:
215 *per tomato*

4 large fresh tomatoes
½ lb. fresh mushrooms, diced
1 medim-size onion, chopped
3 cloves of garlic, crushed
1 medium-size eggplant
2 tbsp. green olive oil
½ tsp. Italian herb seasoning
½ cup black olives, diced
½ cup fresh Italian parsley, chopped
¼ tsp. cayenne pepper
½ cup Romano cheese, freshly grated

Preheat oven at 350°F.

Scoop out the center of the tomatoes and put them aside in a small bowl.

In a large frying pan, sauté the mushrooms, onion, garlic, and eggplant in the olive oil over medium heat for 8 minutes.

Add the tomato pulp, Italian herb seasoning, olives, parsley, and cayenne pepper; stir and cook together for 5 minutes.

Place the tomato shells in an oiled baking dish and fill each shell with the sautéed mixture. Sprinkle each with Romano cheese and bake for 10 minutes.

VARIATION

* Use 1 cup of cooked zucchini, rice, pasta, asparagus, broccoli, or green peppers.

Serve as a hot side dish with an entrée, or serve as an appetizer.

VEGETABLE MISTO ALL' ADELAIDE

Servings:
6
Time:
15 *min.*
Calories:
150 *per serving*

1 large red pepper, chopped
1 large green pepper, chopped
1 large onion, chopped
2 large potatoes, peeled and diced
2 tbsp. green olive oil
2 medium-size zucchini, chopped
1 lb. fresh mushrooms, chopped
¼ tsp. crushed red pepper
½ tsp. Italian herb seasoning
½ cup fresh Italian parsley, chopped
3 cloves of garlic, crushed
¼ cup Parmesan cheese, freshly grated

In a large sauté pan, sauté the red and green peppers, onion, and potatoes in the oil for about 5 minutes; stir often.

Add the zucchini, mushrooms, hot pepper, Italian herb seasoning, parsley, and garlic. Stir thoroughly and cook for 10 minutes.

Toss with Parmesan cheese and serve hot.

VARIATIONS
* Add 3 eggs, slightly beaten (great for brunch).
* Add other vegetables, such as asparagus, eggplant, or spinach.
* Add leftovers.

VEGETABLES BELLA VITA

Swiss Chard, Potatoes, Onions, and Tomatoes

Servings:
4
Time:
15 *min.*
Calories:
140 *per serving*

1 large bunch of Swiss chard
1 medium-size potato
1 cup onion, chopped
3 cloves of garlic, crushed
2 tbsp. green olive oil
1 tsp. Italian herb seasoning
Dash of cayenne pepper
3 plum tomatoes, diced
½ cup fresh Italian parsley, minced

Cut the heavy white stems off the Swiss chard up to the leaf area. Rinse well in cold water, drain, and dry. Break into small pieces.

Boil the potato for 5 minutes, then dice.

In a heavy skillet, sauté the onion and garlic in the oil for a minute. Add the Swiss chard, Italian herb seasoning, and pepper; cover and cook for 6 to 8 minutes.

Uncover and add the tomatoes, potatoes, and parsley. Cook for 5 minutes. Serve warm.

VARIATIONS

* Use spinach if Swiss chard is not available.
* Prepare without tomatoes and use diced pimentos or red pepper for color.
* Eliminate the potatoes for a lighter version.

GRILLED RADICCHIO

Servings:
5
Time:
15 *min.*
Calories:
120 *per serving*

3 lb. radicchio, halved
3 tbsp. green olive oil
Black pepper, freshly ground, and salt to taste
Lemon wedges
Parsley sprigs

Brush the radicchio with the olive oil and sprinkle with the salt and pepper to taste.

Cook over a preheated grill for a few minutes on each side, until slightly browned.

It can also be prepared under a preheated hot broiler for 10 minutes; turn often. Place on a serving platter with lemon wedges and parsley sprigs.

VARIATION
* Add 2 tablespoons of lemon juice and chopped parsley.

This version of grilled radicchio has become a very popular and chic new vegetable dish, served with grilled fish, chicken, or meat. It can be an appetizer, if served with arugula and goat cheese, or with grilled mushrooms.

S T U F F E D   E G G P L A N T   M I S T O

1 large eggplant (2 lb.)
1 tbsp. green olive oil
1 cup shallots or onion, diced
3 cloves of garlic, crushed
1 lb. fresh porcini or domestic mushrooms, diced
½ tsp. crushed red pepper
1 anchovy fillet, rinsed and diced
½ cup celery, diced
1 cup short-shape pasta; or diced chicken; or diced seafood
1 cup plum tomatoes, crushed (fresh or canned)
1 cup black olives, chopped
1 cup fresh Italian parsley, chopped
¼ cup Parmesan cheese, freshly grated

Servings:
4
Time:
30 *min.*
Calories:
368 *per serving*

Preheat oven at 350°F.

Wash the whole eggplant, dry it, and place it on a baking sheet. Bake for 10 minutes or until tender. Remove the eggplant from the oven, and slice it down the center. Scrape out the pulp and set it aside: Be careful not to damage the half-shells.

In a large skillet, heat the olive oil and sauté the onion, garlic, mushrooms, hot pepper, anchovy, celery, and eggplant pulp for 8 minutes. (*Note:* If you use diced seafood, chicken, or a cup of lean ground beef, sauté them with the above mixture.)

Add the tomatoes, olives, and parsley; sauté for 5 more minutes. (*Note:* If using pasta with the vegetable misto, cook it until it is al dente, drain, and add it to the mixture in the skillet. Mix thoroughly.)

Stuff the eggplant shells with the mixture. Top with Parmesan cheese. Bake in a shallow baking dish for 5 to 8 minutes. Serve from the baking dish immediately.

* Use diced chicken, lean ground beef, or diced seafood, such as shrimp, lobster, scallops, calamari, or whitefish. Do not cook the seafood for more than 3 to 6 minutes.

Stuffed Eggplant Misto can be an appetizer, main course, or, with a vegetable misto, an accompaniment to the main course. It's versatile, visually pleasing, and offers an exciting blend of taste.

C A R C I O F I   I N B O T T I T I

Stuffed Artichokes alla Peggi

Servings:
4
Time:
50 *min.*
Calories:
264 *per serving*

1½ cups fresh whole-wheat breadcrumbs
½ cup Parmesan cheese, freshly grated
½ tsp. Italian herb seasoning
2 cloves of garlic, crushed
1 medium-size onion, finely chopped
4 tbsp. fresh Italian parsley, chopped
Black pepper to taste, freshly ground
4 medium-size artichokes, washed, with stalks trimmed and old leaves removed
3 tbsp. green olive oil
½ cup lemon rind

In a large mixing bowl, combine the breadcrumbs, Parmesan cheese, Italian herb seasoning, garlic, onion, parsley, and pepper.

Spread the leaves of each artichoke and fill the space between with the breadcrumb mixture. Press it down firmly with the back of a spoon.

Place the stuffed artichokes in a heavy-based pan large enough to hold them upright. Pour ½ tablespoon of olive oil over the top of each artichoke. Add water to half the height of the artichokes and add the lemon rind. Bring the water to a boil, cover the pan tightly, and reduce the heat. Simmer gently for 35 to 45 minutes or until the outer leaves of the artichokes can be easily removed.

Take the artichokes from the water and serve hot or at room temperature.

VARIATIONS
* Add a little diced white chicken meat to the stuffing.
* Toast the breadcrumbs with a sprinkle of Pecorino cheese.

TORTE FESTIVA

Eggplant, Ricotta Cheese, Swiss Chard, and Roasted Peppers in a Whole-Wheat Crust

FILLING

1 medium-size eggplant
8 cloves of garlic, crushed
1 cup fresh Italian parsley, chopped
1 cup skim-milk ricotta cheese
½ cup Parmesan cheese, freshly grated
¼ cup green olive oil
1 cup onion, chopped
2 lb. Swiss chard, trimmed and diced
2 tsp. Italian herb seasoning
3 large red peppers and 3 large green peppers, roasted (see page 7) and diced
¼ tsp. crushed red pepper

CRUST

2 cups cake flour
1½ cups whole-wheat flour
4 cloves of garlic, crushed
1 cup fresh Italian parsley, chopped
¼ cup green olive oil
¼ tbsp. cold water

TOPPING

Prepare Basic Marinara Sauce and Basic Pesto Sauce (see pages 192 and 197, respectively).

FOR CRUST

Combine the flours, garlic, and parsley. Stir with a fork and add the oil slowly. Blend thoroughly until smooth. Add the water and mix until the dough forms (will be soft). Dough should be moist but not sticky. Cover the dough and refrigerate it for about 45 minutes.

FOR FILLING

Soak the eggplant in cold water after slicing; rinse 2 to 3 times. Dry and dice the eggplant, leaving the skins intact. Place the eggplant under the broiler and brown (if dry, sprinkle with olive oil).

Add the eggplant, 3 cloves of crushed garlic, ½ cup of diced Italian parsley, ricotta cheese, and Parmesan cheese to a food processor and puree.

In a large skillet, sauté the oil, garlic, and onion for a few minutes. Add the Swiss chard and Italian herb seasoning; cover and sauté for 5 minutes. Set the mixture aside.

Yield:
6 *slices*
Time:
105 *min.*
Calories:
848 *per slice*

In another skillet, sauté 2 tablespoons of olive oil, 3 cloves of crushed garlic, the roasted red and green peppers, and the hot pepper for about 5 minutes. Set the mixture aside.

Add a few tablespoons of olive oil to a lightly floured working surface. Place the dough in the center and pound with a rolling pin until the dough is pliable but not too soft. Roll the dough into an 18-by-8-inch rectangle. Spread oil over the top of the dough.

Fold the dough over into three equal sections, removing excess flour. Turn the dough so that it opens like a book. Roll again and fold into thirds. Wrap the dough tightly, and refrigerate for another 45 minutes, or until ready to use.

ASSEMBLING THE TORTE

Preheat oven at 400°F.

On a lightly floured surface, roll about ⅔ of the dough to the thickness of about ⅛ inch. Use a 9½-inch springform pan; allow ⅛ inch of overhang as you line and fit the pan with the dough.

Line the bottom of the pan with the Swiss chard mixture. (Keeping it thin and smooth, use ⅓ of the amount.) Line with the red/green pepper filling next; finally, layer with the eggplant and cheese mixture.

Roll out the remaining dough very thin. Drape the dough over the top and cut off the edges. Trim and score the edges.

Brush the torte with olive oil and sprinkle with more chopped parsley. Make 4 to 5 slits in the center of the torte to allow steam to escape. Bake for 30 minutes; then cover with aluminum foil and bake for 30 more minutes. Let stand for 20 minutes before serving. Cut into 6 wedges: be careful of the fillings.

Prepare the basic tomato sauce and the basic pesto sauce while the torte is baking. Serve each slice of the torte with tomato sauce on one side and pesto sauce on the other side of the dish.

VARIATIONS

* Use pieces of sliced chicken or ham for the filling.
* Use well-drained spinach instead of Swiss chard.
* Use only red peppers and puree with garlic and parsley.
* Use only one kind of sauce, or tomato and ricotta sauce.

A fabulous visually pleasing presentation. This exciting blend of tastes is perfect for entertaining.

EGGPLANT LASAGNA ELEANORA

Eggplant, Red Pepper, Ricotta, and Pesto Sauce

3 medium-size eggplants, peeled and cut into 1-inch slices
2 tbsp. green olive oil
1 cup onion, diced
4 cloves of garlic, crushed
1 tsp. Italian herb seasoning
Dash of pepper (cayenne or black)
6 large red peppers, roasted and puréed (see page 7)
½ cup fresh Italian parsley, chopped
2 cups skim-milk ricotta cheese
¼ cup Parmesan cheese, freshly grated
3 cups of Basic Pesto Sauce (see page 197)

Servings:
8
Time:
25 *min.*
Calories:
689 *per serving*

Preheat oven at 350°F.

Soak the eggplant in cold water for 30 minutes; rinse often. Drain and dry the eggplant slices. Place them on a baking sheet; put a few drops of olive oil on top and broil until they are lightly browned on each side.

In a large frying pan, sauté the onion, garlic, Italian herb seasoning, cayenne pepper, and red pepper puree in the oil for a few minutes. Add the parsley and blend thoroughly.

Mix the ricotta and Parmesan cheeses in a bowl.

Rub a long baking dish with olive oil. Place the eggplant slices on the bottom; spread the red pepper puree on the top, then the cheese mixture, and top with the pesto sauce.

Make 3 layers to the top and finish with the Basic Pesto Sauce. Bake for 10 minutes. Serve immediately.

VARIATIONS
* Add sliced mushrooms to the red pepper purée.
* Eliminate the cheeses.

This dish is great as an appetizer, main course, or lunch.

F A G I O L I
A L L ' U C C E L L E T T O
M O S I A N O

Lima Beans in Tomato Sauce, Mosiano—St. Angelo Style

Servings:
4
Time:
25 *min.*
Calories:
216 *per serving*

1 cup onion, chopped
3 cloves of garlic, crushed
2 tbsp. green olive oil
2 lb. fresh lima beans, shelled; or 3 cups frozen; or 1 16-oz. can
½ tsp. Italian herb seasoning
Black pepper to taste
1 cup fresh plum tomatoes, peeled and diced; or crushed tomatoes, drained
½ cup fresh Italian parsley, chopped

In a large skillet, sauté the onion and garlic in the oil for a few minutes. Add the lima beans, Italian herb seasoning, and pepper, and cook for 3 minutes. Pour in the tomatoes and cook for 15 minutes.

Taste for seasoning; add more pepper if desired.

Serve warm; sprinkle with chopped parsley.

VARIATIONS
* Use diced mushrooms instead of onions.
* Prepare without the tomato sauce.
* Mix with ½ cup of diced prosciutto.

PESCE

Fish, Shellfish, Crustacea

Seafood: The Perfect Choice

Italians eat an enormous amount of fresh fish. It is caught in the Mediterranean on one side and the Adriatic on the other side of Italy.

With the current trend in America toward light and healthy eating, seafood is the perfect choice. There are so many exciting gastronomic adventures you can have with the endless selection of *pesce:* swordfish, calamari, clams, shrimp, crab, mussels, sole, and even eels. Cooking fish is an art in itself, and so this next section is devoted to glorious seafood!

Seafood is a marvelous mixer: It blends well with a huge variety of vegetables, herbs, pasta, rice, and cornmeal, and it blends perfectly with lush, light sauces made from wine, onions, garlic, fresh herbs, and tomatoes.

Whether you have it for breakfast, brunch, lunch, dinner, or supper, seafood is wonderfully versatile. It can be prepared simply or elaborately. From inexpensive tuna to ultra-expensive caviar, there's a fish for all seasons.

The health benefits of eating seafood are too numerous to list here. But since fish is so low in calories, it is a must for anyone who is health- or weight-conscious.

One of the first things to learn about seafood is that it must be fresh. When you buy a whole fish, look for shiny, moist skin, bright eyes, and bright red gills. Fillets and fish steaks should look moist and close-grained. Above all, seafood must not smell fishy. A good rule of thumb: The more it smells, the longer it has been since it swam. When you buy fish, get it into the refrigerator quickly; cover it with ice. Fresh fish can be kept in ice for as long as three days.

Seafood makes an ideal base for soups and stews: Shellfish, vegetables, and seasonings simmered in a wine-and-fish tomato stock make a wonderful stew; add more liquid to make a soup. Seafood soups and stews can easily become a feast in themselves when served with salad, crusty fresh bread, and a fine Italian white wine.

Shellfish, such as clams, mussels, lobster, shrimp, and crab, together with the firm-textured fish, such as cod, sea bass, halibut, swordfish, haddock, or rockfish, give the best flavor to soups and stews. The more delicate fish tend to fall apart in stews; they offer much less taste. Strong-flavored fish, such as sardines, anchovies, herring, or salmon should also not be used in stews or soups since they have an overpowering taste.

A soup or stew can easily be made with just one type of fish, but it will be far more interesting and flavorful if several types of fish *and* shellfish are combined. One of the most important things to remember when preparing any fish recipe is not to overcook. Normally, most fish can be cooked in five minutes or less. If you overcook fish, it will quickly become tough and tasteless. Don't forget, fish goes on cooking after you've removed it from the heat source. Even in a stew, start with fish stock only; add the pieces of fish and shellfish just a few minutes before serving.

Methods of Cooking Fish

Poaching, steaming, and steeping are three methods of cooking fish and shellfish that keep them moist and tender. This kind of cooking eliminates the need for oils or fats and is healthier and less caloric than other cooking methods. The natural taste and texture of the fish are at their peak when the fish has been cooked by one of these three methods.

Firm-textured fish, such as salmon, striped bass, halibut, or swordfish, hold their shape well when poached, steamed, or steeped. High-fat and soft-texture fish, such as sablefish, herring, and bluefish, usually fall apart when cooked in liquid.

Poaching is the term used for cooking food in liquid that moves but does not boil or bubble. Liquid for poaching can be fish stock, wine, tomato sauce, or a combination of water and wine. The ideal way to poach fish properly is, of course, in a fish poacher. However, if you do not have one, an oblong pan with a tightly fitted lid or a large, lidded sauté pan will do. You can also use a roasting pan with a fitted top. It's best to wrap a large fish in cheesecloth; leave the long ends open so that you can easily lift the fish out of the liquid.

Steamed fish and shellfish are cooked *over* boiling liquid *not in the liquid*. Steaming provides a gentle, even heat that preserves the natural juices and delicate texture of fish, keeping it tender and moist. In most cases, steamed fish should be accompanied by a sauce in order to enhance the flavor. Serve the sauce on the side, or lightly coat the fish when serving.

Grilling, broiling, and baking fish are known as dry heat cooking. The best method is to wrap the fish tightly in aluminum foil with a few drops of oil on the bottom to keep it from sticking to the foil. Whole fish fillets, steaks, and chunks of fish can be broiled, grilled, or baked. Skewered pieces, such as skewered swordfish, and high-fat fish, such as mackerel, bluefish, mullet, and tuna, are especially good when broiled or grilled. It should be understood that the process of broiling and grilling dries the fish, so marinating and basting are important to keep the fish moist and tender while cooking.

Broiled fish is cooked *under* intense, direct heat. To avoid excessive drying, adjust the broiling pan so the fish is four to six inches from the heat source. This will prevent burning and give an appetizing, golden brown look to the fish. The piece of fish to be broiled should be one to one-and-a-half inches thick; thinner pieces are more likely to overcook before they brown. For best results, most fillets and fish steaks are cooked only on one side, but a particularly thick piece may require turning.

Grilled fish is cooked *over* direct heat. A gas flame or electric burner can be used, but the trend today is to use charcoal, wood, or, best of all, mesquite, which gives more flavor. Remember, high heat quickly seals the fish and keeps in the natural flavors and juices. Always use the firmer, fatter fish for grilling: salmon, tuna, swordfish, mackerel, bluefish, or trout. Delicate fish, such as flounder or sole, are overwhelmed by the flame and fall apart.

To sauté fish, you need a small amount of oil. The sautéing is done *over* low to medium heat, using a frying pan, skillet, or wok. Steaming can be made part of this cooking process by adding a lid. Sautéing is an excellent way to seal in the flavor of delicate fish; it helps the texture and keeps the fish intact. The numerous possibilities for sauces, herbs, spices, and seasonings make this method of cooking one of the best.

Quick and easy, sautéed foods are not greasy as fried foods are. They do not have the high calorie or cholesterol content produced by the frying process. For these reasons, as well as the resulting lack of taste and texture, I do not recommend deep-frying as a method of cooking fish.

Baking is an ideal way of preparing fish. Baking is quick, easy, and very light for whole fish, stuffed fish, or fish fillets. It should be done in a very hot oven, at 400°F to 450°F. Baking at high temperatures shortens the cooking time and seals in the natural juices and flavor. But it is very important to add enough liquids to keep the fish moist during the cooking process. Adding wine, water, tomato juice, or green olive oil with herbs will protect the fish from the dry oven heat. It is also important to slightly undercook the fish because it will continue to cook for a few minutes after it is removed from the oven. The worst thing you can do to fish is to overcook it—it will become tough and dry. The usual cooking time is three to eight minutes; stuffed fish will take up to fifteen minutes. Cooking time will vary depending on the thickness and type of fish.

Try baking the fish in parchment paper or foil to seal in the flavor and moisture. This method protects the fish from dry heat. Covering the baking dish will help to keep in the moisture; use foil or a lid.

Another great advantage to baking fish is that your time is free to prepare other parts of the meal while the fish is baking. The best types of fish to bake are fillet of sole, bass, halibut, snapper, swordfish, salmon, and codfish. Shellfish is best when sautéed, steamed, or grilled.

Microwave cooking is also a good way to preserve the delicate flavor and texture of fish and shellfish. Cooking time is minimal, and the fish stays moist when marinated and small amounts of liquid are added. Thick cuts are more difficult, and rotation is important to cook the fish evenly.

SEAFOOD AND VEGETABLES ALLA GRILL

Grilled Seafood and Vegetable Kebabs, Served with Two Sauces

Servings:
12
Time:
15 *min.*
Calories:
338 *per serving*

4 medium-size onions
6 cloves of garlic, crushed
1 cup fresh Italian parsley, chopped
4 lb. swordfish or monkfish steaks (cut 2 inches thick)
30 scallops
1 dozen large shrimp (with shells)
3 red peppers
3 green peppers
4 medium-size zucchini
1 lb. large mushrooms
½ cup green olive oil
1 tbsp. Italian herb seasoning
Juice of 2 lemons
½ cup red wine vinegar
20 cherry tomatoes
Pepper to taste
Two sauces (Basic Pesto Sauce, page 197; Salsa Verde, page 200; Mustard Dill
    Caper Sauce, page 201; or Basic Marinara Sauce, page 192)

To prepare the marinade, mix all the ingredients in a large bowl; let stand for at least 2 hours. The grill must be very hot. Add the vegetables first, grilling quickly on each side and basting with the marinade; then add the seafood. Baste the seafood and cook for only a few minutes—it will toughen quickly.

Remove the ingredients from the grill and place on a warm platter. Serve as kebabs, alternating the vegetables and seafood, or serve with the vegetables on one side of the platter and the seafood on the other. Pour the marinade juices over the mixture and serve with a choice of two sauces.

VARIATIONS
* Use lobster instead of shrimp.
* Use eggplant instead of zucchini, and red peppers instead of tomatoes.
* Use pieces of radicchio leaves.

BAKED CODFISH WITH FENNEL AND TOMATOES

Servings:
6
Time:
25 *min.*
Calories:
217 *per serving*

1 lb. codfish fillets
4 medium-size, new potatoes, peeled and cut into 2-inch pieces
2 cups onion, chopped
3 cloves of garlic, crushed
½ cup celery, diced
1 cup fresh fennel, diced (heart of the fennel only)
2 tbsp. green olive oil
1 tsp. Italian herb seasoning
1 tbsp. fennel seeds, crushed
Dash of cayenne or black pepper
1 cup dry Italian white wine
3 cups fresh plum tomatoes, diced, peeled, and seeded; or 2 14-oz. cans of
    Italian plum tomatoes
1 cup fresh Italian parsley, chopped

Preheat oven at 350°F.
Wash the codfish and dry. Cut it into 2- to 3-inch chunks.
Boil the potatoes for 5 minutes.
In a large skillet, sauté the onion, garlic, celery, and fennel in the oil for a few minutes. Add the codfish, Italian herb seasoning, fennel seeds, and pepper; sauté for 5 minutes. Turn the fish carefully to brown on both sides.
Add the wine and cook for 2 to 3 minutes; then add the drained, crushed tomatoes and parsley, and cook for 3 minutes. Pour the mixture into a large baking dish and bake with the potatoes for 15 minutes.
Serve immediately.

VARIATIONS
* Cook with wine only—eliminate the tomatoes.
* Use mushrooms.
* If fennel is unavailable, use more fennel seeds and celery.

PESCE SPADA VILLA IGIA

Swordfish with Sicilian Sauce

6 swordfish steaks
1 cup fresh Italian parsley, chopped
2 cups onions, chopped
4 cloves of garlic, crushed
¼ tsp. crushed hot pepper
2 tbsp. green olive oil
6 small plum tomatoes, peeled, seeded, and chopped; or 1 16-oz. can whole
 plum Italian tomatoes, peeled, drained, and chopped
1 tbsp. small capers, rinsed
½ cup dark raisins
¼ cup pignoli nuts, roasted
¼ cup black Sicilian olives, diced
1 tsp. Italian herb seasoning

Servings:
6
Time:
20 *min.*
Calories:
351 *per serving*

Preheat oven at 350°F.

Rinse the fish and dry it on paper towels.

Oil a baking dish, which should be large enough to line a single layer of fish. Line the fish in the baking dish and sprinkle with the parsley and Italian herb seasoning.

In a large skillet, sauté the onion, garlic, and hot pepper in the oil for 3 to 4 minutes. Add the tomatoes, capers, raisins, pignolis, and olives; cook for 5 to 8 minutes.

Pour the sauce over the fish and bake for 6 minutes. Keep the fish tender and slightly undercooked, so it will not get tough.

Serve immediately.

VARIATIONS

* Use 2 cups of dry white Italian wine instead of tomatoes.
* Add 1 crushed anchovy instead of the raisins and nuts.

CHECKERBOARD PASTA AND FISH COMBINATION

Red, White, and Green Pasta Strips with Whitefish

Yield:
6 *rolls*
Time:
45 *min.*
Calories:
496 *per roll*

6 green lasagna noodles
½ white wine
1 lb. whitefish fillet (sole, halibut, cod, swordfish, etc.)
½ lb. fresh fillet of salmon
¼ tsp. Italian herb seasoning
¼ cup Basic Pesto Sauce (see page 197)
¼ cup Basic Marinara Sauce (see page 192)

Preheat oven at 350°F.

In a large lidded pan, boil water to cook the pasta.

Pour the wine in a shallow baking dish and poach the whitefish and salmon in the Italian herb seasoning for 4 to 6 minutes (keep firm). Drain the fish and let it cool; then cut it into 1-inch strips.

Cook the lasagna noodles al dente, drain, and cool them under cold water. With a sharp knife, carefully cut off the curly sides of the noodles and dispose of them. Cut the remainder of the lasagna noodles into even 1-inch strips.

On two large dinner plates, lattice the whitefish with the salmon and lasagna strips to form a red, white, and green checkerboard effect. Trim any uneven ends to make a neat square.

If you want to serve immediately, place the plates in a hot oven (or microwave) to warm. Add the pesto and tomato sauces at room temperature just before serving. Use them to dress each side of the checkerboard.

VARIATIONS

* Use spinach leaves instead of salmon and use red pasta.
* Strips of pasta (three colors) can be used instead of the fish.
* Try strips of parboiled zucchini with the skin on for the green effect.

This is a special presentation. This recipe can be prepared in advance and kept refrigerated. It's ideal for intimate dinner parties.

MUSSELS FORTUNATO

Mussels in a Wine, Tomato, and Herb Sauce

4 dozen mussels
1 cup onion, diced
4 cloves of garlic, crushed
¼ tsp. crushed red pepper
2 tbsp. green olive oil
1 cup dry Italian white wine
1 tsp. Italian herb seasoning
3 cups fresh plum tomatoes, diced, peeled, and seeded; or 2 cups of canned
   Italian plum tomatoes, crushed
½ cup fresh Italian parsley, chopped

Servings:
4
Time:
15 *min.*
Calories:
186 *per dozen mussels with sauce*

Scrub the mussels with a brush to remove the sand from the shells, and rinse well. Remove the beards. Discard the mussels that are open. Rinse the mussels in cold water and drain.

In a large skillet, sauté the onion, garlic, and crushed pepper in the oil for a few minutes. Add the wine and Italian herb seasoning; cook for 2 to 3 minutes; add the crushed tomatoes and cook for 5 minutes. Add the mussels, cover, and simmer for 4 to 8 minutes or until the mussels open.

Use a large slotted spoon to remove the cooked mussels. Discard any mussels that do not open. Add the parsley to the sauce.

Spoon the mussels into individual shallow bowls, and pour the sauce over the mussels.

VARIATIONS
* Eliminate the tomatoes.
* Use white wine and herb sauce only.

This dish is an excellent appetizer or main course with hard bread.

PESCE POSITANO

Grilled or Baked Fish with Wine, Herb, and Garlic Sauce

Servings:
4
Time:
15 *min.*
Calories:
311 *per serving*

¼ cup green olive oil
2 lb. fish fillets (flounder, halibut, swordfish, bass, sole)
½ cup dry Italian white wine
3 cloves of garlic, crushed
½ tsp. Italian herb seasoning
Dash of black pepper
¼ cup lemon juice, freshly squeezed
½ cup fresh Italian parsley, chopped

Mix all of the ingredients except the fish in a large bowl.

If grilling, prepare the grill and wrap the fillets in foil with the sauce spooned over the fish, and served on the side. Cook in the foil, 4 to 6 inches above the hot coals or high heat. Grill for 2 to 3 minutes; remove from the heat when the fish is slightly undercooked.

If baking, wrap fillets in foil with the sauce and place in a large baking dish. Bake at 425°F for 6 to 8 minutes. Keep the fish slightly underdone. Serve immediately.

VARIATIONS
* Use only lemon juice instead of wine.
* Eliminate the garlic and add diced fresh basil leaves.
* Add diced shallots.

CALAMARI SALAD

Servings:
4
Time:
20 *min.*
Calories:
382 *per serving*

3 lb. squid, cleaned
1½ cups green and red bell peppers, diced
½ cup celery, finely chopped
¼ cup shallots or onion, finely diced
½ cup black olives, chopped
½ cup fresh Italian parsley, finely chopped
¼ cup small capers, drained
¼ cup red wine vinegar
2 small cloves of garlic, crushed
½ cup fresh basil, chopped
½ tsp. Italian herb seasoning

½ cup lemon juice, freshly squeezed
⅛ cup green olive oil
Black pepper to taste
12 lettuce leaves, cleaned and shaped (for decoration)
1 lb. plum tomatoes, thinly sliced

Cut the squid tentacles in half crosswise; cut the bodies into small slices (about ½ inch). Place squid in a pan of boiling water and simmer for about ½ minute until the squid becomes opaque.

Remove quickly with a draining spoon and rinse thoroughly in cold water. Dry the pieces of squid with paper towels.

In a large bowl, toss the cooked squid, bell peppers, celery, onion, olives, parsley, and capers.

In a mixing bowl, combine the vinegar, garlic, basil, Italian herb seasoning, and lemon juice. Beat in the oil a little at a time.

Spoon the dressing over the salad, toss, and season with black pepper to taste.

Place washed lettuce leaves on serving dishes and spoon the salad on top. Add tomatoes to garnish. Serve slightly chilled.

VARIATIONS
* Use a 6½-oz. can of salmon instead of calamari.
* Add 2 tablespoons of Dijon mustard to the olive oil and vinegar mix.

C A P P E   S A N T E   E
G A M B E R I   A L   P E S T O

Bay Scallops and Shrimp with Pesto Sauce

¼ cup shallots, diced
3 ripe plum tomatoes, peeled and diced
1 tbsp. green olive oil
1 lb. bay or sea scallops, diced
½ lb. small shrimp, diced
Dash of cayenne pepper
¼ cup Basic Pesto Sauce (see page 197)

Servings:
4
Time:
20 *min.*
Calories
286 *per serving*

In a large skillet, sauté the shallots and tomatoes in the oil for a few minutes. Add the fish and pepper and mix thoroughly; cook for 2 to 3 minutes.

Pour the pesto sauce over the fish and mix well; cook for 3 to 5 minutes.

Serve warm, or cool, as an appetizer over radicchio leaves.

VARIATIONS

* Use only the pesto sauce with one kind of fish.
* Add 2 cloves of crushed garlic and more hot pepper.

Serve this dish as a sauce over pasta, or as a cocktail food over crostinis.

GRILLED FISH WITH TOMATO AND BASIL SAUCE

Servings:
4
Time:
10 *min.*
Calories:
315 *per serving*

4 5-oz. firm-textured fish steaks (swordfish, tuna, cod, or haddock)
3 cloves of garlic, crushed
¼ cup green olive oil
2 cups fresh plum tomatoes, peeled, seeded, and diced
1 cup fresh basil leaves, chopped; or 2 tbsp. dried basil
½ tsp. Italian herb seasoning

Marinate the fish steaks in the marinade sauce for a minimum of 15 to 30 minutes.

Preheat the grill and grease the rack.

In a sauté pan, sauté the garlic in the oil for a minute; add the tomatoes, basil, and Italian herb seasoning, and cook for 3 to 4 minutes. Remove from the heat and set aside.

Place the fish steaks on the rack about 4 inches above the hot coals or high heat. Brush them with marinade or olive oil. Grill 1 to 2 minutes on each side, turning once. Do not overcook the fish, or it will get tough. The fish should be slightly undercooked.

Place the fish on a serving dish; spoon the tomato and basil sauce over the top of each fillet and serve.

VARIATIONS

* Try fresh dill or dry dill weed if basil is not available.
* Use marinade sauce only (see page 202).

CALAMARI JULIANOVA

Squid in Tomato and Hot Pepper Sauce

½ cup onion, chopped
3 cloves of garlic, crushed
¼ tsp. crushed red pepper
2 tbsp. green olive oil
2 cups canned Italian plum tomatoes, crushed with juice
¼ tsp. Italian herb seasoning
2 tbsp. small capers
½ cup fresh Italian parsley, chopped
1 lb. squid, cut into small strips or circles

Servings:
4
Time:
15 *min.*
Calories:
192 *per serving*

In a large skillet, sauté the onion, garlic, and hot pepper in the oil for 3 to 4 minutes. Add the tomatoes, Italian herb seasoning, capers, and parsley, and cook for 3 to 4 minutes. Add the squid and cook for 3 to 5 minutes. Do not overcook the calamari—it will toughen quickly.

Remove the mixture from the skillet and serve on a serving platter. The calamari will continue to cook, so remove when slightly undercooked.

VARIATIONS
* Use as a pasta sauce.
* Add diced olives.

BAKED SALMON BERNARDO

Salmon with Dill, Mushroom, Wine Sauce

2 tbsp. green olive oil
12 oz. fillet of salmon
½ lemon, juice only
¼ dry Italian white wine
½ tsp. fresh dill, minced; or dill weed
4 large fresh mushrooms
¼ cup fresh Italian parsley, finely chopped
½ lemon, thinly sliced to decorate

Servings:
2
Time:
18 *min.*
Calories:
520 *per serving*

Preheat oven to 425°F.

Coat an 18-by-18-inch strip of aluminum foil with oil.

Cut the salmon into two pieces and place in the foil. Sprinkle the salmon with the lemon and wine, add the dill, mushrooms, and parsley, and seal tightly. Place it in a baking pan and bake for 6 to 8 minutes. Keep the salmon slightly under-cooked for taste and texture, as it will continue to cook after it is removed from the oven.

Serve decorated with lemon slices.

VARIATIONS
* Use 1 tablespoon of small capers.
* Add 1 cup of chopped fresh tomatoes instead of wine and lemon or try using Mustard Dill Caper Sauce (see page 201).

POLLO

Chicken, Turkey, Capon

Chicken Italian Style

Italians prefer chicken to red meat. There are fewer calories, it is plentiful and inexpensive, and there is an enormous variety of ways to prepare chicken: grill, boil, bake, sauté, roast, stuff, roll, chop, fricassee, and braise. Chicken can be used in sauces or salads, or mixed with pasta or rice. It also makes a wonderful stock that can be used in dozens of different recipes.

Every region in Italy has its own vast repertoire of chicken recipes. In the north, chicken is often served with porcini mushrooms and red wine sauces. It's boiled with *salsa verde* and served with cheese toppings. In the south, chicken is served more often with vegetable mistos, tomato sauces, or grilled with herbs and shredded in timbales.

Chicken Italian style offers great variety and exciting, delicious recipes, using fresh herbs, spices, garlic, tomatoes, and wine sauces. Always buy the freshest poultry; try free-range chickens for a healthier product.

In this section, you will find recipes that also feature turkey and capon, focusing on the healthy and light sides of *la cucina Italiana*.

CHICKEN WITH LEMONS, CAPERS, AND GARLIC SAUCE

Servings:
6
Time:
15 *min.*
Calories:
185 *per serving*

2 tbsp. green olive oil
1 cup onions, chopped
4 cloves of garlic, crushed
2 lb. chicken breasts or thighs, skinned
2 cups dry Italian white wine
1 tsp. Italian herb seasoning
Dash of black or cayenne pepper
2 lemons, sliced very thin with the skins
1 cup fresh Italian parsley, chopped
1 tbsp. small capers

In a large, heavy skillet with a lid, sauté the olive oil, onion, garlic, and chicken; cook for 5 minutes, turning the chicken to cook golden brown. Add the wine, Italian herb seasoning, and pepper, and cook for 3 minutes. Add the sliced lemons, parsley, and capers, cover, and simmer for 6 to 8 minutes, until the chicken is soft and tender. Be sure to turn the chicken often in the sauce.

VARIATIONS
* Add ½ cup of mushrooms or olives.
* For a tart taste, use lemon juice with a bit of water instead of wine.

BAKED CHICKEN ALLA MARCO

Servings:
4
Time:
35 *min.*
Calories:
275 *per serving*

3 lb. chicken for roasting (use thighs and breasts)
1 tsp. rosemary
½ tsp. Italian herb seasoning
10 cloves of garlic, crushed
2 cups Italian white wine

Preheat oven at 400°F.
Wash the chicken parts and dry. Remove skin.
Put the chicken in a large baking pan and sprinkle with the rosemary, Italian herb seasoning, and garlic. Bake for 15 minutes, turning the chicken to brown.

Add the wine and cover; cook for 15 to 20 minutes more, depending on your oven.

Place the chicken on a serving platter. Decorate with parsley and serve while hot.

VARIATIONS
* For a stronger wine taste use red wine and add diced onions and mushrooms.
* Use lemon juice instead of wine.

This chicken dish is simple, yet very moist and juicy. It offers the great taste combination of garlic, rosemary, and herbs, and is a classic from Abruzzi.

POLLO ALL'ACETO BALSAMICO

Chicken with Balsamic Vinegar Sauce

4 lb. mixed chicken parts or chicken breasts
3 tbsp. green olive oil
2 cups onion, chopped
4 cloves of garlic, crushed
1 cup warm water
½ cup balsamic vinegar
2 tbsp. small capers
¼ cup black olives, diced
1 tsp. Italian herb seasoning
½ tsp. rosemary
½ cup fresh Italian parsley, chopped
Crushed black pepper

Servings:
8
Time:
20 *min.*
Calories:
404 *per serving*

Wash and dry the chicken parts; cut them into small, 2-inch pieces. (If the parts are drumsticks and larger pieces, leave whole.)

In a large skillet, sauté the oil, onion, and garlic for a few minutes. Add the chicken and brown slightly.

Pour the water and balsamic vinegar over the chicken; add the capers, olives, Italian herb seasoning, rosemary, and parsley. Cover and cook for 10 minutes.

Add black pepper to taste.

VARIATIONS
* Add ½ cup pimentos for color.
* Add 1 cup of mushrooms.

GRILLED CHICKEN
AND PASTA SALAD

Servings:
6
Time:
25 *min.*
Calories:
568 *per serving*

1 lb. short-shape pasta (penne, rotini)
1 tbsp. balsamic vinegar or red wine vinegar
½ cup lime juice, freshly squeezed
1 medium-size onion, thinly sliced
3 cloves of garlic, crushed
¼ cup green olive oil
2 large chicken breasts, skinned and boned
1 medium-size head of lettuce (red leaf, boston, or iceberg)
1 small bunch of arugula leaves
1 small head of radicchio (optional)
3 large ripe tomatoes, peeled and diced
3 red peppers, roasted and julienned (see page 7)
1 cup fresh mushrooms, sliced
½ cup black olives, diced
¼ cup pignoli nuts, roasted
1 cup fresh Italian parsley, chopped
1 tsp. Italian herb seasoning
Dash of black pepper

Boil water to cook the pasta.
Prepare the grill.
In a small bowl, combine the vinegar, lime juice, onion, garlic, and olive oil.
Put the chicken breasts in the marinade while the grill gets hot, and prepare the ingredients for the salad.
Wash and dice the lettuce, arugula, and radicchio leaves and place them in a large salad bowl with the tomatoes and roasted red peppers. Toss with the mushrooms, onion, olives, pignoli nuts, parsley, Italian herb seasoning, and black pepper.
When the chicken is grilled, cut it into bite-size pieces and add it to the salad with the marinade; toss thoroughly.
Cook the pasta al dente, drain, and rinse in cold water. Add the pasta to the chicken misto and mix thoroughly. Serve immediately at room temperature or place the salad in the refrigerator until ready to serve. However, remove the salad ½ hour before use; do not serve chilled.

VARIATIONS
* Use only tomatoes; eliminate the roasted red peppers.
* Try a mustard–herb dressing.
* Make with turkey or capon.
* Use ½ cup of diced cucumbers, celery, or zucchini.

CHICKEN FLORENTINE ALLA ROBERTO

Chicken, Onions, Wine, and Spinach with Rice

1½ lb. chicken thighs, skinned and boned
¼ cup green olive oil
1 large, full bulb of garlic, chopped
2 large onions, chopped
1 tsp. rosemary
½ cup Italian white wine
1 lb. fresh spinach, chopped; or 1 package of frozen chopped spinach
½ tsp. Italian herb seasoning
1 cup fresh Italian parsley, chopped
½ lemon, squeezed
Black pepper to taste
2 cups water
1 cup long-grain rice

Servings:
4 *to* **6**
Time:
35 *min.*
Calories:
175 *per serving*

Preheat oven at 350°F.

Wash and dry the chicken thoroughly; place it in a shallow, oven-proof glass dish. Add ½ of the olive oil and ½ of the chopped garlic and onion, and cook for 15 minutes. Sprinkle with rosemary and ½ cup of wine. Cover tightly with foil and bake for 25 minutes, or until the sauce has thickened and the chicken is soft, moist, and tender.

In a large, covered skillet, sauté the remaining olive oil and garlic and onion over medium heat. After 1 minute, reduce the heat and add ½ cup of white wine. Cook slowly over low heat; reduce until slightly thick (about 3 to 4 minutes). Add the spinach, Italian herb seasoning, parsley, lemon, and black pepper. Cover tightly and cook until al dente (about 6 minutes).

Put exactly 2 cups of water in a separate tightly lidded saucepan, and bring to a fast boil. Add 1 cup of rice and boil for exactly 20 minutes. To serve, pour the cooked spinach in sauce onto a serving platter, and arrange the rice around the outside. Place the pieces of chicken on the bed of spinach. Garnish with thinly sliced tomato, if desired.

VARIATIONS

* Use veal or turkey breast instead of chicken.
* Use broccoli instead of spinach.

P O L L O   G E N O V E S I

Chicken with Dried Tomatoes, Mushrooms, and Leeks

Servings:
4
Time:
15 *min.*
Calories:
230 *per serving*

2 whole chicken breasts, skinned, boned, and halved
1 large leek, diced (white part only)
3 cloves of garlic, crushed
¼ tsp. crushed red pepper
½ cup Italian herb seasoning
1 cup fresh or dried mushrooms
2 tbsp. green olive oil
½ cup dried tomatoes, coarsely chopped
1 cup fresh Italian parsley, chopped
1 cup dry Italian white wine

Slice the chicken breasts in halves; then crosswise on the diagonal, into 6 equal pieces.

In a large skillet, sauté the leek, garlic, hot pepper, Italian herb seasoning, and mushrooms in the olive oil for a few minutes. Add the chicken, dried tomatoes, and parsley; cook for 4 to 5 minutes (slightly undercook the chicken to keep it tender and moist).

Add the wine and cover; cook for 3 to 4 minutes.

Serve immediately.

VARIATION
* Add black olives and use fresh tomatoes if you can't find the dried tomatoes.

This dish from Genoa is very visual and offers an exciting blend of tastes.

P O L L O   C O N
P E P P E R O N C I N I

Chicken with Red and Green Pepper Sauce and Mushrooms,
Olives, and Tomatoes

Servings:
4
Time:
25 *min.*
Calories:
619 *per serving*

1 small chicken or mixed chicken parts (cut into serving pieces)
1 cup shallots or onion, diced
3 cloves of garlic, crushed
3 red peppers, chopped
3 green peppers, chopped
1 lb. fresh mushrooms, sliced
½ tsp. crushed red pepper
2 tbsp. green olive oil
1 cup red wine
1 tsp. Italian herb seasoning
1 cup fresh plum tomatoes, diced and peeled; or 1 cup Italian canned tomatoes,
   crushed and drained
1 cup fresh Italian parsley, chopped
½ cup black Italian olives, diced

Wash and dry the chicken parts.

In a large skillet, sauté the onion, garlic, red and green peppers, mushrooms, and hot pepper in the olive oil for 3 to 4 minutes. Add the chicken parts and brown on all sides (5 to 8 minutes). Do not overcook.

Add the wine and Italian herb seasoning, and cook for 10 minutes, covered, over low heat. Add the tomatoes, parsley, and olives, and cook uncovered for 5 more minutes.

Serve warm.

VARIATIONS
* Prepare with roasted peppers and no tomatoes.
* Use diced eggplant.
* Try chicken breast meat for fewer calories.

This dish is visually pleasing and delicious when served with pasta, rice, or polenta.

CAPON, MUSHROOMS, ARUGULA, AND RED PEPPERS

Servings:
4
Time:
20 *min.*
Calories:
356 *per serving*

3½ cups capon meat, cooked and diced (use breast if possible)
2 tbsp. green olive oil or safflower oil
½ tsp. Italian herb seasoning
2 red peppers, roasted and diced (see page 7)
2 cups fresh mushrooms, sliced
½ cup fresh Italian parsley, chopped
4 marinated artichoke hearts, diced
3 tbsp. shallots, diced
2 bunches of fresh arugula leaves, broken into small pieces
Black pepper to taste
2 tbsp. lemon juice
1 tbsp. red wine vinegar
½ tsp. dried dill weed

Sauté the capon over a low flame in ½ of the oil and Italian herb seasoning for 6 to 8 minutes.

Put all of the remaining ingredients except the vinegar, lemon juice, and dill weed in a large bowl. Mix the ingredients and pour them over the mixture with the capon. Add the red peppers and toss thoroughly to mix well. Add the lemon juice, vinegar, and dill weed to taste.

VARIATIONS

* Use turkey, chicken breast, swordfish, bass, or halibut instead of capon.
* Use tomatoes instead of red peppers.
* Use green beans instead of arugula or radicchio lettuce instead of the peppers.

This dish can be served as an appetizer, salad, or main course.

Serve hot or cold as a salad. Use the vinegar for the salad; toss with more oil and even a dash of dry mustard.

CAPPONE PERINO'S

Boiled Capon with Salsa Verde

1 capon (3 lb.)
1 cup onion, diced
½ cup fresh Italian parsley, chopped
1 tsp. Italian herb seasoning
1 lemon, juice only
4 cloves of garlic, crushed
2 bay leaves
1 cup of Salsa Verde (see page 200)

Servings:
4
Time:
40 *min.*
Calories:
440 *per serving*

Wash and dry the capon. Place it in a large pot with water and all of the ingredients, except the Salsa Verde, and cover. Cook for 25 to 30 minutes, until the capon is tender. Prepare the salsa verde while the capon is cooking.

Remove the capon from the liquid and cool. Slice into serving pieces and line on a serving platter. Spread the slices with the Salsa Verde and serve.

VARIATION

* Use a Red Pepper and Tomato Sauce, Basic Pesto Sauce, or Lemon and Herb Dressing Sauce (see pages 193, 197, and 198, respectively).

This dish is perfect for lunch or dinner, or as an appetizer. It's very light.

CAPPONE AL BRUNELLO

Capon Braised in Brunello Wine Sauce

1 capon (4 lb.)
2 cups shallots or onion, diced
6 cloves of garlic, crushed
2 cups of porcini or fresh mushrooms, sliced
½ tsp. thyme
Pepper to taste
1 cup fresh Italian parsley, chopped
1 tsp. Italian herb seasoning
⅛ cup green olive oil
2 cups Brunello d' Montalcino red wine
1 bay leaf

Servings:
6
Time:
35 *min.*
Calories:
618 *per serving*

Preheat oven at 300°F.

Wash and dry the capon.

In a large skillet, sauté the shallots, garlic, mushrooms, thyme, pepper, parsley, and Italian herb seasoning in the oil for 3 minutes. Slightly brown the capon (do not overcook); then add 1 cup of wine and the bay leaf, and cover. Cook over low heat for 10 minutes.

Transfer the capon and sauce to a baking dish; add 1 cup of wine and bake for 15 minutes. Remove from the oven and let stand for a few minutes.

Serve the capon on a large platter with the sauce and sautéed vegetables on top. Small roasted potatoes or rice are very good with this type of sauce and the capon.

VARIATION

* Add carrots and celery to the sauce when sautéing. Marinate in the wine and herbs for 6 hours before cooking.

T A C C H I N O   S A V O A

Turkey Breast with Caper, Mustard, Dill, and Wine Sauce

Servings:
6
Time:
20 *min.*
Calories:
225 *per serving*

1 red pepper, roasted and diced (see page 7)
2 cups shallots or onion, chopped
3 cloves of garlic, crushed
2 tbsp. green olive oil
6 2-inch-thick cooked turkey breast slices
2 tbsp. small capers, drained
1 cup dry Italian white wine
1 tbsp. prepared Dijon-type mustard
¼ cup fresh dill, diced; or 2 tbsp. dried dill weed
Dash of pepper
½ cup fresh Italian parsley, chopped

In a large skillet, sauté the red pepper, onion, and garlic in the oil for a minute. Add the turkey slices and the capers; cook 2 to 3 minutes, turning the slices.

In a small bowl, mix the wine, mustard, dill, and black pepper, until smooth and creamy. Pour over the turkey slices and cook for 5 minutes.

Transfer the turkey and sauce to a serving platter; sprinkle parsley on top.

VARIATIONS

* Use no mustard, only white wine with capers and dill.
* Add fresh sliced mushrooms.
* Use chicken slices instead of turkey.

This dish makes a great visual presentation. It offers very exciting, tart taste combinations.

It can be prepared in advance and stored in the refrigerator. Serve at room temperature. It's excellent for entertaining.

T A C C H I N O ,   P A S T A ,   E
V E G E T A L E

Turkey, Pasta, and Vegetable Salad

½ lb. short-shape pasta (rotini, penne, elbows, bows)
2 3-oz. slices of cooked turkey breast meat, diced (2-inch thick)
6 ripe plum tomatoes, peeled and diced
1 cup artichoke hearts, diced (jarred, marinated, rinsed, and drained)
1 cup fresh arugula leaves, diced
½ cup black olives, diced
½ cup fresh green onions, minced
1 cup red radishes, sliced
2 tbsp. green olive oil
1 tbsp. red wine vinegar or balsamic vinegar
1 tsp. dry mustard
Dash of pepper
½ cup fresh Italian parsley, chopped

Servings:
4
Time:
25 *min.*
Calories:
390 *per serving*

Boil water to cook the pasta al dente. Drain the pasta.

In a large bowl, mix the turkey, tomatoes, artichokes, pasta, arugula, olives, onion, and radishes; in a separate bowl, mix the oil, vinegar, mustard, and pepper. Pour the oil-and-vinegar mixture over the turkey, pasta, and vegetables. Toss and blend thoroughly. Sprinkle with parsley and serve.

VARIATION

* Use asparagus tips, green beans, or radicchio leaves.

TURKEY WITH PESTO SAUCE AND TOMATOES

Servings:
6
Time:
15 *min.*
Calories:
437 *per serving*

3 cloves of garlic, crushed
1 cup fresh plum tomatoes, diced and peeled
Black pepper to taste
¼ tsp. Italian herb seasoning
1 tbsp. green olive oil
12–14 pieces of leftover turkey; or 6 raw turkey breast cutlets
1 cup Basic Pesto Sauce (see page 197)
6 fresh basil leaves, minced

In a large skillet, sauté the garlic, tomatoes, pepper, and the Italian herb seasoning in the oil for 5 minutes. Add the turkey and cook for 5 to 8 minutes.

Put the turkey in the center of a large serving platter. Put the Pesto Sauce all around the turkey and spread the tomato sauce on top. Sprinkle with the basil leaves.

VARIATIONS
* Use only one of the sauces.
* Try chicken instead of turkey.
* Red Pepper and Tomato Sauce (see page 193) can be used instead of tomato sauce.

GAME

Pheasant, Quail, Rabbit

Since before the days of the Roman Empire, game has been a specialty food in Italy. Today, it's becoming quite popular in America because of its availability and simplified methods of preparation and cooking.

For this section, I have selected some of the more familiar types of game that are easy to prepare and delicious to eat. I would urge you to try some of these classic Italian recipes to add variety to your daily meals and especially for entertaining. Quail, served with *polenta* or *risotto*, or cooked in a wine sauce with mushrooms, has become very chic. You should also try rabbit, pheasant, or game hen: All are very tasty and exciting. Don't be frightened by the tag "game." Believe me, game can be easy to prepare, and it doesn't have to have that strong, "gamey taste" either.

A final point in favor of game: It's very lean and low in both calories and cholesterol, as well as being high in protein and nutrients.

QUAGLIE ALLA SCHIDONATA ARMANDO

Quail on the Spit, Grilled with Herbs

6 cloves of garlic, crushed
8 medium-size quail
10 fresh basil leaves, diced
1 cup fresh Italian parsley, chopped
1 tsp. Italian herb seasoning
Black pepper to taste
¼ cup green olive oil
1 cup red wine
8 slices prosciutto

Servings:
4
Time:
20 *min.*
Calories:
484 *per serving*

Mix the herbs and garlic.

Clean, wash, and dry the quail. Stuff them with chopped basil, parsley, garlic, Italian herb seasoning, and pepper. Mix the oil and wine, and brush over each quail.

Wrap each quail in a slice of prosciutto, secure with thread, pins, or toothpicks. Put them on the spit and baste often with the oil and wine mixture.

Brown the quails over high heat for a few minutes on each side. Do not over-cook, or quail will become dry and tough. Baste before removing from the spit.

Place the quail on a serving platter and remove the prosciutto.

Serve immediately with rice, polenta, or short-shape pasta.

VARIATIONS

* Place the quail in the broiler section; baste and turn often.
* Use bacon slices if prosciutto is unavailable.
* Marinate the quail in the wine, garlic, and herb mixture.

F A G I A N O   A L L A   B E A U   R I V A G E ,   M A L I B U

Pheasant in Wine and Mushroom Sauce

Servings:
4
Time:
45 *min.*
Calories:
671 *per serving*

3 bacon slices
1 3-lb. pheasant, cleaned
2 tbsp. green olive oil
3 cloves of garlic, crushed
1 cup onions, minced
2 cups fresh mushrooms; or 1 cup dried mushrooms (if dried, soak in 2 cups red wine for 30 minutes)
2 cups dry Italian red wine
2 tbsp. sage leaves, minced
1 tsp. Italian herb seasoning
Dash of black pepper

Wrap the bacon around the pheasant.

Sauté the oil, garlic, onion, and mushrooms for a few minutes in a large cas-serole dish. Add the pheasant and brown on all sides. Pour the wine over the pheasant, add the sage, Italian herb seasoning, and pepper. Cover, and cook for 30 minutes.

Remove the bacon slices. Serve immediately with risotto, polenta, or potatoes.

VARIATIONS

* Use carrots, celery, and peas with the pheasant.
* The pheasant can be roasted with potatoes and cooked in a wine-and-herb sauce.

CONIGLIO VERDE
E ROSSO

Rabbit in Red Wine with Green Olives and Garlic

¼ cup green olive oil
2- or 3-lb. rabbit
4 medium leeks, chopped (white part only)
3 medium-size onions, chopped
3 carrots, diced
3 large cloves of garlic, crushed
½ tsp. thyme
¼ tsp. oregano
1 tsp. rosemary
1 tsp. Italian herb seasoning
1 bay leaf
2 cups thick chicken stock
2 cups Italian Barolo dry red wine
1 cup mushrooms, diced
Black pepper to taste
15 green olives, pitted
1 cup fresh Italian parsley, chopped

Servings:
6
Time:
1¾ *hrs.*
Calories:
391 *per serving*

Clean and separate the rabbit into serving pieces: legs, loins, and ribs.

Heat the olive oil in a large, heavy skillet over medium-high heat.

Add the rabbit to the hot oil in skillet and lightly brown it on both sides (about 10 minutes). Remove the rabbit from the skillet and set aside.

Add the leeks, onion, carrots, garlic, thyme, oregano, rosemary, Italian herb seasoning, and bay leaf to the skillet; cover and cook over medium-low heat until the leeks and onion are translucent (about 15 minutes). Stir occasionally and add a little more oil if necessary.

Stir in the stock and the wine, add the mushrooms, and bring the mixture to a gentle boil. Return the rabbit to the skillet, cover, and simmer gently until the rabbit is tender and the stock has been reduced to a thick sauce (about 75 minutes). Add the black pepper, olives, and parsley; cook for a few more minutes.

Serve with rice or pasta.

VARIATIONS

* Use chicken or thinly sliced veal instead of rabbit.
* Use zucchini instead of carrots.

CONIGLIO SELVATICO

Wild Rabbit in Red Wine, Fennel, and Mushroom Sauce

Servings:
6
Time:
25 *min.*
Calories:
323 *per serving*

3-lb. rabbit
2 cups fennel
4 cloves of garlic, crushed
1 cup of onion, chopped
3 tbsp. green olive oil
1 tsp. Italian herb seasoning
Sprigs of fresh thyme; or ¼ tsp. dried thyme
2 cups dry Italian red wine
2 cups porcini or dried mushrooms (soaked 30 minutes in 2 cups red wine)
1 bay leaf

Clean and separate the rabbit into serving pieces: legs, loin, and ribs.

In a large skillet, sauté the fennel, garlic, and onion in the oil for 3 minutes. Add the rabbit, Italian herb seasoning, and thyme, and sauté for 10 minutes, turning the rabbit to brown on all sides.

Add the wine, mushrooms, and bay leaf; cover and cook for 10 minutes. Remove the cover and cook for 2 to 3 minutes. Remove the bay leaf.

Serve warm with polenta, rice, or pasta.

VARIATIONS

* Use white wine.
* Flame in brandy before serving.
* Marinate the night before preparation in wine, herbs, and garlic.

GAME HENS FLORENTINA

Servings:
6
Time:
1 *hr.*
Calories:
555 *per ½ hen*

¼ cup green olive oil
4 cloves of garlic, chopped
1 large onion, diced
½ tsp. crushed red pepper
4 cups fresh spinach, chopped (frozen will do)
½ cup chicken broth
¼ tsp. nutmeg
¼ cup small raisins or currants

1 cup dry Italian white wine
1 small apple, peeled and cut in small cubes
6 slices of whole wheat bread, cut into cubes and lightly toasted
½ tsp. sage
¼ tsp. thyme
1 tsp. Italian herb seasoning
3 small Cornish game hens, cleaned and gutted
½ cup fresh Italian parsley, coarsely chopped

Preheat oven at 400°F.

Prepare the stuffing in a large skillet. Sauté the olive oil, chopped garlic, onion, and hot peppers in the skillet over medium heat, cooking their flavor into the oil. After about 2 minutes, add the chopped spinach. (*Note:* If using frozen spinach, allow it to thaw completely and drain off all the fluid.) Sauté the vegetables together for 2 minutes; then add the chicken broth, bring to a boil, and cook for 3 minutes.

Add the nutmeg, raisins, wine, and apple; cook for 2 minutes. Remove the skillet from the flame, and add the bread cubes, sage, thyme, and Italian herb seasoning, mixing thoroughly. Set the skillet aside and let stand while preparing the hens.

Scald the inside of the hens, removing all the visible fat from the cavities. Fill the cavity of each bird about ⅔ full with stuffing mixture. Close the cavities with a skewer or by tying the legs together. Fold back the wings of each bird, and place them legs up in a shallow, lightly oiled baking dish. Brush each bird lightly with olive oil and roast for about 50 minutes.

Place the extra stuffing in an oven-proof glass dish and bake for about 25 minutes.

To serve, cut the hens in half lengthwise, place them, stuffing side down, on a plate, and garnish with parsley.

VARIATIONS
* Replace whole wheat bread cubes with cooked wild rice.
* Use chopped broccoli instead of spinach.

VITELLO, AGNELLO, CARNE & FEGATO

Veal, Lamb, Beef & Liver

In Italy, the first choice for an entreé is fish or chicken, but, according to per capita consumption, Italians eat more veal than any other people in the world. Next in preference is lamb, liver, and, last of all, beef.

Veal is a young, delicate meat, and there are hundreds of tasty, exciting ways to prepare it; however, you must never forget that to keep veal tender and juicy the cooking time has to be strictly limited.

Like veal, lamb is a delicate meat, and should be handled with great care and respect. When properly prepared with fresh herbs, wine, and lots of garlic, and cooked for the correct time at the proper heat, the taste and tenderness can be a pure gastronomic delight.

The best beef in Italy is said to come from Florence, because the natural cattle fodder is among the best in the world due to the soil and climate. I really enjoy a Bistecca alla Florentina (special grilled steak with porcini mushrooms).

The best cut of beef for roasting is the first three ribs from the small end. I personally prefer to cook these on the bone because it adds enormously to the flavor of the meat. The methods of butchering and cutting beef in America differ from those used in Italy, but the most tasty steaks are the New York cut; the most tender are, of course, the filet mignon.

Liver is another Italian favorite. Liver, prepared "Venetian style," with a wine, onion, and vinegar sauce, tastes exactly like veal scallopini.

Meat is versatile and lends itself to many different methods of cooking, but like so many of the good things in life, the key is careful preparation and moderation in serving.

VITELLO RIPIENO

Veal Stuffed with Fennel

Servings:
8
Time:
2 *hrs.*
Calories:
452 *per serving*

4 small, fresh bulbs of fennel (2 to 2½ lb.)
¼ cup green olive oil
1 cup onion, finely chopped
1 cup vegetable broth

4 lb. veal shoulder roast, boned and dressed
1 tsp. Italian herb seasoning
8 large cloves of garlic, crushed
¼ lb. prosciutto, thinly sliced
1 cup baby carrots, diced
1 medium-size onion, thinly sliced
2 cups dry Italian white wine
2 bay leaves
2 Italian tomatoes, finely chopped
6 sprigs of fresh Italian parsley

Preheat oven at 350°F.

Peel and throw away the outer layers of the fennel, removing the cores and slicing each bulb into sections.

In a large skillet, heat 2 tablespoons of olive oil; add the chopped onion and cook for about 10 minutes. Add the fennel and toss with the onion. Cook for about 2 minutes, and add ½ cup of broth. Cover the skillet and simmer for 30 minutes until the fennel is tender. Remove the lid of the skillet and cook off any remaining liquid. Set the mixture aside and let it cool.

Place the veal on a clean working surface. Sprinkle it with the Italian herb seasoning and ½ of the crushed garlic. Cover the veal with prosciutto, and spread the fennel mixture over it, sprinkling in the remaining garlic. Roll the veal and tie it in several places with cooking twine or string.

In a casserole dish, heat the remaining olive oil over medium flame, and add the carrots and sliced onion. Spoon the vegetables over the oil while stirring to prevent sticking. Add the veal; baste and brown on all sides (about 10 minutes). Remove the veal from the casserole and set it aside.

Add the wine and bay leaves to the casserole, and boil until the liquid is reduced to about 3 tablespoons. Add the tomatoes, and return the veal to the casserole.

Put in the remaining ingredients, and season with a little pepper to taste. Cover the casserole with foil and a lid; bake until the veal is tender (about 1½ hours).

To serve, cut the veal into ½-inch slices, add parsley, baste with juices, and eat immediately.

VARIATIONS
* Try lamb instead of veal.
* Use chicken stock instead of vegetable broth.
* Cook small whole onions around the veal.

VITELLO ALLA SANDRO

Veal Cutlets with Peppers and Capers in White Wine Sauce

Servings:
6
Time:
20 *min.*
Calories:
312 *per serving*

1 cup shallots, chopped
4 cloves of garlic, crushed
1 cup mushrooms, freshly sliced
1 cup red peppers, roasted and julienned (see page 7)
2 tbsp. green olive oil
2 lb. thin veal scallopini (cutlets)
¾ cup dry Italian white wine
2 tbsp. small capers, rinsed and drained
½ tsp. Italian herb seasoning
Dash of hot pepper (crushed red flakes or cayenne pepper)
½ cup fresh Italian parsley, chopped

In a large skillet, sauté the shallots, garlic, mushrooms, and red peppers in the oil for 5 minutes. Add the veal slices and cook for 2 to 3 minutes per side. Add the white wine, capers, Italian herb seasoning, and hot pepper, and cook for another 1 to 2 minutes.

Remove from the heat and transfer to a serving platter. Cover with the sauce and sprinkle parsley on top.

VARIATIONS
* Use green and red peppers and add olives.
* Cook with tomatoes and eliminate the wine.

V E A L   I N   B A R O L O
W I N E   S A U C E
A L L A   V I T O

¼ cup green olive oil
6 cloves of fresh garlic, finely chopped
2 large onions, diced
1 lb. thin veal chops
¼ tsp. rosemary
¼ tsp. dried oregano
¼ tsp. dried thyme
2 cups Italian Barolo dry red wine
1 cup chicken stock
1 bay leaf
2 cups mushrooms, broadly sliced
2 tsp. capers
3 cups cooked Arborio rice
4 sprigs of fresh Italian parsley

Servings:
4
Time:
1 *hr.*
Calories:
508 *per serving*

Preheat oven at 350°F.

In a large iron skillet, heat ½ of the olive oil over medium to high heat. Add the garlic and onion and cook together, constantly stirring. After 2 minutes, as the onion becomes transparent, add the veal chops and quickly sear (about 2 minutes on each side).

Remove the veal chops and sauce from the heat and transfer to a shallow, oven-proof serving dish. Arrange the chops over the onions and garlic; sprinkle with rosemary, oregano, and thyme; and pour in the wine. Bake for about 15 minutes. Remove from the oven and add the chicken stock, bay leaf, and mushroom; sprinkle on the capers.

Return the dish to the oven and cook for 15 minutes until the sauce has reduced and thickened. Add the remainder of the olive oil, cover with a tight lid or foil, and cook for 15 minutes.

Remove the bay leaf and serve over a bed of rice on heated plates; garnish with sprigs of parsley.

VARIATIONS
* To shorten cooking time, sauté the veal chops with the onions and garlic; then add the wine and cook for 15 minutes.
* Eliminate the chicken stock.
* Add porcini mushrooms or sliced celery.

VITELLO GENOVESE ZIA NANNE

Veal Stewed in Wine and Onions

Servings:
8
Time:
45 *min.*
Calories:
362 *per serving*

3 lb. boneless veal shoulder
Black pepper and salt to taste
1 tsp. Italian herb seasoning
4 cloves of garlic, crushed
3 cups onion, diced
2 tbsp. green olive oil
½ cup vegetable or veal stock
1 cup dry white wine
1 cup fresh Italian parsley, chopped

Season the veal shoulder with the salt, pepper, and Italian herb seasoning. Roll the veal tightly and tie with string to hold it together; tie the string circular and lengthwise.

In a large pot, sauté the garlic and onion in the oil for a few minutes. Add the veal shoulder, and pour the veal stock and wine over the veal; bring to a boil, and then reduce to simmer.

Cover the pot and simmer for 30 minutes. Remove the meat from the pan and cut off the strings. Cut the veal into thin slices and place on a serving platter. Spoon the juices over the meat and serve on the side. Garnish with parsley.

VARIATION
* Add sliced mushrooms or diced celery.

VEAL PICCATA ANNA

Servings:
4
Time:
15 *min.*
Calories:
240 *per serving*

8 veal scallopini (about 2 oz. each)
½ cup shallots, diced
1 tbsp. unsalted butter
½ tbsp. green olive oil
3 medium-size lemons
¼ cup fresh Italian parsley, chopped
1 lemon, thinly sliced

Flatten the veal with the flat side of a meat cleaver.

In a large frying pan, sauté the shallots and butter in the oil for a few minutes. Add the veal, lemon juice, and parsley; cook over low heat for about 2 to 3 minutes on each side. Be careful not to overcook; the veal is delicate and will toughen if overcooked.

Serve immediately. Decorate with thin slices of lemon and chopped parsley on top.

VARIATIONS

* Use ½ cup of dry white wine instead of lemon juice.
* Add 1 cup of fresh sliced mushrooms or porcini mushrooms.

VITELLO CON FUNGHI E MARSALA

Veal Steak with Marsala Wine and Mushrooms

1 4-oz. veal steak (lean)
2 cloves of garlic, crushed
¼ tsp. Italian herb seasoning
1 tbsp. green olive oil
1 medium-size onion, diced
½ cup fresh mushrooms, chopped; or dried mushrooms, soaked
½ cup dry Marsala wine

Servings:
1
Time:
15 *min.*
Calories:
375 *per serving*

With a fork, lightly indent the veal steak all over on both sides. Rub with a little of the crushed garlic and Italian herb seasoning. Heat the olive oil in a medium-size skillet, and sauté the onion, garlic, chopped mushrooms, and Italian herb seasoning for 5 minutes.

Add the veal and sear quickly over high heat for 3 minutes on each side. Pour on the Marsala wine and continue cooking quickly for about 3 minutes. (Do not leave the skillet unattended.)

Remove the veal and reduce the wine sauce until it is thick. Serve on a warm dinner plate and eat immediately.

VARIATIONS

* Use an extra onion and 3 garlic cloves; cook down into a strong, thick sauce.
* Marsala wine is a bit sweet, so try a dry red or white wine instead.
* Replace the veal steak with thin slices of veal scallopini in the Marsala and mushroom sauce.

VEAL PAILLARD MARINA

Grilled Veal Scallopini with Lemon-Herb Sauce

Servings:
4
Time:
15 *min.*
Calories:
252 *per serving*

2 tbsp. green olive oil
½ tsp. Italian herb seasoning
Juice of 2 lemons
½ cup dry white wine
2 cloves of garlic, crushed
½ cup fresh Italian parsley, chopped
Crushed black pepper to taste
8 veal scallopini (2 oz. each)

Preheat the grill.

Mix all the ingredients, except the veal, together, and brush the veal slices with the mixture.

Grill the veal slices for 2 minutes on each side, brushing with the oil, lemon, and wine mixture.

Put the veal in a serving dish. Spoon more sauce over the veal. Decorate with the parsley.

VARIATIONS

* If you don't have a proper grill, prepare the veal in a frying pan or quickly broil on each side.
* Use diced fresh tomatoes with basil instead of lemon sauce.

This light and luscious dish is great for lunch or dinner with vegetables and salad.

BRACIOLINE O SCALLOPINI

Veal Scallopini with Artichoke Sauce

Servings:
6
Time:
15 *min.*
Calories:
324 *per serving*

1 large artichoke; or 12 jarred artichoke hearts, drained
Juice of 2 lemons
1 cup shallots or onion, diced
2 cloves of garlic, crushed

½ tsp. Italian herb seasoning
2 tbsp. green olive oil
6 veal scallopini (about 2 lb.)
1 cup dry Italian white wine
1 cup fresh Italian parsley, chopped

If you are using fresh artichoke, soak it in a bowl of cold water and the juice of 1 lemon; then clean and cut into 16 pieces (using the heart only). Steam with lemon juice and water for 10 minutes. If you are using jarred, marinated artichoke hearts, drain, rinse, and dice them.

In a large skillet, sauté the onion, garlic, artichoke, lemon juice, and Italian herb seasoning in the oil for 2 to 3 minutes. Add the veal scallopini and sauté for 2 minutes per side. Remove the veal from the sauce.

Add the wine and reduce the sauce for 3 to 4 minutes. Return the veal to the sauce and heat for 1 minute. Garnish with parsley. Serve quickly. Do not overcook the veal or it will toughen.

VARIATIONS
* Add mushrooms.
* Use asparagus instead of artichokes.
* Dip the veal in a light coating of flour or arrowroot.

L A M B   C U T L E T S
B R A I S E D   I N   R E D   W I N E

4 medium-size lamb chops
1 tsp. Italian herb seasoning
5 cups Italian red wine (Barolo, if possible)
3 cloves of garlic, cut lengthwise in slivers
¼ cup green olive oil
4 carrots, thinly sliced lengthwise
4 stalks of celery
4 small onions, peeled whole
1 bay leaf
¼ tsp. ground nutmeg
4 sprigs of fresh rosemary; or ½ tsp. dried rosemary

Servings:
4
Time:
90 *min. plus marinating time*
Calories:
619 *per serving*

Rub the lamb chops with the Italian herb seasoning. Marinate overnight in the red wine; embed thinly sliced pieces of garlic in the meat. (Make a small cut in the veal with the pointed tip of a sharp kitchen knife, and push the garlic sliver down into the meat.) Make sure that both sides of the meat are covered by the wine.

Warm the olive oil in a large skillet, and add the marinated meat and the vegetables; sear the meat on both sides. Add the red wine marinade. Arrange the whole onions around the lamb chops and add the bay leaf and nutmeg. Put a lid on the skillet and simmer slowly for about 75 minutes, until the meat is tender.

After the meat has been cooking for about 30 minutes, add sprigs of rosemary. Serve with pasta, rice, or polenta.

VARIATIONS

* Use veal instead of lamb.
* Add cloves to the marinade instead of rosemary.
* Marinate the onions in the wine with the meat.

A G N E L L O   C O N   F I N O C C H I E T T I   A L L A   T R E   S C A L I N I

Lamb with Fennel, Tomatoes, Olives, and Herbs

Servings:
4
Time:
25 *min.*
Calories:
376 *per serving*

2 cups onion, diced
4 cloves of garlic, crushed
2 lbs. leg of lamb, boned and diced
2 tbsp. green olive oil
1 cup fresh seedless tomatoes, crushed; or canned Italian plum tomatoes, crushed with juice
1 tsp. Italian herb seasoning
Black pepper to taste
2 lb. fresh fennel, cut into 2-inch pieces
1 cup Italian black olives, diced
¼ cup fresh Italian parsley, chopped

In a flameproof casserole, sauté the onion, garlic, and lamb in the oil for about 3 minutes. Add the tomatoes, Italian herb seasoning, black pepper, and fennel; cook, covered, for 15 minutes over low heat.

Add the olives and parsley, and cook for another 2 to 3 minutes. If the fennel seems tough, cook it for another 3 to 4 minutes.

Serve immediately with rice.

VARIATIONS
* Add mushrooms and cook with wine and tomatoes.
* Add hot crushed red pepper.
* Use celery if you can't find fresh fennel.

This is a typical dish of Sardinia.

A G N E L L O   S I E N A

Lamb Chops in White Wine and Mustard Sauce

1 tsp. dried mustard
1 cup dry Italian white wine
3 cloves of garlic, crushed
2 tbsp. green olive oil
4 lamb chops, trimmed of fat (about 1-inch thick)
1 medium-size onion, chopped
1 tbsp. small capers
¼ tsp. Italian herb seasoning
½ tsp. crushed black pepper

Servings:
4
Time:
20 *min.*
Calories:
219 *per serving*

Mix the mustard and wine until smooth.

In a large skillet, cook the crushed garlic and onions in the olive oil; after a few moments, add the lamb chops and brown them quickly on both sides.

Add the mustard, and wine, capers, Italian herb seasoning, and crushed pepper. Cover the skillet and cook for about 10 to 15 minutes, until the meat is tender.

Serve immediately with vegetables and rice.

VARIATIONS
* Use pork or veal chops.
* Add an extra onion cooked down in an extra cup of white wine, and use as a sauce over pasta, as well.
* Try with sliced mushrooms.

ROAST LEG OF LAMB WITH ROSEMARY AND FRESH MINT SAUCE

Servings:
6
Time:
1½ *hrs.*
Calories:
520 *per serving*

1 leg of young lamb (about 5 to 6 lb.)
5 large cloves of garlic, 4 cut lengthwise in spears, 1 cut in half
¼ cup fresh rosemary leaves, crushed
½ tsp. dried oregano
¼ tsp. black pepper
¼ cup green olive oil
1½ cups dry Italian white wine
3 sprigs of fresh Italian parsley

THE SAUCE

1 large bunch of fresh mint, remove leaves from the stalks and finely chop
1 cup wine vinegar
¼ cup raw brown sugar

Preheat oven at 325°F.

Wipe the lamb with moist paper towels. Scrape the flesh thoroughly with a sharp kitchen knife; then make deep pockets all over, inserting the spears of garlic and the rosemary.

Rub the scraped surface of the meat with the clove of garlic cut in half. Cover the meat generously with the rosemary, oregano, and pepper.

In the oven, warm the olive oil in a shallow roasting pan. Place the meat in the heated oil and cook it for 1¼ hours.

Add the white wine; baste frequently and cook for 30 minutes or until the meat is tender. (*Note:* If you don't have a meat thermometer, test the meat by inserting the tip of a pointed butcher knife into it. When the tip of the knife comes out warm to your moist tongue, the meat is pink on the inside.)

When the meat is cooked, garnish with the parsley, carve in a V-shaped wedge from the center, and serve immediately.

THE SAUCE

Mix the chopped mint with the wine vinegar and stir in the brown sugar. Let the sauce stand while the meat is cooking. Serve in a sauce boat. Stir well to be sure the sugar has dissolved completely.

VARIATIONS

* Replace mint sauce with Mustard Dill Caper Sauce (see page 201) or Salsa Verde (page 200).
* Cook with red wine, instead of white.
* Roast potatoes in the juice of the meat and omit the wine.

FEGATO ALLA VENEZIANA

Calves Liver in Venetian Sauce of Onions and Red Wine Vinegar

1 lb. calves liver
2 cups onion, chopped
1 tbsp. sweet, unsalted butter or safflower oil margarine
2 tbsp. green olive oil
1 tsp. Italian herb seasoning
¼ cup dry Italian red wine
3 tbsp. balsamic vinegar or red wine vinegar
¼ cup fresh Italian parsley, chopped

Servings:
4
Time:
20 *min.*
Calories:
248 *per serving*

Wash and cut the liver into 2-inch strips.

Cook the onions in the butter and oil for 5 minutes. Add the liver and Italian herb seasoning; stir in the wine and cook for 5 to 8 minutes. (Don't overcook or the liver will get tough.)

Add the vinegar and stir thoroughly. Sprinkle with the parsley and serve immediately.

Serve with polenta, risotto, or toasted bread spread with garlic and olive oil.

VARIATIONS
* Add mushrooms and capers.
* Add diced pimentos for red color.

This classic dish is from the region of Venice. It combines a luscious taste of vinegar tartness with onions and red wine sauce.

F E G A T O   D I   V I T E L L O
M I L A N O

Veal Liver Milano Style, with Capers and Lemon Sauce

Servings:
4
Time:
15 *min.*
Calories:
253 *per serving*

1 lb. veal liver, sliced into 2-inch pieces
¼ cup all-purpose flour for coating
1 tbsp. green olive oil
1 tbsp. sweet, unsalted butter
1 tsp. Italian herb seasoning
2 tbsp. small capers
Black pepper to taste
½ cup lemon juice, freshly squeezed
¼ cup fresh Italian parsley, chopped

Coat the liver lightly in the flour.

Put the liver in a large frying pan with the oil and butter and sauté for about 5 minutes. Add the Italian herb seasoning, capers, black pepper, and lemon juice, and sauté for 3 minutes.

Sprinkle with the parsley and serve immediately with rice or polenta.

VARIATIONS
* Coat the liver in egg and breadcrumbs and sauté, Milano style.
* Cook with diced celery and carrots.
* Cook in a veal stock, eliminating the lemon juice.
* Use beef liver instead of veal.

STEAK ALLA EDWARDO

Steak Cooked in Wine and Mustard Sauce

½ tsp. Italian herb seasoning
1 cup onion, chopped
2 cloves of garlic, crushed
1 tbsp. green olive oil
2 5-oz. steaks, lean, New York cut
2 tbsp. Dijon mustard
1 cup Italian red wine

Servings:
2
Time:
10 *min.*
Calories:
565 *per serving*

In a large frying pan, sauté the Italian herb seasoning, onion, and garlic in the oil for 3 to 4 minutes.

Flatten the steaks and serrate both sides with a sharp knife. Add the steaks to the pan and brown over high heat for a few minutes on each side. Mix the mustard with the red wine in a small bowl. Pour the mixture over the steaks and cook over low heat for 3 to 5 minutes (depending on your preference). Use a knife and fork to check the center of the steaks for pinkness. Serve immediately with the sauce poured over the steaks.

VARIATIONS
* Add sliced mushrooms, or omit the mustard.
* Use veal, lamb, pork, or chicken instead of steak.

This method of cooking will actually tenderize the meat and add a great deal of flavor. It's much better than broiling.

SPEZZATO DI MANZO LUIGI

Beef Stew with Vegetables and Potatoes

Servings:
4
Time:
25 *min.*
Calories:
353 *per serving*

1 large onion, finely chopped
3 cloves of garlic, crushed
1 cup celery, chopped
1 large potato, peeled and cubed
1 cup carrots, diced
½ tsp. crushed red pepper
1 cup fresh mushrooms, sliced
¼ cup green olive oil
1 lb. round steak, trimmed of fat and cut into 1-inch pieces
1 cup dry red wine
½ tsp. Italian herb seasoning
1 cup fresh Italian parsley, chopped
1 bay leaf
1 cup canned tomatoes, crushed and drained
1 small onion, sliced and separated into rings
Black or cayenne pepper to taste

In a large skillet, sauté the chopped onion, garlic, celery, potatoes, carrots, crushed red pepper, and mushrooms in the oil for 5 minutes. Add the steak and stir often to brown lightly.

Add the wine and cook for 3 minutes. Add Italian herb seasoning, parsley, bay leaf, crushed tomatoes, and onion rings, and cook for 10 minutes. Taste and season with black or cayenne pepper for a more *piccante* taste.

Remove the bay leaf. Sprinkle with chopped fresh Italian parsley. Serve with a good crusty bread, red wine, and salad.

VARIATIONS
* Eliminate the potato and serve over rice.
* Add diced green peppers, sliced zucchini, eggplant, asparagus, or peeled fresh tomatoes.

INSALATAS

Salads

In Italy, salads are often considered a meal in themselves; they are usually served *after* the main course rather than before. In this way, the salad aids digestion and cleanses the palate. When served with skim-milk Italian cheeses, it helps diminish that sinful desire for a heavy dessert.

In America, it has become the custom, from convenience, to serve a green salad as the initial course: At private dinner parties a salad can be ready on the table when the guests enter, giving the understaffed host or hostess valuable time. In restaurants, a pre-prepared salad served at once gives the appearance of efficient service and allows the cook time to prepare the entrée. Serving the salad first may ease up on the consumption of bread, but the heavy dressings nullify any savings in calories, and the vinegar dulls the palate for both food and wine.

This section offers an interesting variety of greens, vegetables, and fruits that can be accompanied by light Italian cheeses: Bel Paese, Fontina, goat, mozzarella, or ricotta. You can also use small chunks of Parmesan cheese—a perfect combination served with a classic Italian salad dressing.

INSALATA
TRE COLOURE

Italian Salad of Three Colors: Arugula, Endive, and Radicchio

2 bunches of arugula leaves
3 small heads of radicchio
2 heads of endive
2 tbsp. green olive oil
1 tbsp. white wine vinegar

Servings:
4
Time:
15 *min.*
Calories:
86 *per serving*

Break all the lettuce leaves into small pieces.
Place them in a large bowl, and add the oil and vinegar and toss thoroughly. Serve at room temperature.

VARIATION

* If you cannot find the arugula or radicchio, use watercress and add diced tomatoes.

This is a great salad classic in Italy.

The red, white, and green colors represent the Italian flag for great visual effect.

The taste combination is one of the most exciting—from strong to soft to bitter. It's a beautiful balance of tastes.

I N S A L A T A   C A P R I

Tomatoes, Mozzarella Cheese, and Basil

Servings:
4
Time:
10 *min.*
Calories:
112 *per serving*

6 fresh plum tomatoes or very ripe cherry tomatoes, diced
8 fresh basil leaves, minced
2 tbsp. green olive oil
1 tbsp. white vinegar
½ cup fresh mozzarella cheese, diced

Add the tomatoes and basil to a large salad bowl. Toss with the oil and vinegar. Add the mozzarella cheese and blend thoroughly. Let the salad stand for 10 minutes or more before serving. Serve at room temperature.

VARIATIONS:
* Use arugula or endive leaves instead of basil.
* Add goat cheese instead of mozzarella.
* Use ½ cup of shredded skim-milk mozzarella to cut the calories.
* For a stronger dressing, use balsamic vinegar.

This salad is excellent as an appetizer, or as a salad for entertaining.

ENDIVE, WATERCRESS, FENNEL, AND APPLE SALAD

1 large head of fennel, diced (white part only)
2 endive bunches, broken into small pieces
1 medium-size lemon, juice only
1 large bunch of watercress, leaves only, broken into small pieces
1 large red apple, thinly sliced

Servings:
4
Time:
15 *min.*
Calories:
65 *per serving*

Combine all the ingredients in a large bowl and toss well. Chill before serving.

VARIATIONS
* Try the salad with arugula leaves for a very tart and refreshing taste.
* Add finely diced fresh dill.
* Serve without the apple and use diced tomatoes for a first course.

Very refreshing, this salad is the perfect ending to a meal, and lessens the desire for a sweet dessert!

INSALATA DI FUNGHI
Mushroom Salad

1 tbsp. white vinegar
1 tbsp. green olive oil
2 tsp. dill weed, freshly minced
½ tsp. Dijon-prepared mustard
8 large fresh mushrooms, sliced very thin (caps only) (If available, mix 2 to 3 kinds of mushrooms)
1 head of endive lettuce, break into small pieces
1 large red pepper, roasted and diced (see page 7)
2 large Bibb lettuce leaves
Black pepper to taste

Servings:
2
Time:
10 *min.*
Calories:
117 *per serving*

Mix the vinegar, oil, dill, and mustard in a small bowl and blend well. Add the other ingredients, except the Bibb lettuce, to a large bowl, and pour the dressing over the vegetables. Mix well.

Place the Bibb lettuce leaves on two dishes and cover the leaves with the mushroom salad. Add a dash of freshly ground black pepper to taste.

VARIATIONS
* Use diced tomatoes instead of red pepper.
* Try radicchio lettuce instead of endive.
* Try fresh chives or basil leaves instead of dill.
* Eliminate the mustard for a more delicate taste.

G A R B A N Z O   S A L A D

Garbanzo Beans, * *Vegetable Misto*

Servings:
6
Time:
15 *min.*
Calories:
421 *per serving*

2½ cups fresh garbanzo beans, soaked; or canned garbanzo beans, drained
1 cup fresh plum tomatoes, peeled and diced
½ cup red onion or shallots, chopped
½ cup fresh Italian parsley, chopped
¼ tsp. Italian herb seasoning
½ cup black olives, diced
½ cup celery, chopped
1 medium-size green pepper, chopped
Dash of cayenne pepper
Black pepper to taste
¼ cup Parmesan cheese, freshly grated
3 tbsp. green olive oil
2 tbsp. red wine vinegar
2 cloves of garlic, crushed

Combine all the ingredients, except the oil, vinegar, and garlic in a large bowl; mix those 3 ingredients, in a separate bowl with a fork, and pour over the salad. Toss well. Add more oil, vinegar, pepper to taste. Chill before serving, but serve at room temperature to get the full flavors.

VARIATIONS
* Add cucumbers instead of celery.
* Use grated mozzarella cheese or grated zucchini instead of Parmesan cheese.

*Garbanzo beans are also known as chi-chi beans.

GIARDENIA INSALATA

Garden-Style Vegetable Salad

4 large ripe tomatoes, chopped
2 small cucumbers, thinly sliced
½ cup Italian black olives, diced
1 cup fresh Italian parsley, chopped
2 cups arugula leaves, diced
4 endive heads, diced; or 2 red lettuce heads, torn into small pieces
1 cup fresh mushrooms, sliced
2 green onions, sliced
3 tbsp. green olive oil or safflower oil
2 tbsp. red wine vinegar

Servings:
6
Time:
15 *min.*
Calories:
145 *per serving*

   Combine all the ingredients, except oil and vinegar, in a large salad bowl. Toss with the oil and vinegar.
   Serve at room temperature.

VARIATIONS

* Use diced red and green peppers instead of cucumbers.
* Add crushed garlic and a dash of hot pepper.
* Try spinach leaves instead of arugula.
* Use Boston lettuce instead of the endive.

This salad can be made in advance. Serve as the salad course at the end of the meal, or as an appetizer with sprinkled goat cheese and no vinegar.

GREEN BEANS, RED PEPPER, AND MUSHROOM SALAD

Servings:
8
Time:
15 min.
Calories:
78 per serving

2 lb. fresh Italian green beans, trimmed and cut into 1-inch pieces
½ lb. fresh mushrooms, sliced
3 shallots or 1 red onion, diced
1 clove of garlic, crushed
3 red peppers, cleaned, quartered, and roasted (see page 7)
3 tbsp. fresh basil leaves, chopped
½ cup fresh Italian parsley, chopped
3 tbsp. green olive oil or safflower oil
2 tbsp. red wine vinegar or balsamic vinegar

Steam the prepared green beans over boiling water for about 6 minutes, drain, and plunge into ice cold water to cool. (They should be crunchy, but if you prefer them softer cook for a few minutes longer.)

Combine the mushrooms, onion, garlic, roasted red peppers, basil leaves, and parsley in a large glass bowl. Add the cooled green beans. Mix the oil and vinegar and toss thoroughly. Serve chilled or at room temperature.

VARIATIONS

* Use tomatoes instead of peppers.
* Add arugula.
* Add 1 tablespoon of crumbled goat cheese.

INSALATA BOLLA

Roasted Asparagus, Mushrooms, Radicchio, Tomatoes, and Grated Zucchini Salad

Servings:
6
Time:
20 min.
Calories:
154 per serving

3 tbsp. green olive oil or safflower oil
1 tbsp. red wine vinegar
2 tbsp. lemon juice
½ tsp. dry mustard
½ tsp. dill weed
2 lb. fresh, ripe asparagus, roasted (see page 8)
1 lb. fresh mushrooms

2 heads of radicchio
4 medium-size ripe tomatoes, or 12 very ripe cherry tomatoes, peeled and diced
¼ cup sweet red onion, finely chopped
1 medium-size zucchini, grated without the skin
1 medium-size carrot, grated

In a small bowl, mix the oil, vinegar, lemon juice, mustard, and dill, and whisk until smooth.

Combine all of the remaining ingredients, except carrot and zucchini, in a large bowl.

Pour the mixture over the vegetables. Add the grated carrot and zucchini, and then mix thoroughly.

VARIATIONS

* Use roasted red peppers (see page 7).
* Add arugula and diced olives.
* Add goat cheese or ricotta for an appetizer or dessert.

I T A L I A N   T U N A   S A L A D
W I T H   W H I T E   B E A N S

1 20-oz. can cannellini (white beans)
1 6½-oz. can white tuna in olive oil, flaked
¼ cup green olive oil
1 cup red onion, finely chopped
1 tbsp. fresh lemon juice
1 tbsp. red wine vinegar or balsamic vinegar
1 clove of garlic, crushed
Black pepper to taste
¼ cup fresh Italian parsley, chopped

Servings:
6
Time:
15 *min.*
Calories:
216 *per serving*

Drain the beans thoroughly and toss with all of the ingredients, except the parsley, in a serving bowl. After tossing, garnish with parsley and serve at room temperature or slightly chilled. Add extra lemon juice or black pepper to taste.

VARIATION

* Use 2 cups of chopped chicken breast or 1 6-oz. can of pink salmon instead of tuna.

FENNEL, TOMATOES, ROMAINE, AND RED LEAF LETTUCE

Servings:
6
Time:
15 *min.*
Calories:
109 *per serving*

1 head of red leaf lettuce
1 head of romaine lettuce
2 bulbs of fennel celery, diced (use white part only)
6 very ripe plum or cherry tomatoes, chopped
1 clove of garlic, crushed
2 fresh green onions or shallot onions (¼ cup, chopped)
3 tbsp. green olive oil
1 tbsp. red wine vinegar or balsamic vinegar

Wash the lettuce leaves several times with cold water. Dry the lettuce, tear it into small pieces, and put it in a large salad bowl.

Dice the fennel and tomatoes and add to the lettuce leaves with the garlic and onions. Mix the oil and vinegar and pour over the salad. Toss thoroughly.

VARIATIONS
* If you can't find romaine lettuce, use watercress leaves.
* Try arugula instead of red leaf lettuce.
* Radicchio leaves can be used instead of red lettuce.
* Use sliced fresh mushrooms or diced black olives.

I N S A L A T A
D ' F A G O L I N I
M A M A ' ' D ' '

Green Bean Salad with Tomatoes and Herbs

1 lb. green beans, trimmed and cut into 1½-inch pieces
2 lb. ripe plum tomatoes or cherry tomatoes
2 cloves of garlic, crushed
1 cup fresh Italian parsley, minced
¼ cup fresh basil leaves, minced
Dash of black pepper
2 tbsp. green olive oil
1 tbsp. red wine vinegar or balsamic vinegar

Servings:
4
Time:
15 *min.*
Calories:
144 *per serving*

   Blanch the green beans in boiling water for about 2 to 3 minutes. Rinse them in cold water, drain, and pat dry.
   Break them into small pieces.
   In a large salad bowl combine the green beans with the tomatoes, garlic, parsley, basil, and black pepper. Add the olive oil and vinegar and toss thoroughly until well mixed. Serve at room temperature or chill and serve later. Do not prepare more than 4 hours before serving.

VARIATIONS
* Add mushrooms, arugula, olives, or lemon dressing.
* Add a touch (½ teaspoon.) of dill weed.

This salad is perfect after the main course or with the main course as a combination salad and vegetable. It's great for entertaining—colorful, tasty, and easy to serve and eat—and as buffet food.

SALSAS

Sauces, Dressings, Marinade

Glorious sauces are used to enhance the taste of a recipe and to excite the palate, but they should never overpower the basic ingredients. Classic Italian sauces are light, and made with fresh, natural ingredients that consist of herbs, spices, vegetables, wines, lemon juice, onions, and garlic.

Classic Italian sauces are not made with heavy cream, butter, or floury bases. Italian sauces are taste enhancers. In this section, I present a selection of classic Italian sauces, trendy sauces, my creations, and enough variations for you to create your own. On to the *salsas*!

EGGPLANT RED PEPPER SAUCE AND DIP

Yield:
2½ *cups*
Time:
15 *min.*
Calories:
77 *per ¼ cup*

2 medium-size eggplants (1 lb.)
2 tbsp. green olive oil
½ cup onion or shallots, diced
3 cloves of garlic, crushed
3 medium-size red peppers, roasted (see page 7)
1 cup fresh mushrooms, sliced
1½ tbsp. Italian herb seasoning
¼ tsp. cayenne pepper
½ cup fresh Italian parsley, chopped
¼ cup Parmesan cheese, freshly grated
½ cup skim-milk ricotta cheese*

Soak the eggplant. Dice it in ¼-inch pieces, drain, and dry.

Put the olive oil in a large frying pan; sauté the onion, garlic, peppers, eggplant, mushrooms, and Italian herb seasoning for 5 to 8 minutes.

Add cayenne pepper and parsley, and cook for 2 minutes. Add Parmesan and ricotta cheese and purée.

*For a dip, mix ricotta cheese into the eggplant mixture and serve at room temperature, with fresh diced parsley on top.

VARIATIONS
* Add green peppers or diced black olives.
* Use tomatoes instead of peppers.

Serve hot as a sauce or at room temperature as a dip with ricotta cheese—can also be puréed.

B A G N A   C A U D A

Garlic, Olive Oil, and Anchovy Sauce

3 tbsp. green olive oil
3 cloves of garlic, crushed
½ cup dry white wine
3 tbsp. sweet, unsalted butter
1 tbsp. anchovies, finely chopped; or anchovy paste
Pepper to taste (black or cayenne)
2 tbsp. Italian parsley, minced

Yield:
1 *cup*
Time:
10 *min.*
Calories:
60 *per tbsp.*

Cook the oil and garlic in a large saucepan for a few minutes; then stir in the wine and cook until half the mixture is reduced.

Add the butter in small pieces at a time, beating rapidly with a wire whisk. Stir in the anchovy and parsley, and season with pepper.

Serve hot.

VARIATION
* Add more garlic or pepper to your taste or eliminate.

Pour over vegetables, thin spaghetti, or over poached or baked whitefish.

P A R S L E Y   P E S T O

6 bunches of fresh Italian parsley (about 4½ cups)
Dash of pepper
½ cup pignoli nuts
½ cup Parmesan cheese, freshly grated
¼ cup lemon juice
¼ cup green olive oil
3 cloves of garlic, crushed

Yield:
2 *cups*
Time:
10 *min.*
Calories:
75 *per tbsp.*

In a food processor or blender, process the parsley (remove the stems), pepper, pignoli nuts, cheese, lemon juice, oil, and garlic until smooth.

Serve at room temperature or heat for a few minutes.

VARIATIONS

* For a more peppery taste, use cayenne pepper (¼ teaspoon).
* Use walnuts instead of pignoli nuts.
* For a creamy texture, add 3 tablespoons of skim-milk ricotta cheese.
* If you can't find Italian parsley or basil leaves, use fresh spinach leaves.
* A tablespoon of dill weed is good when using over fish.

This sauce can be used over pasta, risotto, frittatas, fish, veal, chicken, or beef. It's also good with vegetables and salads.

B A S I C   M A R I N A R A
S A U C E

Light Tomato Sauce and Sauce for Seafood

Yield:
4 *cups*
Time:
10 *min.*
Calories:
34 *per*
¼ cup

1 cup onion, chopped
2 cloves of garlic, crushed
3 tbsp. green olive oil
3 cups fresh ripe plum tomatoes, peeled, seeded, and diced; or canned Italian
   plum tomatoes, drained and crushed
½ tsp. Italian herb seasoning
½ cup fresh Italian parsley, chopped
Black pepper and salt to taste
6 fresh basil leaves, finely chopped; or 1 tsp. dried basil

In a large frying pan or skillet, sauté the onion and garlic in the oil for a few minutes. Add the tomatoes, Italian herb seasoning, parsley, pepper and salt, and basil, and cook for 5 minutes.

For the seafood marinara sauce, eliminate the basil and add 1 to 2 cups of diced fresh seafood when you add the tomatoes; cook for a few minutes. Do not overcook the seafood. Use clams, shrimp, mussels, lobster, crab, or diced fresh whitefish.

VARIATIONS

* Vary the seasonings.
* Add hot pepper.

RED PEPPER AND TOMATO SAUCE

3 tbsp. green olive oil
2 cups onion, diced
5 large red peppers
4 cloves of garlic, crushed
1 tsp. Italian herb seasoning
3 lb. fresh plum tomatoes, peeled, seeded, and diced
1 cup fresh Italian parsley, chopped

Yield:
2½ cups
Time:
20 min.
Calories:
174 per ½ cup

Put 1 tablespoon of olive oil in a large sauté pan and cook the peppers down until they are tender; stir often. Transfer the mixture to a food processor and purée until smooth.

In the same large sauté pan, sauté the onion and garlic in the remaining oil for a few minutes. Add the Italian herb seasoning and tomatoes, and cook for 5 to 8 minutes. Add the pepper purée and cook together for 3 minutes with the parsley, which is sprinkled in at the last minute.

VARIATIONS

* Mix the red and green peppers with the tomatoes.
* Make a *piccante* sauce: Add ¼ teaspoon of crushed red pepper or cayenne pepper.
* Use ½ cup of chopped, fresh basil leaves.

PORCINI-TOMATO SAUCE

1 oz. porcini mushrooms, dried
1 cup dry Italian white wine
½ cup shallots or onion, chopped
2 tbsp. green olive oil
2 cups canned Italian plum tomatoes, drained and crushed
¼ tsp. Italian herb seasoning
¼ cup fresh Italian parsley, chopped

Yield:
2½ cups
Time:
45 min.
Calories:
48 per ¼ cup

Soak the porcini mushrooms in the wine, covered, for 30 minutes. Drain and reserve the liquid. Squeeze the mushrooms dry and chop into small pieces. Strain the soaking liquid through a sieve lined with a dampened cheesecloth; reserve ½ cup of the liquid.

In a large, heavy frying pan, sauté the onion and mushrooms in the oil for 5 minutes. Add the soaking liquid and cook 2 minutes. Add the tomatoes, Italian herb seasoning, and parsley, and cook for 5 minutes.

Serve over pasta, rice, polenta, chicken, or veal.

VARIATIONS

* Use red wine instead of white.
* Add ½ teaspoon of crushed red pepper.
* Mix 2 or 3 kinds of mushrooms.

R I C O T T A   C H E E S Y
S A U C E

Yield:
2 *cups*
Time:
8 *min.*
Calories:
72 *per ¼ cup*

1 cup skim-milk ricotta cheese
1 tsp. Italian herb seasoning
½ cup Parmesan cheese, freshly grated
¼ cup fresh Italian parsley, chopped
Dash of white pepper
¼ cup warm water

Combine all the ingredients in a small saucepan and stir constantly over medium heat. When mixed thoroughly and hot (not boiling), add more Parmesan cheese and pepper to taste. Serve at once.

VARIATIONS

* Use skim milk instead of water.
* Try Romano or Pecorino cheese instead of Parmesan.
* For color, use cayenne pepper; it adds a zesty taste.

This sauce can be mixed in a blender for a very smooth finish. It can be served uncooked.

ARTICHOKE SAUCE SCARLATTI

4 large artichoke hearts
3 cloves of garlic, crushed
½ cup shallots or onion, diced
½ tsp. Italian herb seasoning
2 tbsp. green olive oil
Dash of nutmeg
¼ cup dry Italian white wine
Black pepper to taste
1 cup fresh Italian parsley, chopped

Yield:
1½ *cups*
Time:
10 *min. (not including time to cook the artichokes)*
Calories:
112 *per ¼ cup*

Remove all the leaves and the stems and cook the artichoke hearts in 2 cups of boiling water for 5 minutes. Chop and mash the cooked artichokes (about 1 cup).

Sauté the garlic, onion, and Italian herb seasoning in the oil for 1 minute. Add the artichoke mash, nutmeg, wine, pepper, and parsley, and cook until the sauce is smooth. Stir often with a wooden spoon. The sauce should be pasty and smooth. (If it's too dry, add more wine.)

Serve hot or at room temperature.

VARIATIONS
* Add 1 tablespoon of ricotta cheese to make it creamy.
* Add crushed red pepper to make it *piccante*.
* Add lemon to make it tart.

This sauce can be used over pasta, risotto, fish, chicken, or veal.
It's also good as a side vegetable when left more chunky in texture.

THREE PEPPER SAUCE ALLA PHYLLIS

Yield:
2 *cups*
Time:
10 *min.*
Calories:
71 *per ¼ cup*

3 cloves of garlic, crushed
2 red peppers, roasted and minced (see page 7)
2 green peppers, roasted and minced (see page 7)
1 yellow pepper, roasted and minced (see page 7)
Dash of cayenne pepper
¼ tsp. crushed red pepper
3 tbsp. green olive oil
¼ cup fresh Italian parsley, chopped
4 tbsp. Parmesan cheese, freshly grated (if using with pasta, risotto, polenta, pizza, or crostini)

In a large skillet, sauté the garlic, red, green, and yellow peppers, cayenne pepper, and hot pepper in the oil for 5 to 8 minutes. Add the parsley and cook for 2 minutes. Sprinkle the Parmesan cheese over the top of the sauce.

VARIATIONS
* Use ¼ teaspoon of Italian herb seasoning for a more "herby" taste.
* Add ½ cup diced mushrooms, or sprinkle with goat cheese on top.

This sauce can be used with medium-size pasta, risotto, polenta, pizza, fish, chicken, or veal, and for crostinis as a cocktail food or appetizer.

SALSA ALLA MICHAELI

Tomatoes, Olives, and Anchovies

Yield:
3 *cups*
Time:
15 *min.*
Calories:
172 *per ¼ cup*

2 anchovy fillets, rinsed and diced
4 cloves of garlic, crushed
3 tbsp. green olive oil
1 lb. fresh tomatoes, skinned, seeded, and diced; or 2 cups canned Italian plum tomatoes, crushed with juice
6 oz. tomato paste
½ cup fresh Italian parsley, chopped
6 fresh basil leaves, snipped into small pieces
10 purple Italian olives (Gaeta), pitted and chopped
2 tbsp. small capers
Black pepper to taste

Sauté the anchovies, garlic, and oil in a large frying pan for a few minutes. Add the tomatoes, tomato paste, parsley, and basil, and cook over medium heat for 10 minutes, stirring often.

Add the chopped olives and capers to the sauce and cook for 5 minutes. Season with pepper to taste.

VARIATIONS

* Use regular olives or stronger black olives if you can't find the Gaeta.
* If you don't like anchovies, eliminate them and add ½ teaspoon of Italian herb seasoning for more taste.

This sauce is great for pasta, fish, chicken, polenta, pizza, crostinis, or frittatas.

B A S I C   P E S T O   S A U C E

2 cups large fresh basil leaves (without stems), packed
2 cloves of garlic, crushed
½ cup Parmesan cheese, freshly grated
¼ cup green olive oil
¼ cup pignoli nuts

Yield:
¾ *cup*
Time:
10 *min.*
Calories:
82 *per tbsp.*

Wash the basil leaves thoroughly and dry. Put all the ingredients into the blender and blend for 5 to 8 seconds, until smooth. Add more Parmesan cheese or garlic to taste.

Serve hot, at room temperature, or cold. Pesto sauce can be stored in the refrigerator with a covering of olive oil to seal, or it can be frozen.

VARIATIONS

* Eliminate the pignoli nuts (fewer calories).
* Eliminate the garlic.
* Use spinach leaves if basil is not available.
* Try Pecorino cheese for a stronger cheese taste.

The sauce can be served over pasta, fish, cocktail foods, chicken, eggs, or polenta.

L E M O N   A N D   H E R B
D R E S S I N G / S A U C E

Yield:
1/2 *cup*
Time:
10 *min.*
Calories:
67 *per 2 tbsp.*

Juice of 2 lemons
2 tbsp. green olive oil
1/4 cup fresh Italian parsley, chopped
1/2 tsp. Italian herb seasoning
2 fresh basil leaves, minced

Pour the lemon juice and oil into a bowl and whisk until smooth. Add the parsley, basil, and Italian herb seasoning, and whisk until blended thoroughly.

VARIATIONS
* Add a dash of cayenne pepper.
* Add a dash of mustard and whisk until smooth.

This sauce can be used over salads, fish, grilled chicken or veal, and vegetables.

P A R M E S A N
V I N A I G R E T T E
D R E S S I N G

Yield:
1 *cup*
Time:
10 *min.*
Calories:
54 *per 2 tbsp.*

1/4 cup Parmesan cheese, freshly grated
1 clove of garlic, crushed
2 tbsp. green olive oil
2 tbsp. red wine vinegar
1/4 cup fresh Italian parsley, chopped
3 tbsp. pimentos, minced
1/4 cup black olives, chopped
Fresh cracked black pepper

Combine all of the ingredients in a large bowl and season to taste. Serve at room temperature or heat a few minutes and serve over vegetables or salads.

VARIATIONS
* Use 1/4 teaspoon of prepared mustard mixed with oil and vinegar.
* Add 1/2 teaspoon of dill weed.
* Use 1 tablespoon of minced shallots or red onion.

BASIC VINAIGRETTE DRESSING

1 tbsp. green olive oil
2 tbsp. red wine vinegar
2 shallots, minced
2 tbsp. prepared Dijon mustard
1 tbsp. fresh dill, minced
½ tsp. Italian herb seasoning
Pepper to taste
¼ cup fresh Italian parsley, chopped

Yield:
¾ *cup*
Time:
10 *min.*
Calories:
30 *per 2 tbsp.*

Combine all of the ingredients in a bowl; whisk until smooth and well blended.
Refrigerate to marinate or serve immediately. Never serve chilled. Serve at room temperature or warm if using as a marinade or sauce blend.

VARIATIONS
* Use dill weed if fresh is not available.
* Add ¼ cup diced black olives or red pimentos.

The sauce can be served over vegetable salads, fish, chicken, or cold pasta salads.

CAPER DRESSING / SAUCE

3 tbsp. green olive oil
1 tbsp. red wine vinegar
1 hard-cooked egg, mashed
2 tbsp. small capers
1 tbsp. pimentos, minced
1 clove of garlic, crushed
3 tbsp. water
Dash of cayenne pepper

Yield:
1 *cup*
Time:
5 *min.*
Calories:
56 *per 2 tbsp.*

Put all the ingredients into a blender and blend for 2 to 5 seconds, or until well mixed and smooth. Chill or serve immediately.

* Add diced olives or chopped, fresh Italian parsley.

This dressing can be served over salads, fish, chicken, veal, or cold vegetables.

S A L S A   V E R D E

Yield:
¾ *cup*
Time:
15 min.
Calories:
59 *per 2 tbsp.*

½ cup fresh basil leaves, minced
2 cups fresh Italian parsley, chopped
6 shallots, diced; or ½ cup onion, finely chopped
2 cloves of garlic, crushed
2 tbsp. green olive oil

Put the basil leaves, chopped parsley, onion, and garlic in a blender or food processor. Add a small amount of the olive oil and purée. Add the remaining oil and purée until smooth and blended.

VARIATIONS
* Add diced and peeled fresh plum tomatoes.
* Eliminate the garlic for a softer taste.

This sauce can be served hot or cold and is great with seafood, chicken, veal, or pasta.

F U N G H I   A L L A   M I M I

Mushrooms in a Wine-Herb Sauce with Red Peppers

Yield:
1½ *cups*
Time:
15 min.
Calories:
62 *per 2 tbsp.*

5 large fresh mushrooms, sliced
Juice of 1 large lemon
½ cup fresh Italian parsley, chopped
3 tbsp. fresh dill; or ½ tsp. dill weed
½ cup dry Italian white wine
½ tsp. Italian herb seasoning
1 cup onion, chopped
2 cloves of garlic, crushed
Dash of black pepper

1 large red pepper, finely diced, or roasted and diced
¼ cup black olives, diced
½ cup celery, finely chopped
2 tbsp. green olive oil

Put the mushrooms in a bowl with the lemon juice, parsley, dill, wine, and Italian herb seasoning, and let stand.

Sauté the onion, garlic, black pepper, red pepper, olives, and celery in the olive oil for 5 minutes. Add the mushrooms and herb mixture and sauté for 5 minutes.

Serve at room temperature.

VARIATIONS
* Use pimentos instead of red pepper.
* Add ¼ cup of freshly grated Parmesan cheese.
* Use fennel instead of celery.

Use this dish as an appetizer to accompany the main course, or as a sauce for pasta, risotto, polenta, frittata, pizza, fish, chicken, or meats.

MUSTARD DILL CAPER SAUCE

½ cup dill, finely chopped
¼ cup Dijon-style mustard
4 tbsp. dry white wine
2 tbsp. small capers, rinsed
2 tbsp. green olive oil

Yield:
¾ *cup*
Time:
5 *min.*
Calories:
95 *per 2 tbsp.*

Put all of the ingredients, except the olive oil, in a blender or food processor. Blend at a slow speed for about ½ minute. When blended, add the olive oil and let thicken slightly.

VARIATIONS
* Replace the capers with a medium-size red onion puréed in a food processor or blender.
* Use balsamic vinegar instead of white wine.

Use this sauce for fish, chicken, lamb, and vegetables.

MARINADE FOR FISH, CHICKEN, OR VEGETABLES

Yield:
1½ *cups*
Time:
minimum, **30**
min.
Calories:
36 *per 2 tbsp.*

1 tsp. Italian herb seasoning
3 cloves of garlic, crushed
1 cup dry Italian white wine
3 tbsp. green olive oil
½ cup fresh Italian parsley, chopped
Juice of 1 medium-size lemon

Place all of the ingredients in a large bowl, and mix well.

Add the fish, chicken, or vegetables and turn a few times to get the marinade into the fibers. Cover and marinate a minimum of ½ hour in the refrigerator.

VARIATIONS

* Eliminate the cayenne pepper if you like a mild taste.
* If wine is not available, use more lemon juice.
* Replace the garlic with ½ cup of diced shallots or onion.

The ingredients in the marinade and the marinating procedure will tenderize, add enormous flavor to, and speed the cooking process of whatever you marinate. Use this marinade as a sauce when grilling, broiling, or baking.

DOLCE

Desserts

If a wonderful soup can be considered the overture and the entrée is the show, then a great dessert must surely be the finale that rounds off a superb meal. Did you realize that this supreme indulgence can be low in calories?

Now don't misunderstand me—I'm not writing about artificially sweetened, chemical-laden cream concoctions—I'm writing about wonderful tasting *dolce* adventures.

Italian-style desserts have traditionally been light and luscious. What about Zuppa Inglese, *tiramisu*, and all those cream-based *gelatas*? They are kept mostly for special occasions, such as birthdays, Christmas, and Easter, when we eat Panetone, a high, puffy breadlike cake filled with raisins and dried fruit. However, for the most part, true Italians end their meals with one of many small, exciting tastes: almond-type cookies and cakes, cheese, fruit *gelata* (ices), and, almost always, fresh fruit.

If desserts are your weakness, remember that a small sample, a delicate titillation of the taste buds that sinfully pampers the palate, may be all that is required to satisfy a craving; the key is moderation. In day-to-day dining, you should end meals the Italian way: with fresh fruit and on special occasions, a small, light, exciting *dolce* and coffee.

To an Italian, coffee means espresso, which is a rich, strong-tasting beverage ideally served in a small, eggshell cup. Coffee made from espresso beans has less caffeine, chemicals, and oil than coffee roasted any other way. Because of its more refined state, it does not interfere with the process of digestion or weight loss.

Some time ago, when I did a feature story on coffee for *House Beautiful*, I discovered that espresso beans are roasted two or even three times to get a really robust coffee taste. During this roasting process, much of the caffeine, harmful oils, and chemicals are burned off, leaving a pure, strong coffee.

TORTA DI RICOTTA KIMA

Italian Ricotta Cheesecake

Servings:
6
Time:
30 *min.*
Calories:
234 *per serving*

3 fresh eggs
2 tbsp. sugar
1 lb. skim-milk ricotta cheese
3 tbsp. all-purpose flour
¼ tsp. baking soda
½ cup fruit, diced and drained (pineapple, oranges, strawberries)
¼ cup lemon rind, grated
4 tbsp. Amaretto
3 tbsp. almonds, toasted and chopped

Preheat oven at 350°F.

Beat the eggs with the sugar in a large bowl; then add the ricotta cheese and continue to beat thoroughly. Slowly add the flour and baking soda; then add all the other ingredients, continuing to mix the batter until well blended.

Butter and flour a 6-cup springform pan. Pour the batter into the baking pan, and bake for 35 minutes.

Let the cake cool, and then run a thin knife around the mold to loosen the cake. Remove the rim of the springform pan and slide the cake, keeping the same bottom, onto a serving plate.

Ricotta cake has a delicate texture. Don't try to remove it from the pan bottom. You can refrigerate ricotta cake to firm up the texture.

Serve the cake with a fruit purée topping or Amaretto liqueur dribbled on the top of each slice.

VARIATIONS

* Use raisins and walnuts with diced oranges.
* Try raspberry or strawberry purée topping.

GRAPEFRUIT AND CAMPARI ICE

1 cup fresh grapefruit, puréed
3 tbsp. lemon juice
4 tbsp. Campari (an Italian liqueur)

Servings:
4
Time:
15 *min.*
Calories:
54 *per serving*

Purée the grapefruit with the lemon juice.

Put the grapefruit purée and the Campari in a large metal bowl. Set the bowl in a large container filled with crushed ice. Stir the mixture with a large wire whisk until it is smooth and creamy. (It never reaches the point of being frozen and hard.)

VARIATION

* Use oranges instead of grapefruit to reduce tartness.

The mixture can be placed in the freezer, but the texture and taste are different. This dessert is a great ending to a wonderful meal. It's so light and refreshing. Serve the ice in a lovely crystal goblet, decorated with fruit on top.

FRITTATA DOLCE AMARETTO CON MERINGUE

Dessert Amaretto Frittata with Meringue Topping

½ cup fruit, diced (strawberries, raspberries, peaches, apples, oranges)
3 tbsp. sweet Marsala wine
6 eggs
1 tsp. sugar
3 tbsp. Ameretto Liqueur
1 tbsp. sweet, unsalted butter
3 egg whites

Servings:
6
Time:
15 *min.*
Calories:
145 *per serving*

Preheat oven at 400°F.
Dice the fruit and marinate in Marsala wine.
Beat the eggs slightly with the sugar and liqueur (be sure the sugar is dissolved).

Heat the butter in a large skillet and pour in the egg mixture. Let it cook for 1 minute; then spoon the fruit mixture into the center and continue cooking for 5 minutes until the top is set.

Beat the egg whites with a pinch of sugar, until stiff peaks form when the beaters are withdrawn.

Gently spread the meringue over the frittata.

Bake for 5 minutes, until the meringue is golden—or broil for 1 minute.

VARIATIONS

* Mix strawberries and oranges for fruit fillings.
* Use Grand Marnier liqueur instead of Amaretto.

ESPRESSO AND SAMBUCA GRANITA

Iced Espresso Coffee with Sambuca Liqueur

Servings:
8
Time:
15 *min.*
Calories:
18 *per serving*

3 cups hot brewed espresso coffee
2 tbsp. sugar
1 cup cold water
1 tbsp. Sambuca Romano liqueur
Twists of lemon peel

Prepare 3 cups of espresso coffee. Pour the espresso into an 8-inch square baking pan.

Combine the sugar, water, and Sambuca in a small saucepan; bring to a boil, stirring until the sugar melts. Boil gently for 5 minutes; then blend into the coffee mixture. Cool the mixture to room temperature.

Freeze on flat surface in the freezer for 4 hours; stir the mixture every 20 minutes.

Garnish with lemon peel as you section the *granita* in dessert glasses or bowls.

VARIATIONS

* Top with Zabaglione Sauce (see page 207).
* Add 2 tablespoons of ricotta cheese and blend thoroughly before freezing.
* Use Amaretto liqueur instead of Sambuca for an almond flavor.

ZABAGLIONE SAUCE

Classic Italian Egg, Marsala Wine, and Coffee Sauce

3 fresh eggs
¼ cup Marsala wine
⅓ cup prepared espresso coffee
2 tsp. sugar

Servings:
4
Time:
10 *min.*
Calories:
85 *per 6 tbsp.*

Separate the eggs. Beat the egg yolks with the Marsala wine and coffee until well combined. Beat the egg whites with the sugar until the meringue forms stiff peaks.

Fold the meringue into the egg yolk mixture. Pour into 4 dessert glasses. Serve immediately over cake or fruit, or serve by itself. Zabaglione Sauce can be frozen.

VARIATIONS

* Use only the egg yolks and pour over cake, or serve by itself.
* Add 1 tablespoon of brandy or Amaretto liqueur.

ITALIAN RUM CAKE

With Strawberries, Rum, and Zabaglione Sauce

1 sponge cake or pound cake (about 8 inches square)
½ cup prepared espresso coffee
¼ cup dark rum
1 tbsp. brandy
1 pint fresh strawberries
½ lemon, juice only
1 tsp. sugar
2 cups prepared Zabaglione Sauce (see page 207)

Servings:
8
Time:
15 *min.*
Calories:
405 *per serving*

Cut the cake into 8 equal pieces and place it on dessert dishes.

Mix the coffee with the rum and brandy. Puncture the cake with a fork, soaking with the coffee mixture. Dice the strawberries and mix with the lemon and sugar and purée.

Place the Zabaglione Sauce over the cake slices, and place the puréed strawberries on top. Place a dab of Zabaglione Sauce on top of each dessert.

VARIATIONS
* Use mixed fruit.
* Use the fruit puree only; eliminate the Zabaglione Sauce.

F R I T T A T A   D O L C E

Sweet Dessert Frittata with Fruit and Liqueur

Servings:
6
Time:
15 *min.*
Calories:
120 *per serving*

3 tbsp. liqueur (Amaretto or Grand Marnier) or orange juice
3 tbsp. Marsala Italian dessert wine
½ cup fruit filling (diced strawberries, raspberries, peaches, oranges, bananas)
6 fresh eggs
1 tbsp. unsalted, sweet butter
1 tsp. white powdered sugar (for topping)

Heat the liqueur and wine separately (to burn off the sugar and alcohol).
Add the Marsala wine to the diced fruit and mix thoroughly to marinate.
Beat the eggs lightly and add the liqueur. Heat the butter in a large skillet and pour in the egg mixture. Let it cook for about 1 to 2 minutes; then spoon the fruit mixture into the center and continue to cook over low heat for 5 minutes, until the top is set.
Sprinkle the powdered sugar on and serve immediately in wedges.

VARIATIONS
* Vary the fruits and liqueurs used.
* Use a fruit purée on top of the frittata.

S T R A W B E R R Y   G R A N I T A

Fresh Iced Strawberries

Servings:
10 *(5 cups)*
Time:
15 *min. plus*
freezer time
Calories:
55 *per serving*

4 tbsp. sugar
¾ cup water
3 pints hulled strawberries
⅓ cup Riunite Peach Wine
8 fresh strawberries
4 mint leaves

Combine the sugar and water in a small saucepan; bring to a boil, stirring until the sugar melts. Boil the mixture gently for 3 to 5 minutes. Let the syrup cool.

Purée the strawberries in a blender or food processor. Stir in the syrup and wine.

Pour the mixture into an 8-inch square baking pan, and cool to room temperature. Cover and store in the refrigerator.

Place the pan level on the freezer surface. Stir the mixture every 20 minutes to combine the partially frozen edges with the soft center, until it freezes solid (about 2 to 3 hours).

When ready to serve, remove the granita from the freezer and place it on a rack in the refrigerator for 15 minutes. Scrape the granita into chilled dessert glasses or small glass bowls using an ice cream server.

Garnish with the strawberries and mint leaves. Granita can be stored in the freezer about 2 days.

VARIATIONS
* Use fresh peaches, raspberries, or melon.
* Add 2 tablespoons of skim-milk ricotta cheese for a creamy textured granita.

Granita may be made 1 day in advance.

F R U I T A   M I S T A

Mixed Fresh Fruit Ice with Brandy

1 cup purée of mixed fruit (strawberries, raspberries, peaches, bananas)
4 tbsp. lemon juice
3 tbsp. brandy or Cointreau liqueur

Servings:
4
Time:
15 *min.*
Calories:
55 *per serving*

Purée the fresh fruits, and squeeze the lemon juice; add them to a large metal bowl with the brandy or Cointreau.

Set the bowl in a large container with crushed ice. Stir the mixture with a large wire whisk until smooth and creamy. (The mixture never becomes frozen.)

Serve immediately in tall glasses or dessert bowls with fresh raspberries or strawberries on top.

VARIATIONS
* Use Marsala wine or Amaretto instead of Cointreau.
* Use one type of fruit only.
* Top with Zabaglione Sauce (see page 207).

BAKED BANANAS
WITH AMARETTO
SAUCE ALLA
LISA

Servings:
4
Time:
15 *min.*
Calories:
134 *per serving*

2 large fresh bananas
1 tbsp. orange rind, grated
1 tbsp. honey
½ cup orange juice
3 tbsp. Amaretto liqueur
1 tsp. unsalted butter (cut into 4 pieces)
Julienned orange rind (optional)
Vanilla bean (optional)

Preheat oven at 350°F. Cut 4 pieces of foil, each 4×6 inches.

Peel the bananas, cut them in half lengthwise, and place each half on a foil rectangle.

In a small bowl mix the orange rind, honey, orange juice, and Amaretto, and spoon over the banana halves.

Top each half with a piece of butter. Fold the foil over once and crimp the ends to seal.

Place each wrapped banana half on a baking sheet and bake for 5 to 8 minutes; if the bananas are very ripe they will cook in about 5 minutes.

To serve, slash the bananas into 5 even pieces along the outside edge and curve into semicircles. Pour the juices over the fruit and garnish with orange rind and vanilla bean.

VARIATIONS

* Add fresh strawberries or peaches.
* Put a cup of Zabaglione Sauce (see page 207) on the side, to add to the top of the bananas.

RICOTTA CAFFE PASQUELINE

Ricotta Cheese, Espresso, and Amaretto Cream

¾ cup skim-milk ricotta cheese
4 tbsp. Amaretto liqueur
1 tbsp. dark-roast espresso coffee, finely ground
4 tbsp. prepared espresso coffee
½ cup fresh or dried fruits, diced (pineapple, peaches, oranges, berries)

Servings:
4
Time:
10 *min.*
Calories:
119 *per serving*

In a large bowl, mix all of the ingredients together. For a smoother, creamy texture, blend the mixture in a blender or food processor for a few minutes.
Serve in dessert dishes, glasses, or as a sauce.

VARIATIONS
* Add ¼ cup shaved dark chocolate.
* Use brandy instead of Amaretto liqueur.
* Make without the diced fruit.
* Add 2 egg whites, stiffly beaten, and fold them into the mixture for a light, fluffy effect.

AMARETTO RICOTTA PUFFS

Ricotta, Eggs, Chocolate Bits, and Amaretto, Served with Zabaglione Sauce or Fruit Purée

1 cup skim-milk ricotta
2 fresh eggs
½ cup dark chocolate bits
¼ cup Amaretto liqueur
½ tsp. espresso grinds
1 cup almond cookie crumbs, finely mashed
Fruit Purée or Zabaglione Sauce (see page 207)

Servings
4
Time:
25 *min.*
Calories:
387 *per serving*

Mix the ricotta, eggs, chocolate, Amaretto, and espresso in a large bowl.

Form the mixture into small balls and roll in cookie crumbs.

Drop the balls into a saucepan and brown lightly in hot safflower oil; turn gently. Place the balls on paper towels and drain.

Serve at room temperature with Zabaglione Sauce or fruit purée.

VARIATIONS

* Use diced dried fruit instead of the chocolate bits.
* Roll the ricotta puffs in powdered milk chocolate.
* Use Grand Marnier instead of Amaretto.
* Use diced oranges and pineapple.

The ricotta puffs can be placed in the refrigerator for a few hours. They are lighter, less caloric, and easier to digest when not fried.

MINI-TORTAS MISTI

Small Cakes with Mixed Toppings

Servings:
6
Time:
10 *min.*
Calories:
215 *per serving*

6 slices of pound cake

1 cup espresso coffee

3 tbsp. Amaretto liqueur or brandy

1 cup fresh fruit, diced (raspberries, strawberries, blueberries, peaches, pineapple, mango)

1 cup prepared Zabaglione Sauce (see page 207)

Place the pound cake on individual dessert dishes.

Mix the espresso with the liqueur. Puncture the cake with a fork; spoon the coffee and liqueur sauce over the cake.

Spread the cake with the Zabaglione Sauce, and top with the fruit or vice versa. Do not spoon too much coffee sauce over the cake.

VARIATIONS

* Use the coffee mixture over the cake and top with fruit ice or *gelato*.
* Try a liqueur base only with Zabaglione Sauce or fruit purée sauce.

L A M P O N E
R I C O T T A
S A L S A

Raspberry and Ricotta Cheese Sauce

½ cup skim-milk ricotta cheese
2½ cups fresh raspberries; or 2 10-oz. packages frozen raspberries, thawed and
    drained
3 tbsp. Framboise (raspberry liqueur)
1 tbsp. superfine sugar

Servings
6 *(½ cup)*
Time:
10 *min.*
Calories:
82 *per serving*

    Purée all of the ingredients in a blender or food processor. Strain the seeds.
Add to a bowl and chill. Serve on cakes and fruits, or plain in small dessert
glasses.

VARIATIONS

* Use Frangelica liqueur or Cointreau instead of framboise.
* Eliminate the cheese and mix with blueberries.

L E M O N   A N D   B A S I L
G R A N I T A

2 cups sweet Italian sparkling wine (such as Moscato d'Asti)
1 cup fresh basil leaves, diced
1 cup fresh lemon juice
3 tbsp. lime juice
6 sliced fresh strawberries for decoration

Servings:
6
Time:
20 *min.*
Calories:
48 *per serving*

    Combine the wine and basil in a small saucepan and bring to a boil. Boil for 2
to 3 minutes, then cool. Mix all of the remaining ingredients, except the strawberries, in a large bowl, and pour in the basil and wine.
    Freeze in an ice cube tray. Remove a few minutes before serving and spoon
into dessert dishes. Top with sliced strawberries.

VARIATIONS

* Use minced fresh Italian parsley leaves.
* Use ½ cup of dry, Brut Italian sparkling wine instead of lemon juice.

CHOCOLATE RASPBERRY CREMA ALLA LYNN

Servings
6
Time:
20 *min. plus*
cooling period
Calories:
202 *per serving*

4 squares of unsweetened chocolate
2 tbsp. confectioner's sugar
2 tbsp. sifted arrowroot
2 tbsp. Framboise liqueur (or cognac)
1 cup skim-milk ricotta cheese
1 cup fresh raspberries, halved (frozen can be used)

Melt the chocolate in a small bowl over warm water and combine it with the sugar, arrowroot, and liqueur. Cook over low heat and stir constantly until the mixture is smooth.

Add the ricotta cheese and continue to stir, keeping the mixture smooth and creamy. (Do not boil.)

Let the mixture cool slightly, stir in the raspberries, and spoon into 6 small, dainty dessert bowls. Cover each bowl with plastic wrap and refrigerate for a few hours or overnight.

Top each dish with a raspberry before serving.

VARIATION

* Use 1 cup of fresh raspberries with the same liqueur and mix in a blender. Add 1 tablespoon of this mixture to the top of each dessert.

POACHED PEARS WITH AMARETTO CHOCOLATE CREAM SAUCE

6 medium-size, soft Bartlet pears, peeled, sliced, and cored
2 cups Amaretto di Saronno liqueur
1 cup water
1½ cups skim-milk ricotta cheese
1 2-oz. Cadbury chocolate bar

Servings
6
Time:
25 *min.*
Calories:
412 *per serving*

Put the prepared pears in a large lidded saucepan with 1½ cups of the Amaretto liqueur and 1 cup of water. Boil the liquid and simmer for 20 minutes until the pears are soft.

Put the ricotta cheese in a small saucepan with the remaining Amaretto and stir constantly over low heat until the mixture is smooth and creamy. (Do not boil.)

Put the pears in dainty, individual serving dishes, spoon the creamy Amaretto sauce over the pears, and sprinkle finely grated chocolate over each pear.

VARIATION
* Use a raspberry or peach sauce.

III. *Entertaining for All Occasions*

Entertaining with A Bella Figura

Entertain with your best—that's what my mother always used to say. When people come to visit you, show them your best and give them your best: Express your love, creativity, and your *casa*. So, from the smallest, most informal functions to the grandest, make a *bella figura*—an expression of you.

I suggest some food and theme ideas in the following pages to help you entertain with a new look and repertoire of food that reflect the current trends and tastes. Quality is the key in entertaining.

Create your *bella figura* for every occasion, and then express your best . . . the "Italian light" way. Your guests will surely applaud you. They will be happy that your food is so delicious and best of all, light and natural. They won't feel bombarded with heavy courses of butter, cheese, and cream that will take days to digest.

They will come away from your dinner party feeling satisfied, yet comfortable, even if you have served three to six courses. Of course, keep the portions to the right amount and serve only wines of good quality.

For a large buffet, use small-shape pasta and bite-size pieces of fish or meat. This makes eating and serving easier. A good choice is a sauce of vegetables or cheese with a fish or meat entrée and salad. You have the vegetable and pasta together, and it is not necessary to make a separate vegetable dish.

Select recipes that are visually pleasing and unusual for dinner parties, especially for buffets. Serve cocktail foods in an unusual tray or bowl, or on a marble pastry board. You can even make various types of cocktail food baskets.

Use colorful tablecloths, napkins, flowers, scarves, ceramic pieces, and so on, to make a special visual setting that will complement the food. It is especially important to tie in the colors and accessories if you have a theme party.

Serving exciting foods that are light and healthy represents the newest trend in entertaining. Present your foods beautifully and the evening will be totally successful. *Bravo!*

Suggested Menus for Entertaining

COCKTAIL FOODS
Mini-Pizzas · Seafood Misto · Crostinis · Eggplant Caviar · Vegetables with Bagna Cauda and Ricotta Dip · Chicken Bits with Pesto Sauce

ANTIPASTI/APPETIZERS/FIRST COURSES
Torte Festiva · Pasta Salmone · Pasta Limone · Pasta with Roasted Pepper Sauce · Risotto Champagne · Risotto Tartufi · Seafood Salad · Eggplant Rolls Stuffed with Ricotta and Herbs · Timballo · Lasagna Rolls · Polenta Pizza · Pasta e Fagiola Soup · Lentil-Pasta Soup · Minestrone with Pesto · Frittata with Cheese, Prosciutto, and Zucchini slices

SECONDI/MAIN COURSES
Spaghetti alla Chitarra · Pasta Pescara · Pasta alla Norma · Risotto with Seafood and Vegetables · Chicken Sarna · Pollo Trevi · Lasagna Verde · Grilled Fish Sicilia · Zuppa d' Pesce · Codfish Livornese · Stuffed Veal Roast · Lamb Sardinia · Beef in Barolo Sauce

CONTORNI/ACCOMPANIMENTS
Pasta · Rice · Polenta · Crostinis · Vegetale Misti · Zucchini–Red Peppers–Mushrooms · Eggplant Rolls · Spinach Florentina · Primavera, Potato Adee · Mashed White and Sweet Potatoes · Pepperonata

INSALATAS/SALADS
Arugula · Endive · Radicchio · Fennel · Mushroom · Spinach

DOLCE/DESSERTS
Granita · *Gelato* · Fruita Marsala · Torte Giuseppe · Ricotta Cheesecake · Zabaglione · Lampone

BREAKFAST/BRUNCH
Frittatas (Cheese, Vegetables, Prosciutto) · Eggs Florentina · Pasta and Eggs · Risotto with Cheese and Mushrooms · Lasagna Rolls · Polenta (Cheese and Tomatoes) · Pizzas · Foccacio Pasta Con Salmone e Vegetale

LUNCH
Pastas · Pasta Salads · Risotto · Polenta · Pizzas · Frittatas · Soups · Fish · Chicken · Veal · Lamb · Vegetale Misti · Seafood Salad · Tri-Coloure Salad · Arugula and Pasta Salad

BUFFETS

Short-Shape Pasta Misti · Risotto · Chicken Sarna · Lamb Sardinia · Vegetables Primavera · Green Bean Salad · Eggplant Caponata · Seafood alla Grill · Foccacio Bread · Polenta Pizzas · Frittata Slices · Rotini Pasta alla Pesto · Stuffed Veal and Capon · Turkey Romana

DESSERT PARTIES

Fresh Fruit Macedonia · Torta Buon Complianno · Ricotta Cheesecake · Raspberries and Zabaglione · Granitas · Ices · *Gelato* · Amaretto Torte

Food Theme Parties

ANTIPASTO PARTIES

"Little tastes of many Italian *Antipasti* foods." It's fun to serve tasty little savories that are visually exciting and easy to prepare. Line the table with many small plates of food, or display the food on a long wooden board or marble surface. Place different shapes of bread, cheese, wine, and colorful napkins around the food. Serve your choice of olives, cheese, marinated vegetables, white bean salad, seafood salad, sardines or tuna fish, ricotta gnocchi, grilled eggplant slices, beets and onions, thinly sliced prosciutto, mini-pizzas, eggplant caviar, or roasted red and green peppers. Make this a buffet of many tastes with good wine and cheese and fruit for dessert.

PASTA PARTY

Use many shapes of pasta and many different pasta sauces. Toss some of the pastas with the sauce and serve immediately. Serve some short-shape pasta with a choice of two or three sauces. (Be sure to toss the pasta with olive oil to keep it from sticking.) Serve the pastas with two or three types of salads, Italian bread, and Italian wines. Use the "segretto method" when preparing the pastas with the sauces.

POLENTA PARTY

A popular dinner party in Italy centers around preparing the "polenta board," using quails in mushroom sauce, or sausages and mixed meats in tomato and cheese sauce. The fun is serving the spread polenta over a large wooden board, and spreading the sauce and cheese on top. Each person gets to take a portion from the board. An old wooden table is traditionally used; each person eats their portion from the side to the center. The fastest eater gets the meat in the center!

PIZZA, FOCCACIO, AND WINE PARTY

Serve a variety of pizzas, foccacio bread, and wines with salad and vegetables.

IV. Vino

"A day without wine is like a day without sunshine" is a favorite expression in Italy. Wine brings light and joy to a simple or elaborate meal, and soothes the soul while complementing the food and aiding the digestive process. Wine is a food in itself; it has vitamins and minerals.

I started drinking Italian wines at the age of three. My father gave me small amounts of red wine at that age because he felt it was good for my blood and general health. This practice is typically Italian: Children start to drink wine while very young and learn to distinguish the good wines from the bad ones. My father made his own wine, so I got involved in the winemaking process at an early age. He knew that good wine was as important as good food; thus, the right care and quality of grapes and the winemaking technique were important. This knowledge has helped me a great deal in life, both personally and professionally. *Bravo, Papa!*

Another custom in Italy is the daily consumption of wine at both lunch and dinner, but never between meals. Usually, only two to three glasses per person at each meal (based on two people sharing a bottle of wine). An aperitif is usually served before dinner and a *digestivo* after. Wine is not served before and after dinner (except champagne, spumante, or a dessert wine) The custom of wine before dinner and at parties was started in America. About ten years ago, when the health, slimness, and fitness movement began, people started substituting white wine for hard liquor. Then, from the sweet, bubbly Lambrusco and the basic Chianti, the knowledge and sophistication grew for fine wines with dinner and at special occasions.

For the past fifteen years, I have personally had the joy of not only introducing real classic Italian food that is light and healthy to America but also teaching Americans about the joys of drinking wine. Many people would say to me, "Oh, I love wine, but I can't drink it anymore, I get a headache, or a stomachache, or feel sleepy."

Such a comment would give me the opportunity to explain the reason for the "ill effects" caused by the type of wine they were drinking. Many mass-produced wines have chemicals and additives that are used to either increase the yield, or to balance the taste. These additives may be harmful to some individuals. To prevent these side effects, *drink only pure wines.*

After years of studying wine with some of the finest enologists in Europe, I found that *Italian wines are proved to be the purest and most natural:* They cause no bad effects to the body (except for those people that do not have the enzymes to digest wines). Italy is the largest wine producer in the world. The climate brings the grapes to the ripest point, so there is no need to add sugar or chemicals to make the wine taste better.

When buying wines, look for private estate and Italian wines: These are the purest. Private estates are small vineyards that make a limited production.

This section on wine contains the most complete and latest information on the production, the regions, and the availability of the fine wines of Italy, and is complete with a glossary, listing the best known and finest wines from each region. An Italian food and wine section advises you on how to combine foods and wine for the best taste results. The information is adapted from the new book by the Italian Trade Commission in New York, which was formulated and written by Burton Anderson, one of the top wine authorities. I will also make reference to further readings about Italian wines; these readings will extend your joy and knowledge of the fine wines of Italy, which are currently rated the premier wines of the world.

In today's social and business world, knowledge about food and wine is as important as social graces and manners. A person is judged the minute they sit down at the table to share lunch or dinner by the food and wine they choose.

Important Facts About Italian Wines

The popularity of Italian wine in the United States has been linked to the growing success of Italian food. Since the two are always at their best together, the exposure, quality production, and new imports have brought Italy to the highest level of success in both areas.

Italy produces, consumes, and exports more wine than any other country. Italian wines have outsold all other imports combined in the United States in recent years. The key to this success has been good quality at reasonable prices.

However, American preference for Italian wines is not based on bargains alone. Consumers have begun to appreciate that Italians produce and export more wines of a better quality and a greater variety than any other people.

The only complaint made about Italy's fine wines is that there are too many to ever get to know them all. Thus, I have selected from the Italian Wine Guide (Italian Trade Commission) only the finest and most popular Italian wines, classified by regions. You will find that most classic Italian restaurants, cafés, and trattorias, as well as wine stores, will feature the wines mentioned in this section. If they do not, ask them to order the wines for you. Venture into the exciting new world of pure, natural wines from Italy, which are recognized as some of the finest quality wines in the world, and are the number-one imports in America today.

HISTORY AND STATUS

Winemaking in Italy advanced rapidly during the nineteenth century. Methods of vinification and aging were improved; special corks were used to seal reinforced bottles; and advancements were made in shipping techniques. Responsible producers had been trying to tighten regulations and to reemphasize premium quality wine. (Up to that time the best wines stayed in Italy; low-cost wines packaged in outlandish shapes and sizes were profitable for some, but did little for the image of Italian wines abroad.) In the mid-1960s, the *denominazione di origine* laws created a new climate of dignity and trust for quality Italian wines only. The government control applied nationwide to wines of "particular reputation and worth" under what is known as *denominazione di origine controllata* (DOC).

There are now 220 DOC wines from Italy, and five of the classified wines have been distinguished as DOCG (the G stands for *garantita*—guaranteed authenticity by government-appointed commissions). These wines are Barbaresco, Barolo, Brunello di Montalcino, Chianti, and Vino Nobile di Montepulciano. Albana di Romagna was recently approved as the first DOCG white wine. This does not mean that the other wines exported from Italy are not of the finest quality; they should be praised on their own merits, and have been. For the first time, a national Italian wine-tasting contest was held in San Francisco in October 1986, and the Italian wines won many gold, silver, and bronze medals, including the whites, reds, and many sparkling wines (referred to as spumante, made by either the sealed-tank or bottle-fermented champagne method). Italy is the largest producer of bubbly wines, whether lightly fizzy (*frizzante*) or fully sparkling spumantes.

Italy now produces a number of wines that have received acclaim with the international elite. And Italy's premium production is constantly improving, thanks to people like Dr. Ezio Rivella, an Italian enologist of international renown. Traditional grape varieties and their methods of cultivation are being improved, new grape varieties are being developed, and highly automated vinification systems are overcoming nature's vagaries and the hazards of chance.

This success story has been a long and difficult one for the Italian wine world, but when you start with the perfect climate, soil, mountain ranges, and the Mediterranean sunshine, nature's favor seems to be a spontaneous culture of wine—the pure, natural, quality wines of Italy.

In the end, the most reliable guide to the quality of any wine from anywhere is the reputation of the individual producer or estate. Certain names are well worth getting to know. Read the labels carefully: All Italian wine imported into the United States must carry the INE seal of approval for export on a red-neck label. Labels must state the bottle size in milliliters, alcohol by percentage of volume, a description of the wine (dry white, red, table wine, or sparkling), the importer's name and location, the producer, and the words "product of Italy."

Salute! Indulge in one of the great joys of life . . . fine wine with fine food. The Italians do it so well! *Vino Vita!*

ITALIAN REGIONS

Southern Regions and Islands
Sicily
Sardinia
Calabria
Apulia
Campania

Central Regions
Latium
Molise
Abruzzi
Marches
Umbria
Tuscany

North-by-Northwest Regions
Emilia–Romagna
Liguria
Lombardy
Piedmont
Valle d'Aosta

North-by-Northeast Regions
Veneto
Friuli–Venezia Giulia
Trentino–Alto Adige

Vallé
d'Aosta

Alto Adige-
Trentino

Friuli-
Venezia-
Giulia

Lombardy

Veneto

TORINO

TRIESTE

MILAN

Piedmont

VENICE

Italy

Emilia-
Romagna

GENOA

Liguria

BOLOGNA

FLORENCE

Tuscany

PERUGIA Marche

Umbria

Sardinia

Lazio

Abruzzi

ROME

Molise

Campania

Puglia

NAPLES

Basilicata

Calabria

PALERMO

Sicily

Italian Wine Terms

The following Italian terms may be found on labels or in literature about wine.

Abboccato: Lightly sweet.
Alcool: Alcohol, usually stated by percent of volume.
Amabile: Semisweet.
Annata: Vintage year.
Azienda agricola or Agraria: Farm.
Bianco: White.
Bottiglia: Bottle.
Brut: Dry—in sparkling wine.
Cantina: Cellar or winery.
Cantina sociale: Cooperative winery.
Casa vinicola: Private winery.
Cerasuolo: Cherry-hued rosé.
Chiaretto: Deep rosé.
Classico: The historic center of a DOC zone.
Consorzio: Consortium of producers.
Dolce: Sweet.
Enoteca: Wine library, public or commercial.
Fattoria: Farm or estate.
Fermentazione naturale: Natural carbon dioxide (CO_2) in bubbly wine.
Frizzante or frizzantino: Fizzy or faintly fizzy.
Imbottigliata: Bottled (*all'origine* implies at the source).
Invecchiato: Aged.
Liquoroso: Wine fortified with alcohol.
Metodo charmat: Sparkling wine by the sealed-tank method.
Metodo classico or champenois: Sparkling wine by the champagne method of bottle fermentation.
Passito: Sweet wine from partly dried grapes.
Podere: Small farm or estate.
Produttore: Producer.
Recioto: Strong, usually sweet wine from partly dried grapes, although Recioto Amarone is dry.
Riserva: Reserve, DOC, or DOCG wine aged a specified time.
Rosato: Rosé.
Rosso: Red.
Secco: Dry.
Semisecco: Medium sweet, usually sparkling wine.
Spumante: Sparkling wine, dry or sweet.
Superiore: Denotes a higher level of alcohol or aging or special geographical origin in DOC wines.
Tenuta: Farm or estate.
Uva: Grape.
Vecchio: Old, rarely used term for specified aging in DOC wines.

Vendemmia: Harvest or vintage.
Vigna or vigneto: Vineyard.
Vino da tavola: Table wine, applies loosely to most non-DOCs.
Viticoltore: Grape grower.

World Wine Production, Export, and Consumption by Nation

Production average
(in millions of liters)

Italy	7,254
France	6,962
Spain	3,577
Soviet Union	3,460
Argentina	2,132
United States	1,745
West Germany	1,212
Rumania	982
Portugal	902

Export average
(in millions of liters)

Italy	1,758
France	994
Spain	603
West Germany	240
Portugal	147
Austria	49
United States	31

Consumption per capita
(in liters)

Italy	90.5
Portugal	84.2
France	82.0
Argentina	66.3
Luxembourg	62.5
Switzerland	49.9
Spain	45.0
Greece	43.9
United Kingdom	9.5
United States	8.7

Italian Regional Wine Guide

Total regional information is included in this guide with the listings of wine production and the most noted wines, from DOC or DOCG to other important and popular wines. Most of the wines are readily available in the United States, or can be ordered. I have selected only the well-known wines of each region, and some of the finest producers in Italy.

The South and the Islands (Sicily, Sardinia, Calabria, Basilicata, Apulia, and Campania) are six regions that produce nearly 40 percent of Italy's total wine. Several of Italy's red wines that are most impressive for long aging originate in the south.

SICILY

Sicily is Italy's largest region in area (9,926 miles) and fourth in population. Vineyards cover 414,387 acres. Average annual wine production is 1.15 billion liters.

DOC Wines (10)
Alcamo or Bianco d'Alcamo—white: dry
Cerasuolo di Vittoria—rosé: dry
Etna—white, red, rosé
Faro—red: dry
Malvasia delle Lipari—white: sweet
Marsala—white: dry, sweet, vergine or soleras, superiore, fine, stravecchio
Moscato di Noto—white: sweet, sparkling, liquoroso
Moscato di Pantelleria—white: sweet, sparkling, liquoroso
Moscato di Pantelleria Passito—white: sweet, extra, liquoroso
Moscato di Siracusa—white: sweet, liquoroso

Other Wines of Note
Corvo Duca di Salaparuta—white, red: dry
Draceno—white, red, rosé: dry
Regaleali—white, red, rosé: dry
Settesoli—white, rosé: dry, sweet
Rincione—white, red, rosé: dry
Carboj-Red—white, red rosé: dry, sweet
Donnafugata—white: dry
Bell'Agio—white, rosé: sweet

SARDINIA (SARDEGNA)

Sardinia ranks third in size among the regions (9,301 square miles) and twelfth in population. Vineyards cover 167,500 acres. Average annual wine production is 225 million liters.

DOC Wines (17)
Arborea: Sangiovese—red, rosé; Trebbiano—white: dry, sweet, frizzante
Campidano di Terralbe—rosé: dry
Cannonau di Sardegna—rosé: dry, superiore secco, dolce, riserva, liquoroso

Carignano del Sulcis—rosé, red, invecchiato: dry

Giro di Cagliari—rosé: sweet, dry, liquoroso

Malvasia di Bosa—white: sweet, aged, liquoroso

Malvasia di Cagliari—white: sweet, liquoroso

Mandrolisai—red, rosé: dry, aged

Monica di Cagliari—rosé: sweet dry, liquoroso

Monica di Sardegna—rosé: dry, superior, aged

Moscato di Cagliari—white: sweet, liquoroso, aged

Moscato di Sardegna—white: sweet, sparkling

Moscato di Sorso-Sennori—white: sweet, liquoroso

Nasco di Cagliari—white: sweet, dry, liquoroso, aged

Nuragus di Cagliari—white: dry

Vermentino di Gallura—white: dry

Vernaccia di Oristano—white: dry, sweet, superiore

Other Wines of Note

Anghelu Ruju—rosé: sweet

Cannonau di Alghero—rosé: dry

Malvasia di Planargia—white: dry, sweet, liquoroso

Rosé di Alghero—rosé: dry

Torbato di Alghero—white: dry, sparkling

CALABRIA

Calabria ranks tenth among the regions (5,822 square miles) and has a population of 2,061,000. Vineyards cover 81,696 acres. Average annual wine production is 115 million liters.

Doc Wines (8)

Ciro—white, red, rosé: dry

Donnici—rosé: dry

Greco di Biano—white: sweet

Lamezia—red: dry

Melissa—red, white: dry, superiore

Pollino—rosé: dry, superiore

Sant 'Anna di Isola Capo Rizzuto—rosé: dry

Savuto—red: dry, superiore

Other Wines of Note

Grecco Rosso—rosé: dry

Lacrima di Castrovillari—rosé: dry, sweet

Moscato di Calabria—white: sweet, sparkling

Pellaro—red, rosé: dry

BASILICATA OR LUCANIA

Basilicata ranks eighteenth among regions (3,858 square miles) and has a population of 610,000. Vineyards cover 41,733 acres. Annual wine production is 45 million liters.

DOC Wines (1)

Aglianico del Vulture—red: dry, sparkling, vecchio

Other Wines of Note

Aglianico dei Colli Lucani or di Matera—red: dry, sweet, sparkling

Asprino or Asprinio—white: dry, frizzante

Malvasia del Vulture—white: sweet

Montepulciano di Basilicate—red: dry

APULIA (PUGLIA)

Apulia ranks seventh among regions in size (7,469 square miles) and has a population of 3,872,000. Vineyards cover 337,393 acres. Annual wine production is 1.15 billion liters.

DOC Wines (23)

Aleatico di Puglia—red: sweet
Alezia—red, rosé: dry
Brindisi—red, rosé: dry
Cacc'e mitte di Lucerea—red: dry
Castel del Monte—red, rosé, white: dry
Copertino—red, rosé: dry
Gioia del Colle—white: dry; red, rosé: sweet
Gravina—white: dry, sweet
Leverano—white, red, rosé: dry
Locorotondo—white: dry, sparkling
Martina Franca or Martina—white: dry, sparkling
Matino—red, rosé: dry
Moscato di Trani—white: sweet, liquoroso
Nardo—red, rosé: dry
Orta Nova—red, rosé: dry
Ostuni—Bianco—white: dry; Ottavianello—red: dry

Primitivo di Manduria—red, rosé: dry, sweet
Rosso Barletta—red: dry, invecchiato
Rosso Canosa—red, rosé: dry
Rosso di Cerignola—red: dry
Salice Salentino—red, rosé: dry, invecchiato
San Severo—white, red, rosé: dry, sparkling
Squinzano—red, rosé: dry

Other Wines of Note

Apulia—red: dry
Cabernet di Puglia—red: dry
Castel Mitrano—red: dry
Chardonnay di Puglia—white: dry
Pinot Bianco di Puglia—white: dry
Rosa del Golfo—rosé: dry
Sauvignon di Puglia—white: dry
Toree Quarto—white, red, rosé: dry

CAMPANIA

Campania ranks twelfth among the regions in size (5,249 square miles) and is second in population (5,463,000). Vineyards cover 117,825 acres. Average annual wine production is 275 million liters.

DOC Wines (7)

Capri—red, white: dry
Fiano di Avellino*—white: dry
Greco di Tufo*—white: dry
Ischia—red, white: dry
Solopaca—red, white: dry
Taurasi*—red: dry, riserva
Vesuvio (Lacryma Christi del Vesuvio)*—white, red, rosé: dry

Other Wines of Note

Aglianico del Taburno or Taburno—rosé: dry
Barbera—red: dry
Falerno—red: dry
Gragnano—red: dry, frizzante
Biancolella—white: dry
Don Alfonzo—white, red, rosé: dry
Forastera—white: dry
Kalimera—white: dry, sparkling

*Wines produced by one of the master wine-makers: Masterberadino.

Central Italy includes Latium, Molise, Abruzzi, Marches, Umbria, and Tuscany.

LATIUM-LAZIO (Rome and surrounding areas)

Latium ranks ninth in size (6,642 square miles) and third in population (5,000,000). Vineyards cover 169,033 acres. Annual average wine production is 570 million liters. The Orvieto DOC zone centered in Umbria also extends into Latium.

DOC Wines (16)

Aleatico di Gradoli—red: sweet, aged

Aprilia—Merlot—red: dry; Sangiovese—red, rosé: dry Trebbiano—white: dry

Bianco Capena—white: dry

Cerveteri—white, red: dry, sweet

Cesanese del Piglio—red: dry, sweet, frizzante

Cesanese di Affile—red: dry, sweet, frizzante, sparkling

Cesanese di Olevano Romano— red: dry, sweet, sparkling

Colli Albani—white: dry, sweet

Colli Lanuvini—white: dry, sweet

Cori—white, red: dry

Est! Est! Est!!! di Montefiascone— white: dry, sweet

Frascati—white: dry, sparkling

Marino—white: dry, sparkling, sweet

Montecompatri-Colonna—white: dry, sweet

Velletri—white, red: dry

Zagaroloa—white: dry, sweet

Other Wines of Note

Castel San Giorgio—white, red: dry

Castelli Romani—white, red, rosé: dry, sweet

Cecubo—red: dry

Colle Picchioni—red: dry

Fiorano—white: dry, sweet; red: dry

Torre Ercolana—red: dry

Maccarese—white, red: dry

MOLISE

Molise ranks nineteenth among regions (1,714 square miles) with a population of 328,000. Vineyards cover 23,309 acres. Average annual wine production is 50 million liters.

DOC Wines (2)

Biferno—white, red, rosé: dry

Pentro di Isernia—white, red, rosé: dry

Other Wines of Note

Bianco del Molise—white: dry

Montepulciano del Molise—red: dry

Moscato del Molise—white: sweet, sparkling

Rosso del Molise—red: dry

Sangiovese del Molise—red: dry

ABRUZZI (ABRUZZO)

Abruzzi ranks thirteenth among regions in size (4,168 square miles) with a population of 1,218,000. Vineyards cover 74,397 acres. Average wine production is 380 million liters.

DOC Wines (2)

Montepulciano d'Abruzzo*—
Cerasuolo—rosé: dry; Rosso—
red: dry

Trebbiano d'Abruzzo*—white: dry,
frizzante

Other Wines of Note

Moscato—white: sweet, sparkling

Rubino—dry: red

Spinello—white: dry

Emidio Peppe*—white, red: dry

MARCHES (MARCHE)

The Marches ranks fifteenth in regional size (3,742 square miles) with a population of 1,412,000. Vineyards cover 78,970 acres. Average annual wine production
is 240 million liters.

DOC Wines (10)

Bianchello del Metauro—white:
dry

Bianco dei Colli Maceratesi—
white: dry

Falerio dei Colli Ascolani—white:
dry

Lacrima di Morro—red: dry

Rosso Conero—red: dry

Rosso Piceno—red: dry

Sangiovese dei Colli Pesaresi—
red: dry

Verdicchio dei Castelli di Jesi—
white: dry, sparkling

Verdicchio di Matelica—white:
dry, sparkling

Vernaccia di Serrapetrona—red:
dry, sweet, sparkling

Other Wines of Note

Fontanelle—white: dry

Montepulciano delle Marche—red:
dry

Rosato di Montanello—rosé: dry

Tenuta di Pongelli—red: dry

UMBRIA

Umbria ranks sixteenth in regional size (3,265 square miles) with a population of
808,000. Vineyards cover 55,691 acres. Average annual wine production is 105
million liters.

DOC Wines (6)

Colli Altotiberini—white, red,
rosé: dry

Colli del Trasimeno—white, red:
dry

Colli Perugini—white, red, rosé:
dry

Montefalco Rosso—red: dry

Sagrantino di Montefalco—red:
dry, sweet

Orvieto—white: dry

Torgiano—white, red, rosé: dry

Other Wines of Note

Assisi—white, red: dry

Bianco d'Arquata—white: dry

Castello di Montoro—red: dry

Rubesco†—red: dry

San Giorgio†—red: dry

Vin Santo—white: sweet

*Leading wine producers: Emidio Pepe and Dino Illuminati.

†Master wine producer: Lungorotti.

TUSCANY (TOSCANA)

Tuscany ranks fifth among the regions in size (8,877 square miles) with a population of 3,581,000. Vineyards cover 219,647 acres. Average annual wine production is 440 million liters.

DOC Wines or DOCG Wines (21)

Bianco della Valdinievole—white: dry; Vin Santo—white: sweet

Bianco di Pitigliano—white: dry

Bianco Pisano di San Torpe—white: dry; Vin Santo—white: sweet

Bianco Vergine della Valdichiana—white: dry, frizzante

Bolgheri—white, rosé: dry

Brunello di Montalcino (DOCG)—red: dry, riserva, aged

Candia dei Colli Apuani—white: dry

Carmignano—red, rosé: dry, riserva; Spumante, Vin Santo—white: sweet

Chianti (DOCG)—Classico, Colli Arentini, Colli Fiorentini, Colli Senesi, Colline Pisane, Montalbano, Rufina—red: dry

Colline Lucchesi—white, red: dry

Elba—white: dry, spumante; red: dry

Montecarlo—white, red: dry

Montescudaio—white, red: dry; Vin Santo—white: sweet

Morellino di Scansano—red: dry

Moscadello di Montalcino—white: sweet

Parrina—white, red: dry

Pomino—white, red: dry, riserva; Vin Santo—white: sweet

Rosso di Montalcino—red: dry

Val d'Arbia—white: dry; Vin Santo—white: sweet

Vernaccia di San Gimignano—white: dry, riserva, spumante

Vino Nobile di Montepulciano (DOCG)—red: dry, riserva

Other Wines of Note

Aleatico—red: sweet

Bianco di Toscana—white: dry, frizzante

Centine Rosso Di Montalcino*—red: dry

Chardonnay di Toscana*—white: dry

Flaccianello della Pieve—red: dry

Fontanelle Chardonnay della Toscana*—white: dry

Galestro—white: dry

La Corte—red: dry

Logaiolo—red: dry

Malvasia di Toscana—white: dry, sweet

Maremma—white, red, rosé: dry

Pinot Grigio di Toscana—white: dry

Predicato di Cardisco—red: dry

Rosato di Cercatoia—red: dry

Sammarco—red: dry

San Angelo Pinot Grigio*—white: dry

Santa Costanza*—light red: dry

Sassolato—white: sweet

Tignanello—red: dry

Torricella—white: dry

Villa Antinori Bianco—white: dry

Vin Santo—white, red: sweet, dry

Vinattieri Rosso—red: dry

*Famed enologist Dr. Ezio Rivella created these wines.

The North by Northwest region includes Emilia-Romagna, Liguria, Lombardy, Piedmont, Valle D'Aosta.

EMILIA-ROMAGNA

Emilia-Romagna ranks sixth among the regions in size (8,542 square miles) with a population of 3,958,000. Vineyards cover 208,952 acres. Average annual wine production is 950 million liters.

DOC Wines (11)

Albana di Romagna—white: dry, sweet, spumante

Bianco di Scandiano—white: dry, sweet, spumante

Colli Bolognesi-Monte San Pietro-Colli Medioevali (8 types)—Barbera—red: dry; Bianco—white: dry, sweet; Cabernet Sauvignon—red: dry; Merlot—red, dry; Pignoletto—white: dry; Pinto Bianco—white: dry, sweet; Riesling Italico—white: dry; Sauvignon—white: dry

Colli di Parma—Malvasia—white: dry, sweet, frizzante; Rosso—red: dry, frizzante; Sauvignon—white: dry, frizzante

Colli di Piacentini—red: dry

Lambrusco di Sorbara—red: dry, sweet

Lambrusco Grasparossa di Castelvetro—red: dry, sweet

Lambrusco Reggiano—red, rosé: dry, sweet

Lambrusco Salamino di Santa Croce—red: dry, sweet

Langiovese di Romagna—red: dry

Trebbiano di Romagna—white: dry, sweet, spumante

Other Wines of Note

Barbarossa di Bertinoro—red: dry

Bianco della Pusteria—white: sweet

Cagnina—red: sweet

Lambrusco Amabile—red, rosé: frizzante

Lambrusco Bianco—white: dry spumante

Malvasia—white: dry, sweet, frizzante, sparkling

Picolit—white: sweet

Pinot Spumante—white: dry, sparkling

Riunite Bianco & D'Oro—white: dry, sweet, frizzante

Riunite Lambrusco & Rosato—white, rosé: sweet, frizzante

Riunite Spumante—white: sweet, sparkling

Ronco dei Ciliegi—red: dry

Ronco del Re—white: dry

Rosso Armentano—red: dry

Sauvignon—white: dry, frizzante

LIGURIA

Liguria ranks eighteenth among regions in size (2,091 square miles) with a population of 1,808,000. Vineyards cover 17,596 acres. Annual wine production is 35,000,000 liters.

DOC Wines (3)

Cinqueterre—white: dry; Sciacchetra—white: sweet

Riviera di Ponente—Ormeasco—red: dry; Pigato—white: dry;

Rossese di Albenga—red: dry; Vermintino—white: dry

Rossese di Dolceacqua or Dolceacqua—red: dry, superiore

Other Wines of Note

Barbera—red: dry
Buzzetto di Quiliano—white: dry
Coronata—white: dry
Lumassina—white: dry
Terizzo—red: dry

LOMBARDY (LOMBARDIA)

Lombardy ranks fourth among the regions in size (9,211 square miles) with the largest regional population (8,892,000). Vineyards cover 76,104 acres. Average annual wine production is 215 million liters.

DOC Wines (13)

Botticino—red: dry
Brut Pinot Spumante—white: dry, sparkling
Ca ' Del Bosco Rosso Franciacorta—red: dry, sparkling
Capriano del Colle: Rosso—red: dry; Trebbiano—white: dry
Cellatica—red: dry
Colli Morenici Mantovani—Bianco—white: dry; Chiaretto or Rosato—rosé: dry; Rubino—red: dry
Franciacorta—Bianco or Pinot—white: dry; Rosso—red: dry; Spumante—white: dry, spumante; Spumante Rossato—rosé: dry, sparkling
Lungana—white: dry, sparkling
Oltrepo Pavese—Barbacarlo—red: dry, frizzante; Barbera—red: dry; Bonarda—red: dry; Buttafuoco—red: dry, frizzante; Cortese—white: dry; Moscato—white: sweet, frizzante, spumante; Moscato Liquoroso—white: sweet; Pinot Grigio—white: dry, frizzante; Pinot

Nero—red, white, rosé: dry, frizzante; Pinot Nero Spumante—white, rosé: dry, sparkling; Riesling Italico—white: dry, sparkling; Riesling Renano—white: dry, sparkling; Rosato—rosé: dry; Rosso—red: dry; Sangue di Giuda—red: dry, frizzante, sweet
Riviera del Garda Bresciano-Chiaretto—rosé: dry; red: dry, superiore
San Colombano or San Colombano al Lambro—red: dry
Tocai di San Martino della Battaglia—white: dry
Valcalepio—white, red: dry
Valtellina—red: dry; Valtellina Sfursat or Sforzato—red: dry
Valtellina Superiore—red: dry; riserve; Grumello, Inferno, Sassella, Valgella

Other Wines of Note

Cabernet—red: dry
Canneto—red: dry
Chardonnay—white: dry, spumante
Colle del Calvario—red, white: dry

PIEDMONT (PIEDMONTE)

Piedmont ranks second among the regions in size (9,806 square miles) with a population of 4,480,000. Vineyards cover 182,691 acres. Average annual wine production is 410 million liters.

DOC or DOCG Wines (37)

Banfi Brachetto d'Acqui—red: sweet, frizzante

Barbaresco (DOCG)—red: dry, riserva

Barbera d'Alba—red: dry, superiore

Barbera d'Asti—red: dry, superiore

Barbera del Monferrato—red: dry, frizzante, superiore

Barolo (DOCG)—red: dry, riserva

Boca—red: dry

Brachetto d'Acqui—red: sweet, frizzante, spumante

Bramaterra—red: dry, riserva

Calusco Passito—white: sweet, liquoroso

Carema—red: dry

Colli Tortonesi: Barbera—red: dry, superior; Cortese—white: dry, frizzante

Cortese dell'Alto Monterrato—white: dry, frizzante, spumante

Dolcetto d'Acqui—red: dry, superiore

Dolcetto d'Alba—red: dry, superiore

Dolcetto d'Asti—red: dry, superiore

Dolcetto delle Langhe Monregalesci—red: dry, superiore

Dolcetto di Diano d'Alba—red: dry, superiore

Dolcetto di Dogliani—red: dry, superiore

Dolcetto di Ovada—red: dry, superiore

Erbaluce di Caluso—white: dry

Fara—red: dry

Freisa d'Asti—red: dry, sweet, frizzante, spumante, superiore

Freisa di Chieri—red: dry, sweet, frizzante, spumante

Gabiano—red: dry

Gattinara—red: dry

Gavi or Cortese di Gavi—white: dry, frizzante, spumante

Ghemme—red: dry

Grignolino d'Asti—red: dry

Grignolino del Monferrato Casalese—red: dry

Lessona—red: dry

Malvasia di Casorzo d'Asti—red: sweet, frizzante, spumante

Malvasia di Castelnuovo Don Bosco—red: sweet, frizzante, spumante

Moscato d'Asti—white: sweet, frizzante; Asti Spumante or Asti—white: sweet, spumante

Nebbiolo d'Alba—red: dry, sweet, frizzante, spumante

Roero—red: dry

Rubino di Cantavenna—red: dry

Sizzano—red: dry

Other Wines of Note

Arneis dei Roeri—white: dry

Barengo—white, red: dry

Berbesco—white: dry

Bonardo del Pimente—red: dry

Bricco del Drago—red: dry

Chardonnay del Piemonte—white: dry

Spanna del Piemonte—red: dry

Spumante-Brut—white, rose: dry, spumante

Vinot—red: dry

VALLE D'AOSTA

Valle d'Aosta is Italy's smallest region (1,259 square miles) with a population of 112,000. Vineyards cover 2,429 acres. Average wine production is 3.5 million liters.

DOC Wine (1)

(Names and labels may also be in French)

Valle d'Aosta or Vallée d'Aoste (15 types)—Arnad Montjovet—red: dry, superior; Bianco or Blanc—white: dry, frizzante; Blanc de Morgex et de La Salle—white: dry, frizzante; Chambave Moscato or Muscat—white: dry, sweet; Chambave Rossoor Rouge—red: dry; Donnaz or Donnas—red: dry; Enfer d'Arvier—red: dry; Gamay*—red: dry; Müller Thurgau—white: dry; Nus Pinot Grigio or Pinot Gris—white: dry; Passito or Fletri—white: sweet; Nus Rosso or Rouge—red: dry; Pinot Nero or Pinot Noir—red: dry; Rosato—rosé: dry, frizzante; Rosso or Rouge—red: dry, frizzante; Torrette—red: dry

Other Wines of Note

Aymaville—red: dry
Blacc de Cossan—white: dry
Petit Rouge—red: dry
Vin du Conseil—white: dry

The Northeast region includes Veneto, Friuli-Venezia Giulia, Trentino-Alto Adige.

VENETO

The Veneto ranks eighth among the regions in size† (7,090 square miles) with a population of 4,345,000. Vineyards cover 233,358 acres. Average annual wine production is 910 million liters.

DOC Wines (13)

Bardolino—red: dry, superior; Chiaretto—rosé: dry

Bianco di Custoza—white: dry, spumante

Breganze (7)—Bianco—white: dry; Cabernet—red: dry; Pinot Bianco—white: dry; Pinot Grigio—white: dry; Pinot Nero—red: dry; Rosso—red: dry; Vespaiolo—white: dry

Colli Berici (7)—Cabernet—red: dry, riserva; Garganega—white: dry; Merlot—red: dry; Pinot Bianco—white: dry; Sauvignon—white: dry; Tocai Italico—white: dry; Tocai Rosso—red: dry

Colli Euganei (7)—Bianco—white: dry, sweet, spumante; Cabernet—red: dry; Merlot—red: dry; Moscato—white: sweet, frizzante, spumante; Pinot Bianco—white: dry; Rosso—red: dry, sweet, spumante; Tocai Italico—white: dry

Gambellara (3)—Bianco—white: dry; Recioto di Gambellara—white: sweet, spumante; Vin Santo di Gamellara—white: sweet

Lessini Durello—white: dry, spumante

Lison-Pramaggiore‡ (12)—Cabernet—red: dry; Cabernet

*A regionwide DOC went into effect with the 1985 vintage, incorporating the two previous DOCs of Donnaz and Enfer d'Arvier.

†The Lugana and San Martino della Battaglia DOC zones, centered in Lombardy, extend into the Veneto; Valdadige extends into the Veneto from Trentino Alto Adige.

‡The Lison-Pramaggiore DOC zone extends from the Veneto into Friuli.

Franc—red: dry, riserva;
Cabernet Sauvignon—red: dry;
Chardonnay—white: dry;
Merlot—red: dry; Pinot Bianco—
white: dry, spumante; Pinot
Grigio—white: dry; spumante;
Refosco del Peduncolo Rosso—
red: dry; Riesling Italico—white:
dry; Sauvignon—white: dry,
spumante; Tocai Italico—white:
dry; Verduzzo—white: dry
Montello e Colli Asolani (3)—
Cabernet—red: dry; Merlot—
red: dry; Prosecco—white: dry,
sweet, spumante
Piave (8)—Cabernet—red: dry;
Merlot—red: dry; Pinot Bianco—
white: dry; Pinot Grigio—white:

Other Wines of Note

Campo Fiorin—red: dry
Capitel San Rocco—white, red:
dry
Chardonnay delle Venezie—white:
dry, spumante
Costozza—white, red, rosé: dry
Fratelle Zeni—Soave—white: dry;

dry; Pinot Nero—red: dry;
Tobaso—red: dry; Tocai Italico—
white: dry; Verduzzo—white:
dry
Prosecco di Conegliano—
Valdobbiadene—white: dry,
sweet, spumante; Superiore di
Cartizze—white: dry, sweet,
spumante
Soave—white: dry, spumante;
Recioto di Soave—white: sweet,
spumante
Valpolicella (also Valpolicella-
Valpantena)—red: dry, superior;
Recioto della Valpolicella—red:
sweet, spumante; Recioto della
Valpolicella Amarone or
Amarone—red: dry

Bardolino—red, rosé: dry
Valpolicella—red: dry
Pinot Bianco delle Venezie—white:
dry, spumante
Rosso San Pietro—red: dry
Torcolato—white: sweet
Venegazzu—red: dry

FRIULI-VENEZIA GIULIA

Friuli-Venezia Giulia ranks seventeenth among the regions in size (3,029 square miles) with a population of 1,234,000. Vineyards cover 53,134 acres. Average annual wine production is 120 million liters.

DOC Wines (7)

Aquileia (11)—Cabernet or
Cabernet Franc or Cabernet
Sauvignon—red: dry; Merlot—
red: dry; Pinot Bianco—white:
dry; Pinot Grigio—white: dry;
Refosco—red: dry; Riesling
Renano—white: dry; Rosato—
rosé: dry; Sauvignon—white:
dry; Tocai Friulano—white: dry;
Traminer—white: dry; Verduzzo
Friulano—white: dry
Carso (3)—Caros—red: dry; Carso

Malvasia—white: dry; Terrano
del Carso—red: dry
Colli Orientali del Friuli (12)—
Cabernet—red: dry; Merlot—
red: dry; Picolit—white: sweet;
Pinot Bianco—white: dry; Pinot
Grigio—white: dry; Pinot Nero—
red: dry; Refosco—red: dry;
Ribolla—white: dry; Riesling
Renano—white: dry;
Sauvignon—white: dry; Tocai
Friulano—white: dry;
Verduzzo—white: sweet, dry;

Remandolo—white: sweet
Collio Gorizano or Collio (12)—
Cabernet Franc—red: dry;
Collio—white: dry; Malvasia—
white: dry; Merlot—red: dry;
Pinot Bianco—white: dry; Pinot
Grigio—white: dry; Pinot Nero—
red: dry; Ribolla—white: dry;
Riesling Italico—white: dry;
Sauvignon—white: dry; Tocai
Friulano—white: dry;
Traminer—white: dry
Grave del Friuli (13)—Cabernet or
Cabernet Franc or Cabernet
Sauvignon—red: dry;
Chardonnay—white: dry;
Merlot—red: dry; Pinot Bianco—
white: dry; Pinot Grigio—white:
dry; Pinot Nero—red: dry;
Refosco—red: dry; Riesling
Renano—white: dry; Rosato—
rosé: dry; Sauvignon—white:
dry; Tocai Friulano—white: dry;
Traminer Aromatico—white:
dry; Verduzzo—white: dry
Isonzo (10)—Cabernet—red: dry;
Malvasia Istriana—white: dry;
Merlot—red: dry; Pinot Bianco—

white: dry; Pinot Grigio—white:
dry; Riesling Renano—white:
dry; Sauvignon—white: dry;
Tocai—white: dry; Traminer
Aromatico—white: dry;
Verduzzo Friulano—white: dry
Latisana (7)—Cabernet—red: dry;
Merlot—red: dry; Pinot Bianco—
white: dry; Pinot Grigio—white:
dry; Refosco—red: dry; Tocai—
white: dry; Verduzzo—white:
dry

Other Wines of Note

Chardonnay—white: dry,
spumante
Furlan Franco Castelcosa
Chardonnay—white: dry
Picolit—white: sweet
Pra Di Pradis Chardonnay—white:
dry
Ronco dell Gneniz—dry: white;
Chardonnay Terre Alte—white:
dry
Stelio Gallo Traminer—white: dry;
Maurus—red: dry
Vintage Tunina—white: dry
Zuc di Volpe—red: dry

TRENTINO-ALTO ADIGE

Trentino Alto Adige ranks eleventh among regions in size, (5,256 square miles) with a population of 873,000. Annual average wine production is 130 million liters.

DOC Wines (12)

(Names and labels in Alto Adige
may also be in German.)
Alto Adige or Sudtiroler (19)—
Cabernet—red: dry; Chardonnay
white: dry; Lagrein Dunkel or
Scuro—red: dry; Lagrein
Kretzer or Rosato—rosé: dry;
Malvasia or Malvasier—red: dry;
Merlot—red: dry; Moscato

Giallo—white: sweet; Moscato
Rosa—rosé: sweet; Muller
Thurgau or Riesling Sylvaner—
white: dry; Pinot Bianco—white:
dry; Pinot Grigio—white: dry;
Pinot Nero—red: dry; Riesling
Italico—white: dry; Riesling
Renano—white: dry;
Sauvignon—white: dry; Schiava
or Vernatsch—red: dry;

Spumante—white, rosé: dry,
spumante; Sylvaner—white: dry;
Traminer Aromatico—white: dry
Caldaro—red: dry
Casteller—red, rosé: dry
Colli di Bolzano—red: dry
Mernese di Collina—red: dry
Santa Maddalena—red: dry
Sorni—white, red: dry
Terlano or Terlaner (7)—Muller
Thurgau—white: dry; Pinot
Bianco—white: dry; Riesling
Italico—white: dry; Riesling
Renano—white: dry;
Sauvignon—white: dry;
Sylvaner—white: dry; Terlano—
white: dry

Teroldego Rotaliano—red: dry,
riserva

Other Wines of Note

Castel San Michele—red: dry
De Vite—white: dry
Foianeghe—white, red: dry
Luna dei Feldo—white: dry
Mori Becio—red: dry
Morlacco—red: dry
Pragiara—red: dry
Quattro Bicariati—red: dry
San Leonardo—red: dry
Spumante Brut—white, rosé:
spumante
Vinattieri Bianco—white: dry

Cooking with Italian Wines

I cringe when I hear someone say, "Oh, I use any jug wine to cook with, or the cooking wine they sell in the supermarkets." Each ingredient is important to the taste of the recipe. A cheap cooking wine will not enhance the taste of the dish and may even change the taste, due to the chemical additives and added sugar and salt. I serve my guests the same wine that I use for cooking. The alcohol and the calories are burned off in the cooking process, and only the taste of the wine remains.

Using pure and natural Italian wines gives you the best taste. A large bottle of dry white or red wine such as Soave or Valpolicella is only $5 to $8. You can keep these wines on hand specifically for cooking and baking; or you can use some of the wine you are serving with the meal in the sauce, so that the same taste carries through from the wine to the food. And you only use a half cup to a cup of wine.

Use sweet wines and liqueurs for desserts. Use the finest quality: So little is used, and the taste matters so much. Remember, you burn off calories and alcohol when you heat the liqueurs.

Combining the right type of wine with the right ingredient is important to enhance the taste:

White wine is used for cooking fish, chicken, veal, *risottos*, light sauces, eggs, soups, vegetables, and marinades.

Red wines are best with veal, lamb, beef, pasta sauces, poaching fruits, and in marinades.

Vermouth is used with fish, chicken, salad dressings, and sauces.

Sweet wines, such as Marsala, Proseco, and Moscato, are used for sautéing veal and chicken; they are also used in desserts and for marinating fresh fruits.

Sparkling wines add a zesty touch to risottos, desserts, chicken, and sauces.

Sweet liqueurs are used with fruits, and in dessert sauces and for baking.

The exciting world of cooking with wine is so much a part of true classical Italian cooking. It's the secret ingredient in many famous recipes. Keep the wines pure and of good quality, and use them in small amounts—and you will have healthy, light, and delicious-tasting food.

Regional Food and Wine Combinations

An Italian cognoscente will insist that the specialty foods of a region should be complemented by the wines of the same region. The combinations of regional food and wine are very complementary, and represent the ultimate in sampling each region's specialties. However, the food of Italy is very adaptable and so are the wines, when such regional combinations are not possible.

A typical Italian meal may range from three to six courses—and sometimes more—of small portions. The prime categories are *antipasti* (appetizers), *primi* (pastas, risottos, soups), *secondi* (main courses of fish, chicken, veal, or beef, and sometimes just vegetables or salads), with the main course *formaggi-frutta* (cheese and fruit), and *dolce* (desserts).

Here are some suggested regional Italian food and wine combinations:

Region	Food	Wine
Sicily (Messina)	Pasta Con le Sarde	Etna Bianco Wine or Corvo Bianco
Genova	Trenette con Pesto	Lumassina white wine or Principessa Gavi
Milan	Ossobuco con Risotto alla Milanese	Barbera from Oltrepo Pavese
Florence	Bistecca alla Florentina	Chianti Classico or Brunello d'Montalcino
Abruzzi	Spaghetti alla Chitarra	Montepulciano d'Abruzzo
Bologna	Tagiatelle con Ragu	Sangiovese di Romagna
Piedmont	Risotto con Tartufi	Dolcetto D'Alba or Barolo

Antipasti	Wine
Bruschetta (Grilled Bread with Tomatoes, Garlic, and Basil)	Vernaccia di San Gimignano
Frutti di Mare (Raw Seafood Salad)	Verdicchio dei Castelli di Jesi
Scampi alla Grill (Grilled Large Shrimp with Herbs and Olive Oil)	Soave Classico or Gavid' Gavi
Mozzarella in Carozza (Breaded and Fried Mozzarella in Anchovy Sauce)	Greco di Tufo or Lacrma Christi
Peperonata (sautéed peppers and eggplant)	Regaleali Rosso
Prosciutto con Melone Fichi (Prosciutto with Cantaloupe or Figs)	Frasti Gatto d'Oro or Bianco di Scandiano (dry)

Primi

Bucatini alla Matriciana (Thick Spaghetti with Tomatoes, Onions, and Panchetta)

Gnocchi di Patate con Ragu (Potato Gnocchi with Meat Sauce or Spinach)

Lasagna con fungchi (Mushroom Sauce)

Minestrone (Vegetable-Pasta Soup)

Ravioli (Envelopes with Meat-Spinach Filling)

Ribollita (Thick Vegetable-Bread Soup)

Risotto alla Parmigiana (Rice with Broth and Parmesan Cheese)

Spaghetti con le Vongole (with Tiny Clams)

Orecchiette con Cime di Rapa (Ear-Shaped Pasta with Italian Bitter Broccoli Sauce)

Wine

Montepulciano d'Aburzzo-Cerasuolo

Bardolino Classico, or Amarone

Pinot di Franciacorta
Vermentino di Liguria
Grignolino d'Asti

Centine–Rosso Di Montalcino
Bianco di Custoza

Colli Albani or Trebbiano d'Abruzzo

Locorotondo

Secondi

Branzino al Forno (Baked Sea Bass)

Pollo al Diavolo (Grilled Chicken in Herb and Vegetable Sauce)

Brasato al Barolo (Beef Braised in Barolo Wine)

Abbacchio or Agnello alla Romana (Grilled Lamb with Rosemary, Garlic, and Wine Sauce)

Costoletta alla Milanese (Breaded Veal Cutlet)

Fegato alla Venegiana (Calf's Liver with Onions and Vinegar Sauce)

Wine

Pinot Grigio

Valpolicella Classico Superiore or Dolcetto d'Alba

Barolo

Fiorano Rosso

Barbera d'Asti

Cabernet di Pramaggiore or Piave or Amarone

Verdura e Insalade (Vegetables and Salads)

For the variety of vegetable and salads included, it is best to select a wine that will go with the main course, unless you are serving only vegetable and salad.

Wine

White, rosé, or light red

Formaggi (Cheese)

Italy has more than 400 types of cheeses. Some of the most popular include: Mild, soft cheeses: Bel Paese, Fontina, mozzarella, ricotta, Caprino

Wine

Light to medium-bodied white: Frascati, Soave, Orvietto, Pinot Grigio, Gavi, Fiano d' Avelino

Lightly ripened or seasoned cheeses: Caciota, Taleggio, Robiola, goat cheese

Ripe and aged cheeses: Parmigiano-Reggiano, Grana Padano, sweet Gorgonzola, Caciocavallo Provolone, Pecorino, Asiago

Light reds or Rosés: Bardolino, Gattinara, Dolcetto d'Alba, Spanna, Castel del Monte Rosato

Robusta Reds: Amarone, Barberad'Asti, Barolo, Brunello di Montalcino, Taurasi, Torgiano Riserva

Frutta (Fresh Fruit)

Italians usually eat the fruit after the cheese and serve a sweet or bubbly wine that will carry into the dessert course.

Wine

Sweet Wines: Moscato, Malvasia, Recioto di Soave, Marsala Doce

Dolce (Desserts, Sweets)

Each region has special desserts that go with the regional dessert wines: For example, in Tuscany the almond biscuits go with Vin Santo. (You can dip the cookies in the wine.) Zabaglione goes with Marsala; Panettone with Asti Spumante. Desserts laced with chocolate, rum, or cinnamon are strong tastes when paired with sweet wines; a liqueur would stand up better, such as Amaretto, Sambucca Romano, Anisette, or Frangelica. You can also end the meal with a *digestivo*: Amara Averna, Grappa, Fernet, or Ramazzoto

Wine

Sweet and sparkling: Vin Santo, Marsala, Asti Spumante, Piccolino, Verduzzo Friulano, Malvasia delle Lipari, Moscato Passito di Pantelleria

Below I have listed three excellent books on Italian wines that you may want to read.

Anderson, Burton. *Guide to Italian Wines*. New York: Simon & Schuster, 1984.
Hazan, Victor. *Italian Wine*. New York: Knopf, 1982.
Johnson, Hugh. *The World Atlas of Wine*. New York: Simon & Schuster, 1985.

For more information on the book *Wines of Italy*, write to:
Mr. Augusto P. Marchini
Director, Wines and Food Center
Italian Trade Commission
499 Park Avenue
New York, New York 10022

Calorie Chart

Please keep in mind that the calorie counts for each recipe are based on the tables of the United States Department of Agriculture and were worked out before the ingredients were cooked. As a result, reduction through cooking can vary the figure. The calorie counts, therefore, should be regarded as very close, though perhaps not absolutely accurate. The calorie count is approximate, but accurate enough to give you an idea of how many calories each recipe represents. Thus, calorie-conscious people will be satisfied with the low-calorie foods presented in this book—no-guilt Italian Foods!

FOOD	AMOUNT	CALORIES
alcoholic beverages		
beer	12 oz.	150–170
distilled spirits (bourbon, gin, Scotch, vodka)	1 oz. 80–100 proof	70–85
liqueurs		
brandy	1 oz.	80
Grand Marnier	1 oz.	100
Tia Maria, Kahlúa	1 oz.	92
wine		
champagne, dry	4 oz.	100–115
Marsala, dry	4 oz.	160
Marsala, sweet	4 oz.	200
vermouth, dry	4 oz.	135
red wine, dry	4 oz.	95–100
white wine, dry	4 oz.	85–95
anchovy	1 fillet	9
apple	1 unpeeled 5 oz.	80
artichoke	1 fresh, 8 oz.	35
	3 frozen hearts	28
arugula	½ lb., raw	50
asparagus	1 lb.	62
beans		
green or wax	½ cup, fresh, cooked	16
Italian	½ cup, fresh, cooked	45
beef		
chuck	3½ oz., lean, braised	265
club steak	3½ oz., lean, broiled	280
ground beef	3½ oz., lean, broiled	228
round, bottom	3½ oz., lean, broiled	240
steak, lean	3½ oz., raw	164

FOOD	AMOUNT	CALORIES
bread		
wheat	1 slice	60
Italian	1 slice, 1-inch thick	55
white	1 slice	75
whole wheat	1 slice	56
broccoli	1 lb., raw	113
	½ cup, fresh, cooked	25
butter	1 tbsp.	100
carrot	½ lb., raw	80
celery	1 cup raw, diced	15
cheese		
ricotta	½ cup, skim-milk,	80
mozzarella	1 oz.	80
Parmesan or Pecorino	1 tbsp. grated	30
chicken		
breast	3½ oz., raw	100
	3½ oz., without skin, broiled or poached	135
dark meat	3½ oz., roasted	180
white meat	3½ oz., roasted	165
clams	3½ oz., fresh meats	88
	3½ oz., canned meats, drained	98
cod	3½ oz., fresh	78
	3½ oz., salted	130
cornmeal	2 oz., dry	210
	5 oz., cooked	210
cornstarch	1 tbsp.	30
crab	3½ oz., fresh	98
	3½ oz., canned	104
crackers		
saltine	1	22
Venus Wheat Wafers	1	18
cream	1 tbsp., light whipping	45
	1 tbsp., sour	30
egg	1 large	80
	1 large egg white	15
	1 large egg yolk	60
eggplant	3½ oz., raw	25
	½ cup, simmered pieces	19
endive and escarole	3½ oz.,raw	20
flounder	3½ oz., raw	79
flour		
whole wheat	3½ oz., hard wheat	333
enriched all-purpose	3½ oz.	368
garlic	1 clove, 3 gm.	3

FOOD	AMOUNT	CALORIES
gelatin	1 envelope, 7 gm., unflavored	28
gingerroot	½ oz., fresh	7
grapefruit	½ white, 7 oz.	50
	1 cup, fresh sections	75
grapes	1 cup, green, raw, seedless	95
haddock	3½ oz., raw	80
halibut	3½ oz., raw	100
honey	1 tbsp.	64
lamb		
leg	3½ oz., lean, roasted	195
loin chop	5 oz., lean, with bone	225
rib chop	5 oz., lean, with bone	325
shoulder	3½ oz., lean, roasted	220
leek	1 large, raw	17
lemon	1 tbsp., fresh juice	4
lettuce		
loose-leaf	½ lb., raw	26
romaine	½ lb., raw	26
liver		
beef	3½ oz., raw	125
	3½ oz., broiled	180
calf's	3½ oz., raw	140
	3½ oz., broiled	220
chicken	3½ oz., raw	110
	3½ oz., simmered	165
lobster		
American	3½ oz., raw meat	91
spiny	3½ oz., raw meat	72
milk		
skim	1 cup, 8 oz.	90
whole	1 cup, 8 oz.	160
mushrooms	½ lb., raw	60
mussels	3½ oz., raw meats, no shells	66
mustard	1 tbsp., prepared	11
oil		
green olive	1 tbsp.	120
vegetable	1 tbsp.	120–130
olives		
black (ripe)	1 small	5
green	1 large	5
onion	½ lb., raw	80
	1 3-oz.	30
	1 tbsp., raw, chopped	4
	½ cup raw, chopped	32

FOOD	AMOUNT	CALORIES
orange	1 Florida, 7 oz.	75
	1 California, 6 oz.	60
oysters	3½ oz., fresh	72
parsley	1 tbsp., chopped	2
pasta	2 oz., uncooked	210
noodles	½ cup, cooked al dente, no sauce	100
spaghetti	½ cup, cooked al dente, no sauce	95
peach	1 fresh, 4 oz.	35
pear	1 fresh, 7 oz.	100
peas	½ cup, cooked, fresh green	57
pepper (sweet bell)	1 green, 5 oz.	25
	1 red, 5 oz.	35
pignoli (pine nuts)	1 tbsp.	50
pimento	1, canned	10
pineapple	½ cup, fresh, diced	36
	3½ oz. canned, packed in natural juices	58
potato	1, 3½ oz., raw	78
	1, 3½ oz., peeled and boiled	65
quail	3½ oz., raw, without skin and bones	168
rabbit	3½ oz., raw, without skin and bones	162
radishes	3½ oz., 1 cup, about 15 small	25
raisins	½ cup	230
raspberries	½ cup, fresh, raw	35
rice		
white, long-grain	3½ oz., raw	369
	½ cup, cooked	92
brown	3½ oz., raw	360
	½ cup, cooked	100
salmon	3½ oz., raw	220
	3½ oz., poached	210
	4 oz., canned	160–240
sardines	3½ oz., raw	160
	3½ oz., canned in brine	196
	3½ oz., canned in oil, drained	205
scallops	3½ oz., raw	81
	3½ oz., steamed	112
shallots	1 oz.	18
shrimps	3½ oz., fresh	91
	3½ oz., canned	116
snapper	3½ oz., fresh, without skin or bones	90

FOOD	AMOUNT	CALORIES
soft drinks		
club soda	8 oz.	0
cola	8 oz.	95
sole	3½ oz., fresh, without skin or bones	79
spinach	3½ oz., raw	26
	½ cup, boiled, drained	21
squash		
yellow summer squash	3½ oz., raw	20
	½ cup, cooked, drained	16
zucchini	3½ oz., raw	17
	½ cup, cooked, drained	13
squid	3½ oz., raw	75
stock		
chicken	1 cup	30
veal	1 cup	35
vegetable	1 cup	10
strawberries	3½ oz., fresh, raw, about ⅔ cup	37
striped bass	3½ oz., raw, without skin and bones	108
sugar		
brown	1 tbsp.	50
white	1 tbsp.	45
tomato paste	1 tbsp., canned	15
tomato puree	¼ cup, canned	24
tomatoes		
cherry	1 cup	42
plum	1, 8 oz. to 1 lb.	13
	½ cup, canned	25
round	1 3 oz. to 1 lb.	35
trout	3½ oz., raw, fresh, brook	101
tuna	3½ oz., canned in oil	285
	3½ oz., canned in water	175
turkey	3½ oz., raw, white meat, without skin and bones	116
	3½ oz., roasted, white meat, without skin and bones	170
veal		
loin chop	6 oz., with bone, raw	210
scallop (scalopini)	1 scallop, 2 oz.	120
shoulder or rump	3½ oz., with no fat	163
vinegar	1 tbsp.	2
watercress	3½ oz.	17
	5 sprigs	1
yogurt	1 cup, part-skim, plain	125

Source: Based on information published by the United States Department of Agriculture.

CALORIE CHART

Glossary

Al Dente: To the tooth, that is, with texture to chew, not mushy; used for pasta, rice, vegetables.

Antipasto: Before the pasta; appetizer, hors-d'oeuvre, or first course.

Aperitivo: Aperitif; a drink, often before a meal, that is usually wine, or a fortified or aromatized wine.

Arrabbiata: Literally, furious or raging; used for a sauce made spicy with hot peppers, or for a dish that is prepared with hot peppers (chicken, pasta, etc.).

Blanch: To dip into boiling water briefly, to remove the skin (almonds, tomatoes); or to parboil, to end enzyme action and set the color (vegetables, especially green leafy kinds).

Boil: To cook in water to cover at a temperature of 212°F.

Braciole: Thin slices of meat, usually flattened, filled with a small amount of stuffing, rolled up, and fastened with string or skewers; they are sautéed, then the cooking is finished with wine, stock, or sauce.

Braise: To cook in moist heat, covered, on top of the stove or in the oven; the amount of moisture is minimal, often only the natural juices of the food to be braised.

Cacciatora: Literally, hunter style; a way of preparing chicken, rabbit, or quail; the meat is sautéed, then the cooking is finished with a sauce made of wine, onion, and usually a small amount of tomatoes.

Cannellini: Large white shell beans, like kidney beans; in the United States usually found only canned or dried.

Celery Rib: One piece, the fleshy base ending in leaves, broken from a stalk; a celery stalk is an entire plant.

Chicken Breast: The entire breast portion of the bird; this divides at the breastbone into two half-breasts; each half-breast has two fillets, a larger and a smaller. All poultry breasts are similar in construction.

Cholesterol: A fat-soluble crystalline steroid alcohol, synthesized in the human body; when there is too much, it is deposited in the blood vessels.

Chop: To reduce any food to bits of random size; usually all the pieces are less than one-half inch; chopped pieces are larger than minced pieces. See also, CUBE and DICE.

Clarify: To remove all solid particles, however small, from stock for aspic or consommé to give a clear transparent liquid; or to separate milky particles from butter to give only the clear butterfat, so that butter will not burn when used for cooking.

Contorni: Vegetables used as accompaniments to meat, poultry, or fish.

Crostini: pieces of toast, especially toasts with some sort of topping used for antipasto.

Crush: To flatten or mash, usually said of raw foods, especially garlic; garlic is crushed with the flat side of a chef's knife.

Crustaceans: Marine creatures with segmented exterior skeletons—crab, lobster, shrimp.

Cube: To cut into cubes—pieces of equal dimensions on all sides; unless the size is specified, a cube is usually more than one-half inch but less than one inch in size. See also, DICE.

Devein: To remove the intestinal tract of a shrimp.

Dice: To cut into cube-shaped pieces of less than one-half inch; cubes indicates pieces are larger. Both CHOP and MINCE indicate pieces of random size, but dice of the same size.

Dolce: Sweets, cakes, etc.; desserts generally.

Doppio: Double strength, as in consommé concentrated to make it more flavorful and nutritious; like French *consommé double*.

Drain: To pour off liquid, which is not retained for future use, as draining cooked pasta; the solid food retained in the colander or strainer is used. See also, STRAIN.

Dress: To prepare fish and crustaceans for cooking and eating; each style of preparation has a specific name, as drawn, filleted, pan-dressed, whole-dressed.

Dried: Used for a product that is made dry by artificial heat or by the sun's heat to make it possible to store it for later use, as dried beans, dried apricots, dried herbs.

Dry: Used for a product that is dry in its natural mature state, as mustard seeds, whole or ground; hence "dry mustard."

Dry (wine): Not sweet; however, all such "flavor" terms are relative.

Durum Semolina: Flour or meal made from the grain *Triticum durum;* the flour, high in gluten-producing proteins, is used for the best pasta, center of the wheat.

Enzyme: A substance of the nature of a protein produced by living cells, as in fruits, meats, vegetables, which promotes reactions such as combination with water or oxygen.

Espresso: Black coffee made by forcing steam through finely ground dark-roast coffee beans.

Fennel Rib: See CELERY RIB. A stalk or head of fennel is the whole plant.

Filet: The tenderloin of beef, running through the short loin and sirloin; it is boneless and very tender; similar but much smaller tenderloins are found in other meat animals.

Filet Mignon: A slice, one to one-and-a-half inches thick, cut from the beef filet; one of these weighs six to eight ounces. See also, TOURNEDOS.

Fillet: The boneless flesh cut from one side of a fish; it may retain the skin or not; larger fish may be divided along the center line to make quartercut fillets. Or, one of the parts of the half-breast of chicken; see also CHICKEN BREAST.

Fiorentina: In the style of Florence. When recipes use the English word "Florentine" it almost always means "with spinach."

Flake: To separate cooked fish along its natural lines of division, making small, thin, flattened pieces; when this can be done with the touch of a fork, the fish is cooked.

Flambé: To spoon or pour an alcoholic liquid, usually brandy or other high-proof liqueur, over a food and to ignite it; this can be done during cooking or at serving time.

Frittata: An egg dish similar to an omelet, but usually cooked on both sides and having any filling mixed into the beaten eggs.

Fritto: Literally fried; also a dish of fried food.

Fritto Misto: A mixed fry; a mixture of different ingredients all fried and served together.

Garlic Clove: One bulblet separated from a head of garlic; before peeling one clove may weigh about one-tenth of an ounce.

Gelato: Ice cream; because Italian ice cream is made with less fat, it is more like an American ice or sherbet.

Gluten: A stretchy and tough protein found in wheat flour; to keep piecrust from being tough, it is chilled at some stage to allow the gluten to relax.

Grand Marnier: An orange-flavored brandy-based liqueur made in France; the 80-proof yellow liqueur, which is sweeter than the red, is used for sweetening in some desserts.

Grate: To reduce to small particles by rubbing against a grater; the bits can be very small, as when nutmeg is grated, but they are always smaller than shreds. See also, SHRED.

Grind: To reduce to small bits in a mechanical grinder, powered by hand or electricity; the size of the bits depends on the size of the holes in the grinding plate. One can also grind by hand using a pestle in a mortar.

Herb: A flavoring ingredient based on the leaves of plants of temperate climates; there are a few seed herbs, and garlic (a bulb) and horseradish (a root) are also counted as herbs. See also, SPICE.

Legumi: Legumes; peas, beans, etc., used fresh in pods or fresh shelled or dried shelled.

Lemon Rind: The outer yellow portion of the peel; this contains the aromatic lemon oil. It is usually grated for use; in this state it can be dried or frozen for future use.

Limone: Lemon in Italian.

Macerate: To soak fruits in an acid (lemon juice or wine) or a liqueur, to soften and flavor them.

Marinate: To soak meat, poultry, fish, occasionally vegetables, in an acid (wine, vinegar, lemon juice) and various flavorings to tenderize and flavor it.

Meringo: Meringue in Italian.

Mince: To reduce to very tiny pieces of random size by chopping; especially said of parsley and other herbs. See also CHOP.

Mineral: One of several chemical elements essential to life, found in foods in varying amounts; some that we know to be necessary to us are iron, calcium, potassium, phosphorus.

Minestra: Soup, generally thick, made of vegetables and often including a small variety of pasta.

Minestrina: A thin, clear soup, like consommé.

Minestrone: A thick vegetable soup, also containing either rice or pasta.

Misto: Mixture in Italian; as in *fritto misto,* a "mixed fry."

Monounsaturated: Able to form only one additional product with another nutrient; olive oil is an example. See also, POLYUNSATURATED.

Mozzarella: Literally, cheese that can be cut; a mild, moist cheese, good for eating plain or in cooked dishes; made of cow's milk in the United States.

Oil-Steam: To steam with a small amount of oil, the rest of the needed moisture being supplied by the ingredients being cooked; especially for vegetables.

Parmesan: Literally, of Parma; an aged, grainy cheese produced in a strictly delimited area of Italy; it is an excellent eating cheese when young, but is used more as a flavoring cheese when well aged; true Parmigiano-Reggiano is not exported until aged for two years.

Pasta Asciutta: Dry pasta, the kind one buys in packages in the market.

Pasta Fresca: Pasta freshly made at home, usually cooked soon after.

Pasta In Brodo: Small pasta shapes, cooked and served in broth.

Pastina: Tiny pasta shapes, especially for *pasta in brodo*.

Pavese: Literally, of Pavia; decorated; used of soup garnished with a whole poached egg on a piece of fried bread or toast.

Pecorino: Cheese made of ewe's milk; this is aged for grating just as Parmesan is; Pecorino Romano is the most familiar kind in the United States.

Pesto: Literally, pounded or bruised; the name of a sauce made with fresh basil leaves, grated cheese, and olive oil, sometimes with additional ingredients. Originally the ingredients were pounded in a mortar with a pestle.

Piazziola: Literally, in the style of the piazza or marketplace; a sauce for cooking meat, made of tomatoes, herbs, and sometimes other vegetables.

Piccante: Literally, piquant; appetizing, spicy, with a slight hot taste from hot peppers, ginger, or cayenne.

Pignoli: Pine nuts, the seeds of several varieties of pine trees.

Pimento: A canned, roasted sweet red pepper; the mature pepper has its skin peeled off after roasting; a pimento is softer than a roasted fresh red pepper.

Poach: To cook in water to cover at a temperature just lower than boiling, about 200°F.; a good method for all protein foods, as it does not toughen them.

Polyunsaturated: Able to form many additional products in combination with other materials in the body; corn, soybean, safflower, and sesame oils are examples; recommended for people on low-cholesterol diets. See also, MONOUNSATURATED

Prosciutto: Dry-cured raw Parma ham, dried in air-swept caves; delicate, delicious, flavorful; there is an American version.

Provatura: Cheese made from buffalo's milk; like mozzarella, but made in smaller sizes; tender and juicy.

Purée: To reduce to a smooth homogeneous thick paste, in an electric blender, or by pushing through a food mill or sieve; especially for fruits and vegetables.

Rib: See CELERY RIB and FENNEL RIB. The ribs of a pepper are inner membranes that are always trimmed away, as they are peppery.

Ricotta: A smooth soft cheese, without curds, made from whey, with a rather sweet taste. American ricotta is made with milk.

Risotto: Rice cooked with other ingredients.

Ristretti: Reduced; used for clear soup concentrated to make it more flavorful. See also DOPPIO.

Sauté: To cook in a small amount of oil over medium heat for a short time; the pan must be hot and the food must not be crowded.

Scallop: A small piece of boneless meat, *scallopini*; usually applied to a slice cut from the round of the veal leg.

Scampo: A lobsterette or langoustine, also called prawn, but not a shrimp; similar to a lobster in body shape; available frozen in U.S. markets.

Seafood: Fish, shellfish, and crustaceans found in saltwater, used for food.

Shallot: An onion with a mild but intense flavor, which grows in a cluster of bulblets similarly to garlic. Each little bulb has a reddish or purple skin: before peeling one bulb may weigh about one-quarter ounce.

Shellfish: A hard-shelled creature, such as an oyster, clam, or mussel. Although the shell of a squid is rudimentary, it is also a shellfish. Crustaceans are another kind of shellfish.

Shred: To reduce to small pieces of random size and ragged shape; this can be done in a food grinder or an electric blender, or by hand with a chef's knife.

Simmer: The same as poach as far as temperature is concerned, although it does not necessarily indicate that the food is covered with water.

Slurry: A thin mixture of water and a starch (cornstarch, flour), which is added to other ingredients to thicken them.

Snip: To reduce to small bits with a scissors; useful for chives and other herbs that are difficult to chop.

Soufflé: Originally a baked dish, sweet or savory, containing beaten egg whites, which rose in the baking dish as air trapped in the beaten mixture expanded; later a cold dish piled up to resemble the baked dish and chilled, sometimes frozen.

Spice: A product of a tropical plant—the flower bud, seed, fleshy covering of the fruit, the root or tuber, bark, etc.; available whole (always preferred) and ground; most are dried, but some can be found fresh, e.g., gingerroot. See also, HERB.

Steam: To cook in steam rising from beneath the food; the liquid used can be water or stock. See also, OIL-STEAM. Steaming is not recommended for leafy greens, as they will lose color.

Stock: A liquid food made by extracting flavor and nutrients from various solid ingredients cooked in water for a long time; the basis of good soups and sauces, and useful as an ingredient in other recipes.

Stracciatella: Literally, rags; long, thin strands of egg cooked in a broth, like Chinese "egg-drop soup."

Strain: To remove solid particles from a liquid; often the solid particles are discarded; the liquid is used. See also, DRAIN. Stock that is strained is often treated further to remove minute particles. See also, CLARIFY.

Torta: Tart, pie, cake, or pudding can all be called *torta;* it most nearly resembles a *quiche* in being baked in a shallow layer with no top, but a *torta* usually has no crust on the bottom either; a *torta* can be a first course, main course, or dessert.

Tortina: Literally, a mini-*torta,* or tartlet, but usually a *tortina* is as large around as a *torta;* a *tortina* is an egg pie, made with vegetables, with or without a bottom crust of pastry or bread.

Tournedos: A slice cut from the beef filet; usually about one-inch thick, a tournedos weighs about four ounces. See also, FILET MIGNON.

Vegetable Oil: An oil, liquid at room temperature, made from corn, cottonseed, peanut, safflower, sesame seed, soybean, etc.

Verde: Green; as in *salsa verde,* green sauce, indicating a sauce made from green herbs and vegetables.

Verdure: Green vegetables, such as broccoli, escarole, spinach; leafy greens.

Vitamin: An organic substance contained in foods, essential to the nutrition of humans; some are made in the body, but most need to be taken from food; vitamins regulate the body's metabolism.

Zabaglione: A frothy mixture of eggs, or just egg yolks, with wine or liqueur and other flavoring; served as a dessert, hot, cold, or frozen.

Zest: The outermost layer of citrus rind, orange, lemon, lime, grapefruit, peeled off or grated off to use for flavoring.

Zuppa: Soup; used also for main-course "soups" with relatively little liquid, such as *zuppa di pesce.*

Index

Notes